D1015586

THE COLONISING ACTIVITIES OF THE ENGLISH PURITANS

The Colonising Activities of the English Puritans

The Last Phase of the Elizabethan Struggle with Spain

By

ARTHUR PERCIVAL NEWTON

Lecturer in Colonial History, University of London

With an Introduction

by

CHARLES M. ANDREWS

New Edition with an Introduction by

Ellis A. Johnson

KENNIKAT PRESS, INC./PORT WASHINGTON, N. Y.

THE COLONISING ACTIVITIES OF THE ENGLISH PURITANS

Reissued in 1966 by Kennikat Press

Library of Congress Catalog Card No: 65-20471

Manufactured in the United States of America

INTRODUCTION TO THE 1966 REISSUE

In 1600, Europeans, separated by vast expanses of unexplored coast, occupied three regions of the New World. Thirty years later French, English, Spanish, Dutch, and aboriginal changes of more than shoreline significance had taken place. By mid-century the Providence Company, principal purpose of Mr. Newton's labors, was officially dissolved. This was not necessarily inevitable for, as a great historian of our time points out, "it would have been easy to predict the coming conflict between them for the possession of the interior, but the most far-sighted observer then alive would not have been likely to hit the mark if he had been asked, in 1650, to pick the winner."[1] The Expansion of Europe was a game of hemispheres—and inches:

> What certain nations had secured honestly or dishonestly, by persuasion or agreement, by fraud or by force, could be acquired by other nations equally competent, equally determined or equally unscrupulous. Jealousy, fear, irritation, resistance, hostility and war have followed naturally in the train of all this.

The work in hand is minutely illustrative of this classic pattern.[2]

Bermuda came almost immediately to mind, and, indeed, the new colony of Providence was an engrossing topic for conversation among those of the oldest British Crown Colony in this hemisphere around 1630. Some of the same people were involved in both operations in a comparable time span, but differences soon outweighed similarities (both in challenge and response). Santa Catalina was situated so as to offer "the foundation of very great enterprise by annoying the Spaniard and intercepting his treasure, whereby he hath troubled and endangered most of the States of Christendom and doth foment the wars against the professors of the reformed religion"; the land was "as rich and fertile as any other part of the Indies" and "facility of transporting colonies from thence to the Main Continent" was present; still, as far as the Puritans were concerned, Providence was past history in only a dozen years. The forty-five miles of foot-deep soil on a coral base, now abounding in aircraft (over half of which are American since the destroyer-bases exchange of World War Two) is, on the other hand, still strategic and English in the age of space.[3]

Another comparison soon suggested itself. At precisely the time—1629—the company of prominent Puritans was incorporated to settle Santa Catalina Island and found Providence in the heart of the Caribbean Sea, the grant giving Puritans opportunity to establish a Wilderness Zion on Massachusetts Bay was confirmed by royal charter. By 1635, however, the Providence Company clearly recognized the failure of their attempt to provide a second home for Puritan refugees on the Spanish Main, and although the idea of migration to the Caribbean was still making headway among the Massachusetts people in 1639, little came of it.[4] Internal difficulties inherent in the venture are neatly summarized by the author in considering the case of capable Captain Samuel Axe; he became so disgusted with the state of affairs that he sought (temporary) refuge on the "Moskito" coast!

> Constant little disagreements were arising in the council on questions of precedence and the use of heated language; even a slight knowledge of New England history would convince us that a seventeenth century Puritan was a very touchy person and the numerous

discomforts of the West Indian climate did nothing to lessen this touchiness in Providence. To a modern mind, the amount of trouble the company gave themselves in clearing up some of these silly disputes seems an egregious waste of energy.[5]

Much, of which constant encroachment upon the civil authority by ministers of the Gospel was by no means least, conspired to make Providence "very different from the ideal Puritan community aimed at by its English founders." This was also true in New England but the Caribbean Providence—bound lock, stock, and barrel to the company at home—could not offer a comparable prospect of freedom, and such a prospect "must have been a most potent inducement to emigration to a generation that had begun to think for itself."[6]

At first the enterprise showed considerable promise in planting. This last collective effort of those who had been active in both Bermuda and Virginia came to show, once more, that "in order to make colonists use their best endeavours for the cultivation of the soil, it was needful to give them proprietary interest in it, and to make their obligations fixed and certain." One is reminded of the celebrated observation of "Plimoth Plantation":

> The experience that was had in this comone course and condition, tried sundrie years, and that amongst godly and sober men, may well evince the vanitie of that conceite of Platos & other ancients, applauded by some of later times;–that ye taking away of propertie, and bringing in comunitie into a comone wealth, would make them happy and florishing; as if they were wiser then God. For this comunitie (so farr as it was) was found to breed much confusion & discontent, and retard much imploymet that would have been to their benefite and comforte.[7]

The Providence program was worked out by John Pym and accepted at his suggestion. "King Pym" of Parliamentary fame and Robert Rich, Earl of Warwick (who figured in the first cargo of Negroes ever sold in Virginia and through whose agency abolitionist Massachusetts was chartered), were most influential in formulating company activities which subsequently became part of Cromwell's Western Design and Spanish War.[8]

For both religious and commercial reasons the Puritans were chief Spaniard-haters in England, and in extending operations to Tortuga, renamed the "Island of Association" in 1631, those of the Providence Company entered into the buccaneering phase. Spanish capture of Association (later taken by the French and made the base of efforts culminating in the purchase of Louisiana) and the narrow escape of the entire enterprise turned Providence from a mere plantation into a base for privateering operations against the wealth of Spanish America.[9] In 1641 the might of Spain prevailed and a solemn high Mass was followed by a festal Te Deum in the town square of what had been Puritan Providence. The colonizing successes of English Puritans lay in very different latitudes.[10]

"The Last Phase of the Elizabethan Struggle with Spain" might have been accurately titled *Puritans and Pirates in Providence*, but Mr. Newton reminds the reader that, "The purposes and activities of the Providence Company are not isolated forces operating in the backwaters of the historical current." His extremely detailed and scholarly study brings to mind a thought best expressed by an eminent brain surgeon:

> The wise man does not have to see the ocean to know it. He can deduce every quality of the ocean from considering one drop of water. That which is true with respect to one drop is true with respect to the ocean.[11]

The following story, as Professor Andrews remarked in 1914, is part of the great frontier.[12]

Ellis Allen Johnson

State University College of New York
State College at Cortland
September, 1965

* * *

[1] Arthur Percival Newton, pp. 17, 84, and 308 below, and Arnold Joseph Toynbee, "The Struggle for North America," Chapter VII Part I of *A Study of History,* Abridgment of Volumes I-VI by D. C. Somervell (New York & London: Oxford University Press, 1953), p. 96.

[2] William R. Shepherd, "The Expansion of Europe III," *The Political Science Quarterly,* XXXIV (1919), p. 408, is the classic statement.

[3] See William E. S. Zuill, "Cast Away on Bermuda, July 1609-May 1610," *Bermuda Historical Quarterly,* XVI (1959), pp. 49-67; I was fortunate enough to have been present during observance of the three hundred and fiftieth anniversary of the founding of Bermuda. The "Sommer Ilands XII," first coin minted in British North America, has a pig on the face, the *Sea Venture* on the obverse, and is of particular interest in connection with notes 5 and 6, p. 104 below. Minutes of the Company are quoted in Chapter XI.

[4] Daniel Joseph Boorstin, "A City Upon a Hill: The Puritans of Massachusetts Bay," Book I Part 1 of *The Americans: The Colonial Experience* (New York: Random House, 1958), and pp. 164-71, 287-93 below.

[5] The Axe observation is on p. 156; also see pp. 160-63 and inserted maps; James Truslow Adams, "Some Aspects of Puritanism," Chapter IV of *The Founding of New England* (Boston: Little, Brown & Co., 1927) amplifies this admirably and his Frontispiece, "New England in 1640," is also relevant.

[6] The "Providence Plantations" of New England are given sympathetic treatment in Chapters XV and XVI of Ola Elizabeth Winslow, *Master Roger Williams: A Biography* (New York: The Macmillan Co., 1957). Relationship between England and all the colonies in this period is given in Chapter XI of Curtis P. Nettels, *The Roots of American Civilization: A History of American Colonial Life* (New York: Appleton-Century-Crofts, Inc., 1938)—Providence, Tortuga, and Jamaica are specifically treated on p. 281—and pp. 310-13, below.

[7] Newton's *(The) Colonising Activities of the English Puritans*, p. 223 and *(William) Bradford's History "Of Plimoth Plantation" from the Original Manuscript* (Boston: Wright & Potter, State Printers, 1900), p. 163.

[8] Power was uppermost in the minds of the theorizers and practitioners of English mercantilism because it seemed that wealth was contingent upon it. It is with a minute examination—comparable in thoroughness to the work here introduced—of the mercantilist proposals for its augmentation in single components—and Providence was certainly one of these—that Klaus E. Knorr's *British Colonial Theories, 1570-1850* (University of Chicago: Docotoral Dissertation, International Relations, 1941) concerns itself; see pp. 324-29 below.

[9] Chapter IV and pp. 196-200 of the present work reflect the brilliance of Garrett Mattingly's Epilogue to *The Armada* (Boston: Houghton Mifflin Co., 1959), while note 9, p. 280 might be profitably considered with "Jefferson and the Purchase of Louisiana, 1801-1803," Chapter VII of Thomas A. Bailey's admirable survey, *A Diplomatic History of the American People* (New York: F. S. Crofts & Co., 1947).

[10] The place of Providence in world history is suggested by J. H. Parry in *Europe and a Wider World 1415-1715* (London & New York: Hutchinson's University Library, 1949), p. 115, on which Chapters XI-XVI below are starkly outlined.

[11] Mr. Newton's conclusion finished Chapter XV; Dr. L. J. Meduna, Professor of Psychiatry and Medicine, University of Illinois and Chicago College of Medicine, continues, "Similarly, that which is true with respect to one nerve cell is true with respect to that aggregate of nerve cells, the whole brain." Preface, *Carbon Dioxide Therapy: A Neurophysiological Treatment of Nervous Disorders (Springfield:* Charles C. Thomas, 1950).

[12] The most celebrated recent treatment (political considerations aside) is Walter Prescott Webb, *The Great Frontier* (Boston: Houghton Mifflin Co., 1952), Chapters I-VI of which are especially valuable in affording the present monograph proper perspective.

TABLE OF CONTENTS

INTRODUCTION

The first forty years of the seventeenth century in England, primarily of interest as a period of constitutional conflict, was marked by an outburst of romantic activity that sent hundreds of Englishmen out into the western seas in search of adventure and profit. Coincident with the later days of these half-piratical expeditions and organised commercial enterprises were the migrations of those who, moved by impulses that were partly religious, partly political, and partly economic, sought independence of worship and permanent homes in the New World. Though differing widely in purposes and results, these journeyings into the unknown West were often closely related in origin, and were supported by groups of men, aristocrats, commoners, merchants, and adventurers, who were ready to promote any undertaking, whether commercial or religious, that promised a profitable return. It is difficult to grasp the full significance of the settlements of Virginia, Maryland, Massachusetts, and Saybrook, without a knowledge of the circumstances under which the colonies of Bermuda, Barbadoes, and Old Providence were established; for all represented in different forms and proportions the influences at work in the motherland which were arousing in men of all classes the spirit of adventure and revolt. No single motive governed the men who voyaged over seas during this romantic period. The zeal of the viking and the lust of the capitalist were inextricably interwoven with the hopes of the godly in the task of opening and occupying the great frontier which stretched westward from the maritime states of Europe.

INTRODUCTION

In dealing with the events of this period the historian cannot isolate a part of his subject and observe it, as it were, *in vacuo*. Such treatment is illogical in ignoring the unity of causes which provoked colonial enterprise, and incomplete in omitting many phases of the larger movement that are essential to a proper understanding, not only of the whole, but of any of its parts. Hitherto, the picture of our settlement in the period from 1607 to 1640 has been left provokingly incomplete, and, in consequence, estimates and conclusions have been reached that are often exaggerated, sometimes even grotesque. Writers on early American history have been accustomed, as a rule, to segregate individual efforts at colonisation and to deal with them as independent phenomena, thus giving to our era of beginnings the appearance of a running track, laid out in separate and mutually exclusive courses. However agreeable this form of procedure may be to those whose interest is limited to the history of a single colony, and whose chief concern is a microscopic examination of the incidents of that colony's career, it cannot be satisfactory to those to whom settlement on the American seaboard was but part of a larger commercial and colonising movement in the wider world of the Atlantic basin, where all the maritime enemies of Spain were engaged in the effort, successful in the end, to break the monopoly of the great Colossus.

As a contribution to this aspect of our early history, I welcome Mr. Newton's book. Though dealing primarily with the colonising experiments of the English Puritans in the Caribbean, the author ranges over the larger field of English activity during the eventful years from 1604 to 1660 and gives us a point of view from which to observe the happenings in the New World. Thus to no small extent his work fills in the missing parts of our picture and renders intelligible aspects of the scene that had hitherto remained obscure. Though many phases of the subject still need to be investigated with the same painstaking care that is here expended on the history of the Puritan movement, yet the angle of observation is rightly selected and the character of the period is determined with accuracy and skill. At many points the narrative touches the "original" colonies and throws needed light on details of their history. This is particularly true of the origins of Virginia and Massachusetts and the short-lived settlement of Saybrook, but it is also true of the later history of New England and of the relations of the Puritans of Massachusetts Bay with the aristocratic and conservative Puritans at home. Many passages in Winthrop's journal take on a new meaning, and the unity of Puritan activity, in England and New England and the Caribbean, manifests itself with striking significance. In short, we get glimpses of ourselves from the outside and an opportunity of comparison that cannot but be beneficial. Self-contemplation is never conducive to soundness of judgment, if indulged in without regard to the world around us.

Mr. Newton has done more than fill in our picture and set before us a new point of view. He has presented an exceedingly interesting account of a colonial settlement, hitherto almost unknown and, except in one or two features, entirely unstudied. The ample material that exists for the history of the Providence Company and its colonising ventures enables the author to deal fully with the company, its organisation, personnel, and methods; with the colony, its types of settlers, manner of settlement, forms of cultivation, staples, labour, difficulties, quarrels, and other hindrances to success; and, lastly, with the relations between the two, government, defence, supplies, and distribution of profits. Not only is such a study of interest as showing the prevailing ideas of the period regarding a plantation, but it is particularly suggestive as a Puritan experiment, similar in its inception and spirit, during the early years of its career, to the colony of Massachusetts. As Mr. Newton says, "The founders of both wished to provide a refuge for the oppressed victims of Laud's ecclesiastical régime, each was to be a sanctuary where the Puritans might worship God after their own fashion, each was to be a society ordered according to the dictates of religion and governed with justice and equity, but upon the strictest Puritan pattern." That the Providence settlement failed was in part due to its location in the heart of the Spanish Main, and in part to the fact that "the founding of an ideal community and the pursuit of a profitable investment for trading capital are incompatible aims." The student of New England history cannot but profit from a study of an experiment that presents so many points in common with the Puritan settlements there.

Of equal importance with the light thrown on the colonising activities of the period is the information furnished regarding the political situation in England and the connection of the members of the company, particularly John Pym and the Earl of Warwick, with organised resistance to the personal government of Charles I. The English Puritans formed a veritable clan, intimately bound together by ties of blood, marriage, and neighbourhood, and they acted together in all that concerned colonisation on one hand and autocratic rule on the other. The genealogical features of the book form an impressive commentary upon the religious and political groupings of the period, a commentary the more significant in that the company, which became the nucleus of resistance, was active as a chartered body during the very years when Charles I was endeavouring to rule without parliament. In the months of 1637, at a critical time in the constitutional conflict, "nothing less was in process of formation," says Mr. Newton, "than the first organised political party of opposition to an English government," and of this party John Pym, the treasurer of the company, was the leader and energising force. To the life of King Pym, the author has contributed a valuable chapter, disclosing the importance of his activities during a period of obscurity, to which Gardiner was able to devote but a few lines in his elaborate article on Pym in the *Dictionary of National Biography*. As this period coincided also with the great migration to New England, so careful a study of Puritan plans and purposes furnishes a needed background to New England history, and sets forth for the first time the facts regarding the proposed withdrawal of the Puritan "Lords and Gentlemen" from the Old World to the New.

In the larger field of international relations, the Providence Company played a conspicuous part. Starting as a Puritan colony, it merged into a privateering centre of warfare upon Spanish possessions in the West Indies and on the Main. Mr. Newton shows clearly that the Puritan company perpetuated the Elizabethan tradition of hostility to Spain, which continued for more than seventy years after the Armada, partly because religious warfare was still a vital force during the first half of the seventeenth century, and partly because with the opening of the colonising era a new rivalry arose for the possession of profitable vantage points in the West. The story of the Providence Company is, therefore, the story of organised opposition to Spain in the Caribbean; and its leaders, after the failure of their settlement, by handing on the traditional policy to Cromwell and the men of the Protectorate, prolonged the conflict to the very eve of the Restoration. Apart from the main theme of the book, this abiding hostility to Spain is perhaps the most conspicuous feature of the narrative, and furnishes the connection between the deeds of Elizabethan seamen, the commercial enterprises of the Earl of Warwick, the work of the Providence Company, the voyages of William Jackson at the time of the Long Parliament, the Jamaican expedition of Cromwell, and the plans for an anti-Spanish West Indian company drafted by the merchants and sea captains at the close of the Interregnum. In this respect, as in many others, Mr. Newton has been able to gather scattered threads into an orderly narrative and to give unity and meaning to many events hitherto treated in isolation. His book is of importance to English and American readers alike.

CHARLES M. ANDREWS.

Yale University,

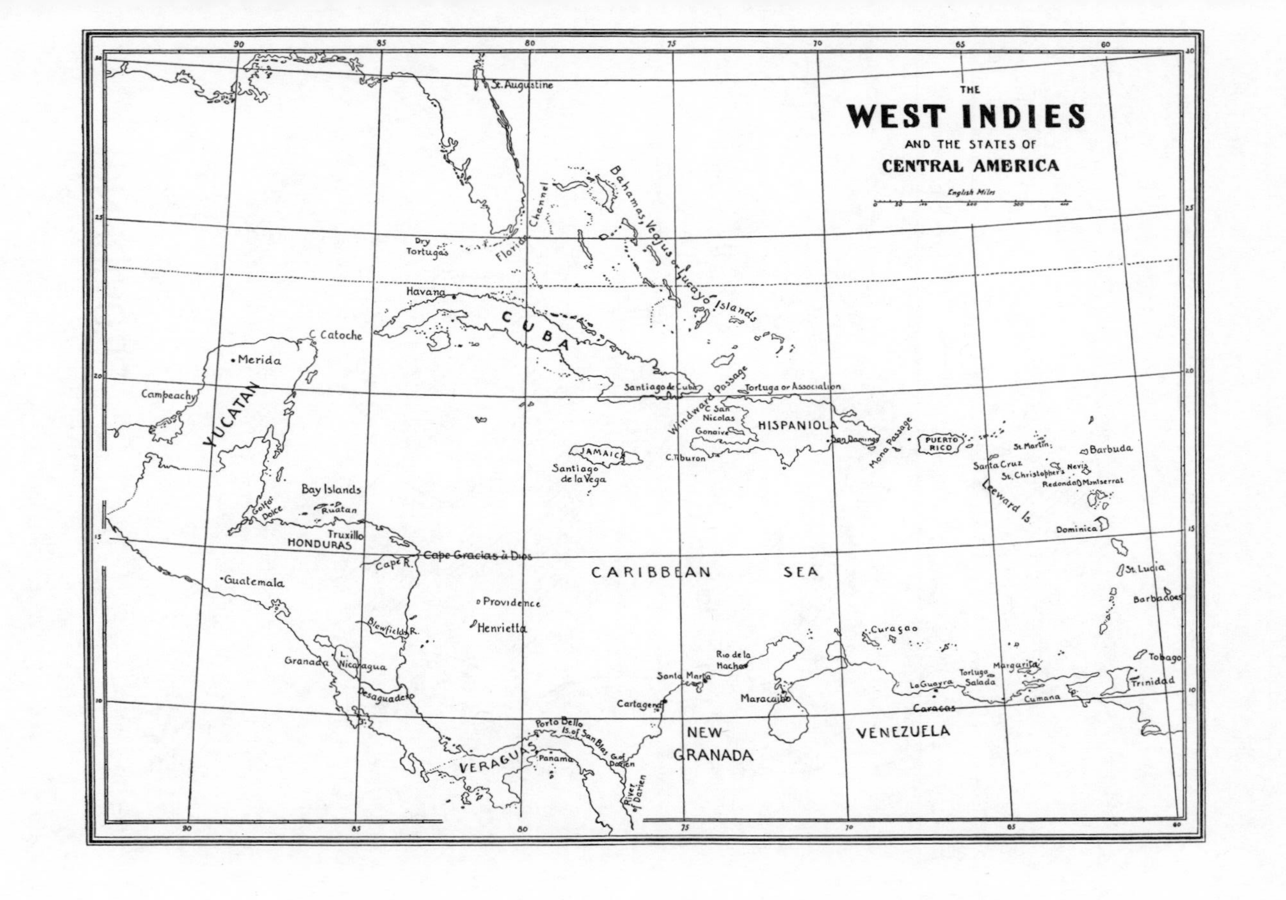

THE
WEST INDIES
AND THE STATES OF
CENTRAL AMERICA
English Miles
St. Augustine
Dry Tortugas
Florida Channel
Bahamas, Veajus or Lucayo Islands
Havana
CUBA
C. Catoche
Merida
Campeachy
YUCATAN
Santiago de Cuba
Windward Passage
Tortuga or Association
C. San Nicolas
Gonaive
HISPANIOLA
San Domingo
Mona Passage
PUERTO RICO
St. Martin
Barbuda
Santa Cruz
Nevis
St. Christopher's
Redonda
Montserrat
Leeward Is.
Dominica
JAMAICA
C. Tiburon
Santiago de la Vega
Bay Islands
Golfo Dolce
Ruatan
Truxillo
HONDURAS
Cape Gracias à Dios
Cape R.
CARIBBEAN SEA
St. Lucia
Barbadoes
Guatemala
Providence
Henrietta
Blewfields R.
Curaçao
L. Nicaragua
Granada
Rio de la Hacha
Santa Marta
Margarita
Tortuga
Salada
Tobago
Trinidad
LaGuayra
Caracas
Cumana
Desaguadero
Maracaibo
Cartagena
Porto Bello
Is. of San Blas
G. of Darien
NEW GRANADA
VENEZUELA
VERAGUAS
Panama
River of Darien

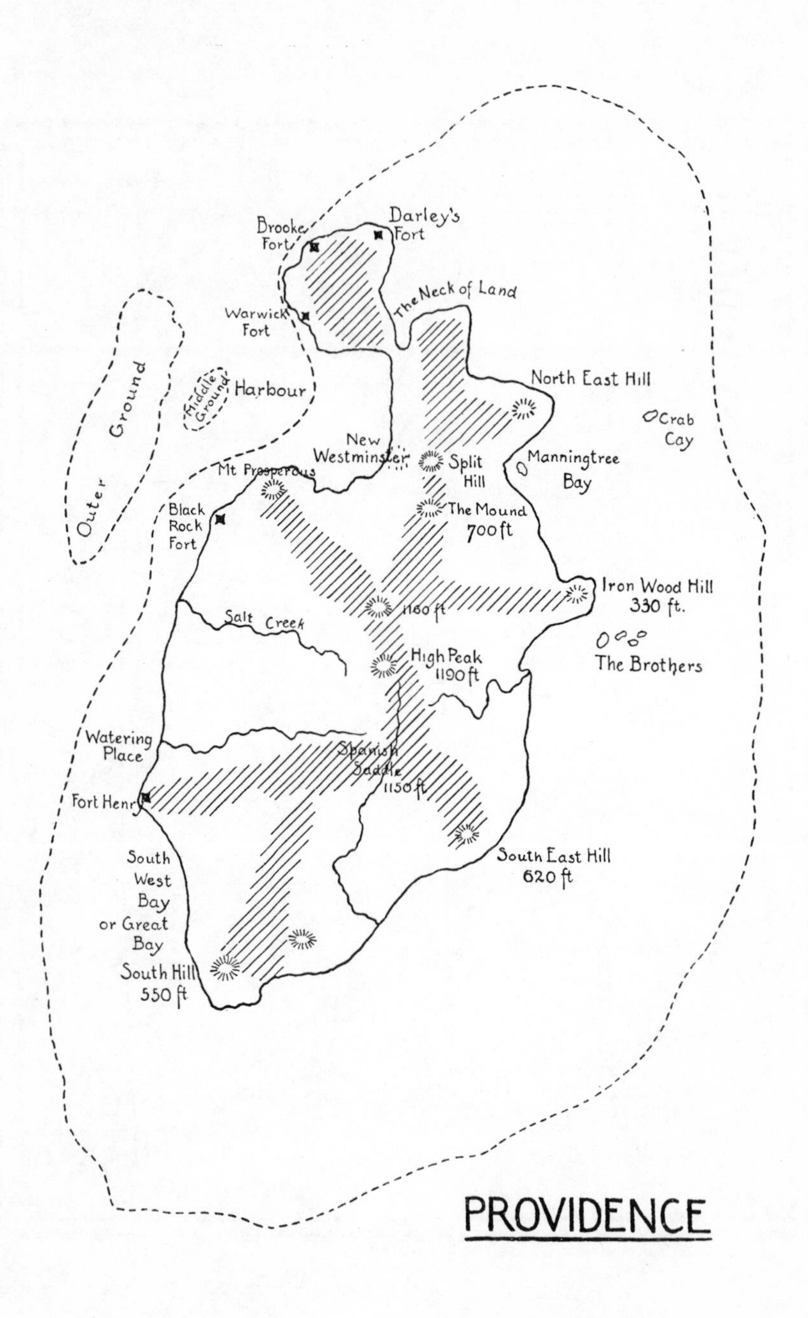
Brooke Fort
Darley's Fort
The Neck of Land
Warwick Fort
Outer Ground
Fiddle Ground
Harbour
North East Hill
Crab Cay
New Westminster
Split Hill
Manningtree Bay
Mt Prosperous
Black Rock Fort
The Mound
700 ft
Iron Wood Hill
330 ft.
1160 ft
Salt Creek
High Peak
1190 ft
The Brothers
Watering Place
Spanish Saddle
1150 ft
Fort Henry
South West Bay or Great Bay
South East Hill
620 ft
South Hill
550 ft

PROVIDENCE

THE MOSKITO COAST

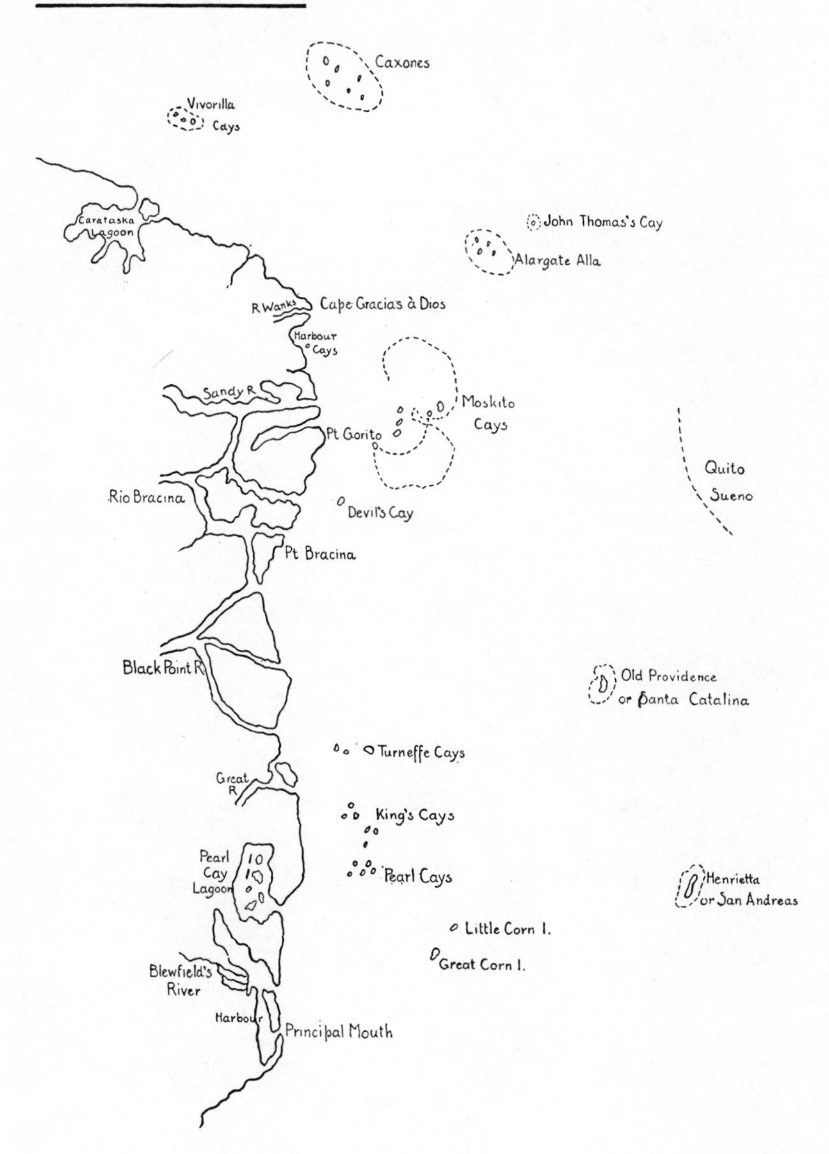

THE COLONISING ACTIVITIES OF THE ENGLISH PURITANS

AUTHOR'S INTRODUCTION

Nowhere, perhaps, in the great field of historic enquiry has there been during the past half-century more patient searching than in that corner where were laid the foundations of the modern constitutional liberties of two great nations, the English and the American. Writing now nearly thirty years ago, one of the most diligent of historical investigators said of the period he had peculiarly made his own: "The subject-matter has been already attempted by writers of no mean reputation, some of whom succeeded in convincing their readers that there is nothing more to be said about the matter; but even the richest materials fail to yield all that the historian requires. Again and again, however the frontier of knowledge may be advanced, the enquirer is confronted by darkness into which he cannot safely penetrate."[1] The frontier of knowledge has been advanced beyond the point where Gardiner left it, and yet the darkness surrounds the seeker after truth who strays but a little from the well-trodden highways of Stuart history. It is in the hope of illumining some portion of this outer darkness that we engage ourselves in the following pages with the story of a long-forgotten attempt to colonise some insignificant West Indian islands, and shall endeavour to show that light sought even thus far from the scene of great events, may yet aid us to see those events in a more balanced perspective and a little more in their own true colours.

In our enquiry it will be borne in upon us again and again that the history of English colonisation in the first half of the seventeenth century is peculiarly a part of the history of England itself; colonising attempts were

[1] Gardiner, *Fall of the Monarchy of Charles I*, I, p. v.

blessed or frowned upon according to the exigencies of European politics, the jealousies and rivalries of English courtiers or merchants involved similar rivalries of their servants abroad, and the quarrels that began at Whitehall or in Change Alley have swayed in a marked degree the destinies of colonists on the banks of the Chesapeake, in bleak New England, or among the tropic Caribbees. But, as in nature all action involves a reaction, so the course of English domestic politics under Charles I was materially influenced by the colonising schemes of the time. The leaders of the parliamentary opposition acquired their power of working harmoniously together in the joint schemes of colonisation that interested them; men who had for years discussed questions of policy round the board of a chartered company, were more capable of acting in concert than had they only met one another in the hunting field, upon the bench or during the rare and brief sessions of parliament. The work of the Long Parliament, that broke forever the power of absolute monarchy in England, and made possible Cromwell's schemes of world politics, was begun in the courts of the Virginia, the Saybrook, and the Providence companies. It is in connection with the story of the last of these, the Company of Adventurers to the Island of Providence, that we shall pursue an attempt to trace out once more some parts of the oft-told tale of the great Puritan migration, and to enter upon the little-explored field of West Indian history in the seventeenth century.

The story of the company that undertook the colonisation of the islands of Providence, Henrietta, and Association, and engaged in various attempts at trade and colonisation upon the mainland of Central America, is of interest from several points of view. The adventurers in the company included amongst their number almost every important member of the inner circle of leaders in opposition to the arbitrary rule of Charles I. The Earl of Warwick, Viscount Saye and Sele, and Lord Brooke took a most active part in the company's affairs throughout; John Pym was its treasurer and the prime mover in every design; while Sir Gilbert Gerrard, Sir Benjamin Rudyerd, and Sir Thomas Barrington, all active members of the Puritan party in the Long Parliament, were unremitting in their attention to its business. Other well-known names met with are those of Oliver St. John, John Gurdon, the intimate friend of John Winthrop, John Robartes, the Earl of Radnor of Charles II's reign, John Hampden, and Sir William Waller, and we shall find that the company provided an outlet for the energies of the parliament men who were thrust out from national affairs during the long eleven years of personal government. On the 2d of March, 1629, Charles I's third parliament was dissolved amid scenes of unprecedented violence and on the 28th of April, Sir Nathaniel Rich received from Bermuda the letter that led to the formation of the new company. On the 3d of November, 1640, the Long Parliament met and the last act of the great constitutional struggle began, while on the 28th of March, 1641, the last letters to Providence were signed, letters that were never to be received, for the island was taken by the Spaniards in May of the same year. The eleven years of the company's activity therefore coincide almost exactly with the eleven years of Charles I's autocracy. This coincidence will seem the more striking when we show that between 1636 and 1640 many of the plans of opposition to the government were matured in security under cloak of the company's meetings.

Through the history of the Providence Company and the allied designs of the Earl of Warwick in the West

Indies it is possible to trace the development of the Elizabethan tradition of hostility to Spain down to the capture of Jamaica in 1655 and the foundation on a firm basis of the West Indian empire, that during the eighteenth century was of such paramount importance to England. The semi-legal piracy that was carried on under the ægis of the company, connects the freebooting enterprises of Drake, Cumberland, and the Elizabethan sea-dogs with Cromwell's "Western Design," a plan that had its inspiration from the minds of Pym and of Warwick. Cromwell himself took no part in the work of the Providence Company, though there is no doubt that he was intimately acquainted with it. His aunt Joan was the mother of Sir Thomas Barrington, and some of his most intimate friends were deeply interested in the company's affairs; the Earl of Warwick was lord high admiral of the parliamentary fleet till 1649, while William Jessop, who had been secretary of the Providence Company, was clerk of the Council of State which took over the lord high admiral's functions after Warwick had resigned.

There is an intimate connection between the Providence Company and the strictly contemporary colonisation of New England. In its beginnings the Massachusetts enterprise was dependent for its influence with the ruling powers upon the members of the Providence Company. The original patent of the Saybrook settlement was issued to them, and, though in later years the company's aims and those of the rulers of Massachusetts were seen to be hopelessly divergent, it was through the Providence leaders that the principles which led to the Massachusetts migration were brought to bear upon the development of the English nation. It is possible to trace in the company's records the ideas of colonisation that animated the English country gentlemen who were the Puritan leaders, and the development of their design of founding a refuge for the Nonconformists from the Laudian persecution. The ideas of John White of Dorchester, expressed in widely circulated pamphlets and letters, commended themselves to the leaders as well as to the rank and file of the Puritans, but while the eyes of Warwick, Saye, Rich, and Pym were turned to the West Indies as the proper home for a Puritan colony, the leaders of the great migration, Winthrop and Dudley, whose names before 1630 were hardly known outside their immediate circle, dared to differ from their powerful friends and, defying precedent, directed the ever-swelling stream of emigrants to the shores of Massachusetts Bay, there to found rather a commonwealth than a colony.

We have concerning Providence a wealth of detail, which is lacking for the colonies in St. Christopher and Barbadoes. It is possible to trace the course of its development from the early ideal of the colony as a home for Englishmen to the realisation of a tropical plantation where all manual labour was performed by negro slaves for the profit of a few white planters, a plantation such as Barbadoes became, after the introduction of the cultivation of sugar on a commercial scale gave to the West Indies the profitable staple commodity that had so long been sought. Interest of a more personal character is not lacking from the records, which in many ways illuminate the views and aspirations of the time and especially those of John Pym, the great protagonist of the constitutional struggle, whose organising capacity and steadfastness of purpose guided the company in every emergency. Pym's life outside parliament has been very little studied, and it is of interest therefore to trace in these records the application of his views of statesmanship to the government of a colony, and to catch here and there a glimpse of his ideas concerning England's true foreign policy as the unrelenting opponent of Spanish power, ideas which his successor, Cromwell, was able to carry into effect when the times were propitious. The career of Robert Rich, Earl of Warwick, will also demand a share of our attention and rightly, for to him, perhaps more than to any of his contemporaries, is credit due for a persistence in colonising enterprise through good or evil fortune, that has written his name large in the records of every English colony of his time.

The story of the Providence Company falls naturally into two portions; from its foundation down to the year 1635 the company was endeavouring to build up a Puritan community, but at the same time by the raising of saleable crops to make a profit on the capital invested; in 1635 this design, having proved impracticable, was to a large extent abandoned and the colony became openly, what before it had been secretly, a base for privateering against the Spaniards. Our attention will first be directed to the circumstances that gave rise to the formation of the company and to the history of Providence as a Puritan settlement. As such it failed miserably, but its story is worth study from this point of view, if only as showing that Puritanism was not necessarily as successful a colonising force as might be supposed if New England only were considered. The second portion of our enquiry will be concerned with Providence as a centre of buccaneering enterprise and as a fortress whence were directed efforts to plant an English colony upon the mainland of Central America. The company's endeavours to found a Puritan colony during this period were at first directed to the banks of the Connecticut River, but, when they again proved unsuccessful, attempts were made to people the Central American colony from New England, and our attention must be directed to the resulting hostility of the rulers of Massachusetts to the English leaders of the Puritan party, a hostility which will show us how far even in those early days Massachusetts had diverged from the normal course of English development.

The sources of our information of the company's affairs may be briefly stated. The Providence Company and its efforts to colonise its islands and to establish English trade upon the mainland of Central America lasted, as we have seen, only for the eleven years from 1630 to 1641 and have been quite forgotten by succeeding generations. So much has this been the case that the chief colony, established upon the small island of Santa Catalina off the Moskito Coast, has, owing to its English name of Providence, been confused since the middle of the eighteenth century with the Island of New Providence in the Bahamas, the colonisation of which was not seriously undertaken till 1670. The earliest instance of confusion concerning the colony appears to occur in John Josselyn's *Account of two Voyages to New England,* published in 1675, where Providence is said to be one of the Somers or Bermuda Islands, and in the same author's *Chronological Observations of America,* the mistake occurs in a similar form.[2] In Hutchinson's *History of Massachusetts Bay,* published in 1760, the accounts of the dealings of New England with the Providence colony that had been derived from Hubbard's manuscript history of New England (1680), are misapplied to New Providence in the Bahamas.[3] The same con-

[2] *An Account of two Voyages into New England* by John Josselyn, London, 1675. *Chronological Observations of America,* London, 1673. Both reprinted in Mass. Hist. Soc. *Coll.,* 3d Series, Vol. III. See p. 381 under date 1637. "The Spaniards took the Island of Providence, one of the Summer Islands, from the English." Both date and position wrong.

[3] Hutchinson, *History of Massachusetts Bay,* London, 1760, p. 96, "The

fusion can also be traced in Churchill's *Voyages* (1763) and has passed thence into Pinkerton's *Voyages* (1810) and Southey's *Chronological History of the West Indies* (1827), though the latter speaks of the colony in some places as Santa Catarina or Old Providence,[4] and in others of it as New Providence in the Bahamas. The *Calendar of State Papers, Colonial,* 1574-1660, in which the records of the colony are calendared, continues the confusion and speaks throughout of the Bahamas, under which title the papers were then catalogued in the Public Record Office. From the *Calendar* the error has crept into many modern works which speak of the colonisation of the Bahamas as having taken place in 1630.[5] Owing to the enquiries of Major General Sir J. H. Lefroy, the author of the *Memorials of the Bermudas,* the true version of the matter was finally arrived at by W. N. Sainsbury, the editor of the *Calendar,* and placed on record in the *Athenæum,* May, 1876. He showed conclusively that the records of the company are quite inconsistent with the history of New Providence in the Bahamas, and that they refer to the island of Old Providence off the Moskito Coast, whose later occupation by the buccaneers in the reign of Charles II is well known. The Bahamas or Veajus Islands were included within the

Lords and others concerned in this attempt to settle the Bahama Islands spent £60,000.''

4 Southey, *Chronological History of the West Indies,* London, 1827, I, 279, ''1637. The English were in possession of Santa Catarina or Old Providence.'' I, 293, ''1641. The Spaniards attacked the English at New Providence.''

5 See for instance Cunningham, *Growth of British Industry. Modern Times,* I, 332 n. C. J. Hoadly, *The Warwick Patent.* The Acorn Club, Hartford, Conn., 1902. Brown, *Genesis of the United States,* II, 979, etc. Many difficulties arise in the short biographies annexed to this work from the confusion of Sa. Catalina with New Providence. See especially the life of Daniel Elfrith.

limits of Sir Robert Heath's Carolana patent of 1629, but no steps were taken for their colonisation.[6]

The records of the Providence Company are contained in two thick folio volumes preserved in the Public Record Office.[7] They are entitled respectively "Journal of the Governor and Company of Adventurers for the Plantation of the Island of Providence" and "Book of Entries of," etc., and contain, as these titles imply, minutes of the meetings held by the company and copies of the letters despatched to the colony. We have in the two volumes a complete and unbroken record in the greatest detail of the proceedings of the company from its foundation in 1630 to the capture of the island of Providence by the Spaniards in 1641 and the abandonment by the company of all its designs in the West Indies owing to the absorption of its moving spirit, John Pym, in the struggles of the Long Parliament and to his early death. It is suggested in the preface to the *Calendar of State Papers, Colonial,* 1574-1660, that the volumes were written most probably between 1640 and 1650, when several proceedings were being taken concerning the debts of the company. So far as the company's journal is concerned, this would appear to be correct, but the entry book of letters is written throughout in the hand of William Jessop, the secretary of the company, and it is annotated by him in the same way as his own private Letter Book, containing in shorthand the drafts of less important letters written to the colony and now preserved in the British Museum.[8] The volumes of the Historical MSS. Commission contain many references to the company and from them it is

[6] *C. S. P. Col.,* 30 Oct. 1629, Grant to Sir Robert Heath of a territory in America betwixt 31 and 36 degrees of North Latitude, "together with the Islands of Veajus or Bahamas and all other islands lying southerly or near upon the said continent."

[7] P. R. O., C. O. 124, 1 and 2.

[8] Brit. Mus., Add. MSS., 10615.

possible to throw some additional light upon its doings. From the Manchester Papers,[9] now in the Public Record Office, we learn something of the beginnings of the company as an offshoot from the Somers Islands Company, and among these papers are also preserved a few letters written from the islands to Sir Nathaniel Rich, or to Viscount Mandeville, the Earl of Manchester of the Civil War. Most of the extant letters from the colony in its early days are to be found among the Barrington MSS., now in the British Museum,[10] but once the property of Sir Thomas Barrington, for some time deputy governor of the company and one of the leaders of the parliamentary party in Essex during the Civil War. Scattered references to the company are also to be found among the Bouverie MSS.,[11] once the property of John Pym, and the Hulton MSS.,[12] which come to us from William Jessop, the secretary of the company and afterwards clerk to the Council of State and the Restoration House of Commons. Repeated references to the company and colony are to be found in the Winthrop Papers and Winthrop's Journal printed in the Collections of the Massachusetts Historical Society.[13] In the British Museum[14] is the manuscript Diary of Capt. Nathaniel Butler, who was governor of the colony in 1639 and this gives us in detail a picture of Providence as a privateering stronghold.

Printed references to the colony are not very numerous, but we hear of its beginnings in the diary of John

9 Very briefly calendared in Hist. MSS. Comm., *Eighth Report,* Appendix 2. In this study only the original papers themselves have been used.

10 Brit. Mus., Eg., 2643-51.

11 Hist. MSS. Comm., *Seventh Report,* Appendix.

12 *Ibid., Twelfth Report,* Appendix.

13 Mass. Hist. Soc. *Coll.,* 3d Series, Vol. IX, 4th Vols. VI and VII, 5th Vol. I, 6th Vol. III.

14 Brit. Mus., Sloane MSS., 758.

Rous (1625-1641),[15] and many details concerning the relations of the colonists with New England from Hubbard's history of Massachusetts.[16] Some light is thrown upon the later history of the colony by the life of the Rev. Mr. Leverton, a minister there, in Calamy's *Nonconformist's Memorial.*[17] The colony appeared to the Spaniards as a mere nest of pirates and their views concerning it can be gathered from Gage's *New Survey of the West Indies,*[18] written about 1638, but not published till later. Gage was himself an eyewitness of some of the piratical exploits of the Providence colonists, and had personal relations with those of them who had been taken prisoners by the Spaniards. Much light on the island's story is also thrown by the many Spanish MSS. relating to the West Indies preserved in the British Museum; some of these are originals,[19] while others are copies made from the originals at Simancas for the purposes of the Venezuelan Arbitration.[20] They include many letters from the Spanish officials in the Indies, bewailing the constant depredations of the English and Dutch corsairs and pleading for assistance to clear the Caribbean of their presence. Other Spanish sources of information are mentioned in the text. The only modern account of the company that affords reliable information is contained in Scott's learned work on joint stock companies,[21] where, for the first time, the importance of Providence in English colonial history is properly appreciated.

15 Camden Soc., Vol. XLII.

16 Printed in Mass. Hist. Soc. *Coll.*

17 Ed. Calamy, D. D., *The Nonconformist's Memorial.* Palmer's edition, 1802.

18 T. Gage, *The English American, his Travail by Sea and Land.* London 1648.

19 Especially in the Kingsborough Collection. Add. MSS., 13977, etc.

20 Venezuela Papers, Add. MSS., 36314-36327.

21 W. R. Scott, *Joint Stock Companies to 1720.* London 1911.

The island of Santa Catalina, or Providence, is situated off the eastern coast of Nicaragua upon the edge of the Moskito Bank about equidistant from Porto Bello, Cartagena, and the island of Jamaica, and lies very close to the track of vessels sailing from Porto Bello or Cartagena to Mexico and Havana. The island is about six miles long and four wide, and is described by Alcedo[22] as one of the best of the West India islands, notwithstanding its small size, as well from the salubrity of its climate as from its fertility. It is exceptionally easy of fortification, abounds in fine water, and is said to contain no serpent or venomous insect. It now forms part of the Republic of Colombia and is inhabited by a few hundred negroes. San Andreas or Henrietta, which was also granted by patent to the company, lies some sixty miles southwest of Providence and is about sixteen miles in length by four in width. It is a long, low island abounding in fine timber, but neither as easily fortifiable nor as fertile as Providence. It also is now a possession of the Republic of Colombia. Tortuga or Association, the third island which will concern us, lies off the northwest coast of the island of Hispaniola or Hayti, within a few miles of Cape San Nicolas and the entrance to the Windward Passage between Hispaniola and Cuba. It is surrounded by rocks and shoals, which render access to its fine harbour difficult. Tortuga had been a rendezvous for the rovers of all nations, at any rate since the time of Drake; from 1640 on it became the headquarters of buccaneering enterprise in the West Indies under the ægis of the French. It now forms a part of the negro republic of Hayti.

[22] A. de Alcedo, *Geographical and Historical Dictionary of America and the West Indies.* Transl. by G. A. Thompson, 5 vols., and *Atlas.* London 1812-1815.

CHAPTER I

BEGINNINGS OF ENGLISH COLONISATION

In August, 1604, the treaty of peace was signed that brought the long war between England and Spain to an end. War had been officially waged between the two powers since 1587, but ever since Hawkins' ill-fated voyage of 1567-1568 the preying of English privateers upon the Spanish shipping and towns in the West Indies had proved a constant source of profit to the merchants who financed them. Since the "Islands Voyage" of 1597 the war had remained in the hands of the privateers,[23] who were waxing ever bolder, and their daring attacks both on the coast of Spain and in the East and West Indies had been returning handsome profits to their owners. The romance of their bolder strokes, so vividly described in the pages of Hakluyt and Purchas, must not blind us to the fact that in the main this privateering was a sordid and prosaic business, which was expected to return its proper percentage of profits to the owners without involving an unnecessary amount of risk. The settled policy of the Spanish government to regard the Indies as the private property of the crown involved of necessity the official view that every foreigner, or, for that matter, every unauthorised Spaniard, found within the Indies was to be looked upon as a trespasser and a robber. But the Spanish fleets that formed the only authorised means of communication between the Indies and Europe were to a considerable extent navigated by Flemings and by Englishmen, who thus acquired a thor-

23 Sir J. K. Laughton in *Camb. Mod. Hist.*, III, 327.

ough acquaintance with American waters and had many friends in every port. The unofficial Spaniard, therefore, could not brand all foreigners as criminals and in many instances we find a considerable amount of good feeling existing between the Spanish colonists and the visitors to their shores. In the last years of the war period the greater part of the Spanish shipping had been driven from the sea and only very small profits would have been returned by mere privateering. A far more profitable way of employing capital was to carry out from Europe a full cargo of manufactured goods to be disposed of secretly in the Indies either to Spaniards or to the natives, and to return laden with the tropical products for which they had been exchanged. An even more prosaic trade which reached large dimensions about 1600, was the carrying of salt to Europe from Punta Araya on the coast of Venezuela. The ships, both Dutch and English, came out laden with goods for barter and after disposing of them met at the great salt pans some fifty miles from Margarita, where their holds were filled with salt, which was then conveyed to England and to Flanders and sold at an excellent profit. Between June, 1602, and May, 1603, one hundred and seventy-two salt vessels and thirty barter vessels of large size came to Araya, and at one time in January, 1603, sixty salt vessels and four barter vessels were lading salt at one time,[24] thus showing that the trade had reached large dimensions.

With the conclusion of peace, the facilities for fitting out these ships in English ports and the ease of disposal of their cargoes on their return were at an end. King

[24] Venezuela Papers, Add. MSS., 36318, fo. 191. Governor of Cumana to King. The letters from the Indies abound with complaints of the clandestine trade. Far more harm was done to the royal revenue by this barter than by all the more shown exploits of Cumberland, Parker, and Sherley.

James, it was well known, regarded the war as at once concluded by his accession, for as king of Scotland he had always been on terms of peace and amity with the Spanish crown. The terms of the treaty itself were a complete surrender of the English right of trade to the Indies,[25] the recognition of which Elizabeth had always insisted upon as a necessary condition of peace. It was no longer possible for a reputable merchant to engage openly in the West Indian trade and large amounts of capital began to be withdrawn and turned to other uses. Capt. John Smith, writing in 1629, puts the matter clearly: "After the death of our most gracious Queen Elizabeth of blessed memory, our Royal King James, who from his infancy had reigned in peace with all Nations, had no employment for those men-of-war, so that those that were rich, rested with that they had; those that were poor and had nothing but from hand to mouth, turned Pirates; some, because they had got much wealth; some, for that they could not get their due; some, that had lived bravely, would not abase themselves to poverty; some vainly, only to get a name; others for revenge, covetousness or as ill; and as they found themselves more and more oppressed, their passions increasing with discontent made them turn Pirates."[26] That a very large increase of the evil of piracy ensued after the signing of the peace may be very roughly proved from the *Calendar of State Papers, Domestic.* In the four years, 1603-1607, only eleven mentions of piracy occur and most of these are concerned with the granting of pardons to English sailors accused of technical piracy against French and Venetian ships. In the four years, 1607-1610, piracy is mentioned twenty-eight times and mostly in connection with outrages on English ships. So acute

[25] *Camb. Mod. Hist.,* III, 537.
[26] Smith's *Works* (ed. Arber), p. 914.

had the evil become in 1609 that a royal commission was appointed to find some means of putting a stop to the pirates' depredations. Many of the more far-seeing London merchants had long realised the precariousness of privateering enterprise and had endeavoured to engage solely in legitimate trade,[27] but others in alliance with men of high rank such as George Clifford, Earl of Cumberland, had expended in it large amounts of capital and had organised what were in reality small navies, most of the ships sailing under the English flag, but others under that of the states of Holland or of Zeeland. One of the foremost of the wealthy men of high rank engaged in schemes of this description, was Lord Rich, who had numbers of ships always at sea. The cessation of hostilities between England and Spain made little difference to his fleet, which merely changed its letters of marque from English to Dutch and made its home ports Middleburg or Flushing instead of the port of London.[28] When the twelve years' truce of 1609 suspended hostilities between the States and Spain and withdrew Dutch letters of marque, Rich's operations continued as before, but under different colours, and some years later we find his ships sailing the Channel with commissions from the Duke of Savoy and still returning a handsome profit to their owner.[29]

The withdrawal of the greater part of the English capital invested in privateering set it free for employment in other directions, and the first five years of the seventeenth century saw the despatch of many private

[27] Cunningham, *English Industry, Mod. Times*, I, 70.

[28] The many ramifications of the schemes of the Rich family lie beyond the scope of this enquiry, but sidelights will be thrown on their later developments in subsequent chapters. From at any rate 1600 onwards the Rich family always had a commercial agent at Middleburg or Amsterdam.

[29] Hist. MSS. Comm., *Fourth Report*. *C. S. P. Dom.*, 1609-1618. *C. S. P. East Indies*, 1617-1621, p. lxxxvi.

expeditions for exploration to the Northwest, mostly financed by the merchants who had fitted out the expeditions of the late sixteenth century;[30] the acute economic difficulties of the time, caused by the growth of population, induced publicists like Popham to join hands with these great merchants and to suggest that the time was now propitious for the carrying out of the ideas of colonisation that had so long been expounded by Gilbert and Raleigh. It is to this conjunction of interests that the founding of the Plymouth and London Companies for Virginia was due.

Previous attempts at English colonisation had been made in each of three directions, and it is of interest to note that geographical conditions had a good deal to do with the location of the first successful colony. In 1600 the shores of the American continents were inhabited by Europeans in three regions separated by enormous stretches of unexplored coast; the Hispano-Portuguese empire of Brazil was divided from the Spanish territory round the Caribbean by the no man's land of Guiana. The shores of the Caribbean and the islands of the Antilles were all occupied in a loose kind of way by the Spanish power or rendered inaccessible by the presence of the fierce and cannibal Caribs, while to the northward Florida, the scene of the long-remembered massacre of Ribault and Laudonnière's Huguenot colonists, was sundered by Raleigh's deserted Virginia from the regions round the Gulf of St. Lawrence, where the French fur-traders were beginning to found a regular trade with the Indians, and where Newfoundland was already a temporary home for fishermen of all the northern nations. The route to all these regions, save the last, was in the main the same; coasting down the shores of Spain and Africa till Cape Cantin was reached,

30 Kingsbury, *Introd. to Records of Va. Co.*, p. 14.

a course was made for the Canaries[31] and thence, after watering, a due westerly course was steered for the Island of Deseada or for Dominica. For Brazil a south-westerly course from the Canaries was taken.[32] The direct and more northerly route to Virginia was only discovered by Argall in 1614 and was not regularly used until some years after that date. The homeward course by the Gulf stream lay through the Florida Channel and across by the Azores, so that the shores of Virginia would be the last point seen upon the American continent. Gilbert's attempts at colonisation had followed the northerly fishing route to Newfoundland[33] and were long remembered for the extreme hardships that had been encountered; Raleigh, however, had taken the usual southern course and had endeavoured to plant his colonies either in Guiana, the first unoccupied portion of the mainland met with, or in Virginia, the last left. Now we shall show later that, notwithstanding Raleigh's double failure in Guiana, repeated efforts were made by Englishmen to establish trading stations there during the early years of the seventeenth century, though the conditions were too precarious to attract the attention of the larger capitalists, who had to keep King James's pro-Spanish predilections in view. England could show a plausible claim of right to Virginia by the ancient discoveries of the Cabots, and the region was more attractive to the merchant adventurers as affording a hope of discovery of the long-sought channel leading westward into the Sea of Cathay. It was Virginia that was therefore chosen with the royal sanction as the scene of the new effort at colonisation.

The two branches of the Virginia Company received

[31] Hakluyt's *Voyages* (Everyman Edition), VII, 246.
[32] Purchas's *Pilgrims* (Maclehose's Edition), XVI, 179.
[33] Hakluyt, VI, 8.

their patents from the king in April, 1606,[34] and the London Company, among whose members were most of the merchants in whom we are interested,[35] and notably Sir Thomas Smythe and the Riches, at once took steps to fit out a pioneer expedition. The North Virginia Company contained fewer men of practical business experience and soon fell into a moribund condition, but the London Company succeeded by 1609 in enlisting in their work the sympathies of almost every rank of society. Englishmen saw in the new colony the only means open to them of continuing the efforts to curb the overweening power of Spain, that had been abandoned by King James and his advisers, but this widespread interest soon failed before the prosaic difficulties of the undertaking, and before long the management of the company's affairs fell into the hands of a small number of men of high rank and of a group of well-to-do London merchants, many of whom had long been interested in privateering enterprises. The Spanish ministers regarded the Virginia colony as a perfidious device of the English government for continuing English piratical enterprise in defiance of the recently concluded treaty, and we can read in the letters of the Spanish officials[36] the same complaints against the new colony that had so often been penned from Venezuela and the same suggestions for nipping the infant community in the bud.[37]

Lying directly in the path of ships northward bound

[34] Brown, *Genesis of the United States*, I, 52-62.

[35] Kingsbury, *Introd. to Records of Va. Co.*, p. 14.

[36] Brown, *Genesis*, I, *passim*.

[37] Add. MSS., 36317, fo. 372. Diego Suarez de Amaya, Governor of Cumana, writes to the King on Dec. 8, 1600, suggesting that the salt at Punta Araya should be poisoned in order to destroy the Dutch and English pirates wholesale. Zuniga repeatedly suggested that the whole of the Virginia colonists should be wiped out to avoid further growth of the colony.

through the Florida Channel, the Bermuda Islands had had an evil reputation throughout the sixteenth century as a place of storms, and were in consequence always avoided by mariners. But after Sir George Somers's shipwreck there in July, 1609, and the subsequent furnishing of Virginia with much-needed provisions, the islands were claimed as lying within the grant of the Virginia Company and as forming a likely field for colonisation. Their importance was so little appreciated, however, that the active members of 1612 bought out the Virginia Company's rights and formed a fresh company of only one hundred and twenty adventurers to undertake the plantation. The new company entered on its operations with vigour and secured a fresh charter on June 29, 1615.[38]

For some years matters proceeded smoothly in both companies, the most active part in their management being taken by those who had, along with the Rich family, an interest in pseudo-privateering enterprise in the West Indies. Gradually, however, we find that two factions were forming in the companies and by 1619 matters were rapidly moving to an open breach.

In May, 1619, Sir Thomas Smythe, who, as treasurer, had been the executive head of the Virginia Company since its foundation, was displaced and Sir Edwin Sandys was elected in his stead.[39] The complete story of this quarrel in the Virginia Company has never yet been written from the standpoint of the Warwick faction, and we can here only deal with those aspects of it that bear directly upon our subject. It must be noted, however, that Sir Thomas Smythe and his supporters represented the privileged merchants of the Merchant Adventurers, the East India, the Turkey, and other

[38] *C. S. P. Col.*, 1574-1660, p. 17.
[39] *C. S. P. Dom.*, 1619, p. 44.

companies who believed in carrying on Elizabethan traditions and had been interested in privateering in earlier years, while Sandys had, since his chairmanship of the Commons committee on the free trade bills of 1604,[40] definitely committed himself to hostility to the privileged companies. Personal rivalries and family feuds were to a considerable extent responsible for the ranging of the aristocratic members of the company on opposite sides and for their bitterness one against another.[41]

Sir Thomas Smythe after his displacement still retained the leadership of the Somers Islands Company, but this did nothing to assuage ill-feeling, and Alderman Johnson, one of his warmest supporters in the City of London, attempted to organize an attack upon Sandys, the new Virginia treasurer. He did not secure much support at first and was censured by a committee of the Virginia Company held at Southampton House[42] on July 8, 1619, of which both the Earl of Warwick and Sir Nathaniel Rich were members. About the beginning of 1620, however, rumours began to spread abroad of some mysterious exploit against the Spaniards achieved by a certain Capt. Daniel Elfrith in a ship called the *Treasurer;* Elfrith seems to have been in a sense acting under the orders of Capt. Samuel Argall, who had been

40 Hewins, *Trade and Finance in the 17th Century,* ch. III.

41 The groupings of the parties in the quarrel recall the scandal that divided society into two hostile camps in the previous generation. Penelope Devereux, Lady Rich, Warwick's mother, lived for years in open adultery with Charles Blount, Earl of Devonshire, and the bitterest hostility reigned between her legitimate offspring and the children of her illicit union, of whom the eldest, Mountjoy Blount, afterwards Earl of Newport, was received into high favour at court in 1617. Southampton, Sackville, and the Cavendishes sided with the Blounts and it seems to be a legitimate hypothesis to assume that this added another to the many causes of the quarrel.

42 Manch. Pap., nos. 250, 251.

governor of Virginia and was using the Earl of Warwick's name as a bolster to his unwarrantable actions.[43] Elfrith brought his vessel to Bermuda in an unseaworthy condition and with her a number of negroes. That the Earl of Warwick was not entirely unconnected with the *Treasurer's* piratical proceedings can be seen by a letter written to him from Bermuda by his protégé, Capt. Nathaniel Butler, the governor, to the effect that he had disposed of his lordship's negroes according to instructions, but that the *Treasurer's* people were dangerous-tongued fellows and had given out secretly that, if they were not paid to their uttermost penny of wages, they "would go to the Spanish Ambassador and tell all."[44] It is a mistake to suppose with some modern writers that anything very terrible lay behind this threat and that the mariners of the *Treasurer* and her sister ship, the *Neptune,* were bloodthirsty ruffians of the type of the legendary Capt. Kidd, sailing beneath the skull and cross-bones and ready for any deed of darkness. The Spanish ambassador of the time was Diego Sarmiento d'Acuña, Conde de Gondomar; in 1620 the broken thread of negotiation for the Spanish Match had just been picked up, and King James was ready to do anything to propitiate the Spanish monarchy. Only two years before, Raleigh, in spite of the semi-approval with which James had regarded his proceedings, had been sent to the block on a similar charge of piracy, and a threat of disclosure, therefore, was no idle one.

The council of the Virginia Company was informed by Capt. Yeardley, the governor, that the *Treasurer,* which was admitted to be the Earl of Warwick's property, was supposed to have "gone to rob the King of

[43] Manch. Pap., no. 262, 20 Jan., 1620.

[44] *Ibid.,* 9 Oct., 1620, no. 275. A very full list of the documents connected with this affair is contained in Kingsbury's *Rec. of Va. Co.*

Spain's subjects in the West Indies by direction from my Lord of Warwick."[45] Sir Edwin Sandys and the council agreed that it was necessary to communicate the information to the Privy Council, but only after having "first blotted my Lord of Warwick's name out of the letters." No action was taken at the time and the Warwick party succeeded in hushing matters up. Further letters arrived from Virginia with details as to the ship's proceedings derived from one of the crew, who had been left behind in the colony; Sandys at once, on receipt of these depositions, reopened the matter by assembling the council and persuading them to acquaint the Spanish ambassador and the lords of the Privy Council with the facts. This step was bitterly resented by the other side, for its effect was "to put upon my Lord of Warwick suddenly ere he was aware," a confiscation of the ship and goods. The quarrel was henceforward irreconcilable, and now became a matter of common scandal.

Things were going none too well with the Somers Islands Company. Daniel Tucker, the first governor, was superseded in 1619 in consequence of his constant disagreements with the adherents of Sir Nathaniel Rich and the Warwick party, and Capt. Nathaniel Butler, one of Warwick's followers, was sent back to the islands as governor; the two factions in the colony were always quarrelling and constant accusations were made against the governor of fostering pirates, most of whom seem to have pretended to hold commissions from the Prince of Orange, the familiar old commissions of the "Sea-beggars." Space will not admit of an examination of the rights and wrongs of the case, but Butler's dealings with a Spanish wreck in 1621 provided specific grounds of complaint and Gondomar, much to the satisfaction of the Sandys party, appealed to the Somers Islands Com-

[45] Manch. Pap., no. 279.

pany[46] and the Privy Council for redress. This appeal and the news of the terrible massacre of the Virginia colonists that reached England in July, 1622,[47] determined the king and his ministers that something was radically wrong and a complete enquiry into the affairs of both companies was ordered April 13, 1623. A variety of evidence was brought before the commission of enquiry, on one side by the Earl of Southampton, Lord Cavendish, Sir Edward Sackville, afterwards Earl of Dorset, Sandys, and the Ferrars, and on the other by the Earl of Warwick, Sir Nathaniel Rich, Sir Thomas Smythe, and Alderman Johnson. After a long and careful investigation, the Virginia Company's charter was surrendered October 20, 1623, and the colony taken under the direct management of the crown, very much to its own benefit. Attempts were made to reopen the matter in the House of Commons, but these were put an end to by a royal message, to the general satisfaction. The Somers Islands Company was permitted to continue along the old lines, and the struggle for control was maintained with varying fortunes, each succeeding treasurer reversing the policy of his predecessor and sending out a fresh governor.

It has been necessary to enter on this very brief outline of the quarrel in the two companies, because to it the genesis of the Providence Company can be traced. The orthodox view concerning the quarrel and the ensuing surrender of the Virginia Company's charter, as expressed by Doyle and other writers, is entirely hostile to the Warwick faction and represents them as mere tools of the court. This is far too simple an explanation of the matter, and the causes would appear to be more complex, for the careers both of Warwick and

[46] *C. S. P. Col.*, 1574-1660, p. 27. 6 Feb., 1622.
[47] *Ibid.*, p. 31. 13 July, 1622.

Sir Thomas Smythe are completely opposed to their assumed subserviency. The idea that in the two factions we have in embryo the parties of the Civil War[48] is almost grotesque, for in truth, as our subsequent pages will show, there were no more ardent opponents of an absolutist régime and no stronger or more definite Puritans than were the Earl of Warwick and Sir Nathaniel Rich, the so-called "subservient tools" of the court. Neither side in the quarrel could claim a monopoly of virtue and it is a mistake to allow the connection of the Earl of Southampton with Shakespeare, the legendary saintliness of the character of Nicholas Ferrar, or the high spirit of Sir Edwin Sandys to blind us to the many solid merits of Sir Thomas Smythe, Sir Nathaniel Rich, Gabriel Barber, and their other opponents.

The abandonment of the West Indian trade after the conclusion of peace in 1604 by the more prominent English merchants did not by any means bring to an end English dealings in Guiana and the Caribbean. Clandestine trade was still carried on and to such an extent as to involve the Spanish authorities in continual anxiety. The vessels engaged in the trade, however, were now of small burthen and were equipped and set forth mainly from Irish ports and from Barnstaple and Dartmouth, where there was less likelihood of coming into conflict with the authorities than in ports nearer the seat of government. So great was the damage done to Spanish commerce that in 1607 the cultivation of tobacco was forbidden in the provinces of Caracas and Venezuela for

[48] This idea has astonishing vitality. In the recently published "England in America" (Vol. 4 of *The American Nation,* p. 76) the author speaks of the "Court" party with Sir Robert Rich at its head, while the "Country" or "*patriot*" party is led by Southampton, Sandys, and Ferrar. For a juster view of the matter see Scott's *Joint Stock Companies to 1720,* II, 269-287.

ten years owing to the large numbers of English and Dutch who were attracted to purchase it.[49] Little effect was produced by the prohibition, for from 1610 to 1620 the Island of Trinidad seems to have been a regular emporium for the illicit tobacco trade,[50] and firms like the Reskeimers of Dartmouth, the Delbridges of Barnstaple, and, on a larger scale, the Courteens of Middleburg made large sums in the trade. Nor did the trade with the Indians languish; repeated attempts to found English trading stations on the Guiana rivers were made and it has been shown[51] that such Dutch firms as the Courteens were building up a perfect network of trade-routes in the interior of South America. Leigh's colony upon the Wiapoco in 1604-1606 was a disastrous failure,[52] but Sir Thomas Roe saw the beginnings of his life of adventure in a couple of years' trading (1606-1607) upon the Guiana coast and several of the pioneer Virginia colonists gained their experience with him in exploring the swamps of the Wiapoco and the Cuyuni.[53] Robert Harcourt in 1608 obtained a patent from Henry, Prince of Wales, and set sail from Dartmouth with ninety-seven men to attempt a trading colony on the Wiapoco;[54] the attempt was a failure and in 1610 the remaining colonists were scattered among the Indians, and for eight or nine years subsisted in native fashion and with occasional supplies obtained from the Dutch.[55] Raleigh's last voyage in 1617 ended, as is well known, in utter disaster,

49 Venezuela Papers, Add. MSS., 36319, fo. 141. Sancho de Aljuiza to the King. June 15, 1607.

50 Add. MSS., 36319, *passim.*

51 G. Edmundson, Arts. in *Eng. Hist. Rev.*, 1896-1903.

52 For an account of this attempt see Purchas, XVI, 316 sqq.

53 Smith's *Works*, p. 896, and Brown, *Genesis of United States*, I, 375, re Roe's voyage of 1610.

54 Purchas, XVI, 358.

55 Smith, p. 897.

but the breaking off of the Spanish negotiations in 1618 and the downfall of the king's pro-Spanish favourites, the Howards, seemed to the Earl of Warwick and his associates a propitious opportunity to undertake the colonisation of Guiana in a more ambitious way than had before been tried. The company undertaking the project was largely organised by Warwick,[56] a patent for the colony was obtained[57] and Capt. Roger North, brother of Lord North and Warwick's cousin, was despatched to Guiana with one hundred and twenty men; there they joined forces with the remnant of Harcourt's colonists and tobacco planting was begun. But, early in 1620, Gondomar returned to England, the broken thread of negotiation for the Spanish Match was taken up, and on May 7, 1620,[58] Warwick was ordered by the Privy Council to deliver up the commission on which North had sailed and compelled to disavow his proceedings. Gondomar's protests to King James were so effective that on North's return to England in December, 1620, to secure fresh supplies he was imprisoned in the Tower and his goods confiscated. His men, abandoned in Guiana, dispersed themselves among the Indians or joined forces with the Dutch. Among the colonists thus abandoned was one Thomas Warner,[59] who, having remained in Guiana about two years, returned to England by way of the Caribbee Islands with two companions. Watering at St. Christopher on the homeward voyage, Warner became friendly with Togreman, the Carib chief

[56] *C. S. P. Dom.*, 30 April, 1619, Locke to Carleton.

[57] *C. S. P. Col.*, 30 April, 1619, p. 21.

[58] *Acts of Privy Council, Col.*, I, 36.

[59] The outline of Warner's proceedings in the text is based upon three sources of authority: Smith's account, 1629, *Works*, p. 898 sqq., John Hilton's account, 1675, Brit. Mus., Eg., 2395, fo. 503; and Sloane MSS., 3662, fo. 45a, written by Major Scott, 1667. For a discussion of the reliability of this last authority, see Edmundson, *Eng. Hist. Rev.* (1901), XVI, 640.

of the island; on his return to England he succeeded in securing some capital from one Merrifield, a merchant interested in the clandestine West Indian trade, and with fourteen companions sailed at the end of 1622 for Virginia and thence to St. Christopher, where they commenced planting tobacco on January 28, 1623.[60] Warner's small band lived in amity with the Caribs for some time, but difficulties at length arose, and it was only by a series of fortunate happenings that the infant colony was saved from destruction. To secure assistance against the Caribs,[61] Warner acquiesced in the division of the island between his men and a band of Frenchmen under D'Esnambuc, who had landed there not long after him.

The breaking off of the Spanish Match in 1623 and Buckingham's hostility to Spain removed the difficulties that had lain in the way of early colonising attempts. The foundation of the Dutch West Indian Company in 1621 put into practice the ideas of colonisation at the expense of Spain as opposed to freebooting that Willem Usselincx had so long been urging and its early success pointed out to the general public both in England and France that the West Indies offered a profitable field for colonisation. Within a month or so of the rupture with Spain we find Secretary Conway proposing[62] that a colonising enterprise should be undertaken in the West Indies in concert with Holland in order to draw off idle people from the kingdom without cost to the king. In April, 1625, Sir John Coke proposed to the king[63] to

60 Smith, p. 900.

61 This is the version of the story given in 1675 by one of the first English settlers. (Eg., 2395, fo. 509.) A good deal of dispute raged in 1675 about the whole sequence of these events, but the facts appear to be as given. Du Tertre is our authority on the French side.

62 *C. S. P. Dom.*, 1623, no. 64.

63 *Ibid.*, 14 April, 1625.

incorporate a company for defence and protection in the West Indies and to develop English trade thither; in the same month Attorney General Heath drew up a memorandum[64] for Charles I, stating that it was neither safe nor profitable for the Spaniards and Dutch to be absolute lords of the West Indies and suggesting English intervention, either openly or underhand. Preparations for the war with Spain were now in full swing and any suggestions for weakening the Spanish power were listened to by Charles and Buckingham with the utmost readiness. Among the Clarendon State Papers[65] there has been preserved a remarkable plan, presented to Buckingham by a fugitive Spaniard, showing how England, without the expenditure of much capital, might found an English empire in the heart of the Spanish Indies. There are reasons for supposing that the plan was introduced to Buckingham's notice by Warwick's mediation, and we have here probably the first germ of some of the ideas animating the Providence Company a few years later. Among the bustle of the war preparations no steps could be taken for a West Indian expedition, but the change of circumstances now made it easy for adventurous spirits to find capitalists ready to finance their colonising schemes. Warner returned to England in September, 1625, and with Ralph Merrifield obtained from the crown letters patent[66] for the colony of St. Christopher, and for the colonisation of Nevis, Barbadoes, and Montserrat; in the same year, Capt. John Powell in the *William and John* with thirty settlers financed by Sir William Courteen, made the first permanent English settlement in Barbadoes.

When grants and privileges had to be obtained from

[64] *C. S. P. Col.*, [April] 1625, p. 73.
[65] *Clar. State Pap.*, vol. I.
[66] *C. S. P. Col.*, 1574-1660, 13 Sept., 1625.

the crown, it was useful to have on one's side a persona grata at court; Merrifield and Warner succeeded in interesting in their cause James Hay, the Earl of Carlisle, and 1626 saw the grant of rights of government over the whole of the Caribbee Islands to the earl, who at once took effective steps to enforce his rights. In 1627 he and the merchants associated with him despatched several emigrants and a store of ordnance to St. Christopher and the first English colony in the West Indies was fairly launched. Courteen, not to be outdone, secured the patronage of Lord Treasurer Ley, Earl of Marlborough, for his colony in Barbadoes, but in 1627 a wholesale grant covering many islands was bestowed upon the lord chamberlain, Philip, Earl of Montgomery, and considerable confusion ensued. The further fortunes of these grants and of the colonies established in virtue of them need not detain us here, but we shall have to return to the early history of St. Christopher and Nevis in a later chapter.

Between 1623 and 1628 the affairs of the Somers Islands Company had been steadily going from bad to worse; John Bernard, the governor sent out in 1622 to investigate Capt. Butler's proceedings, died within a few weeks of his arrival, and his successor, John Harrison, a nominee of the Sandys faction, only held office for a year (1623). He was succeeded by Capt. Henry Woodhouse (1623-1626), and he again by Capt. Philip Bell, a man of good family and an adherent of the Warwick party. Constant complaints were received in England of the monopolist proceedings of the company's agents, who bought the planters' produce cheap and sold in return the necessaries of life at exorbitant rates, while the company were engaged in a perpetual struggle with a merchant, John Delbridge of Barnstaple, who desired to secure the right of trade to the islands without paying the very high license duties demanded. The colonists at length in 1628 appealed to the House of Commons for redress and a committee of enquiry was appointed numbering among its members John Pym,[67] whose name now appears for the first time in connection with colonial affairs. The committee prepared a petition to the king in the colonists' favour, but little appears to have come of it save an order of the Privy Council for an abatement of the tobacco duty in favour of the adventurers.

On April 28, 1629, Sir Nathaniel Rich, one of the most active members of the Somers Islands Company, received from Capt. Philip Bell, the governor of the islands, a long and closely written letter[68] of four quarto pages. The writer expresses grief and surprise that he had been blamed by the company at home without having had an opportunity of defending himself. He describes the many difficulties against which he has had to contend and the factions existing in Bermuda, and then proceeds to the main business of his letter. This is of so much importance in our enquiry that his words must be reproduced *in extenso:*

> Now to the main business I come without further interruption, which is that two of your ships, the "Earl of Warwick" and the "Somers Islands" are now returning home again and in the "Earl of Warwick" is Daniel Elfrith himself coming, who hath put himself out of his own ship into it because she hath neither captain nor master left for her safe conduct home. The other is furnished still with the full company that brought her out, though no present purchase is returned according to hopeful expectation, for it was unhappily lost and missed of. Capt. Cammock with thirty odd men is left upon an island called St. Andreas, which is a very fertile and hopeful place and such as is hoped will give the adventurers good satisfaction.

67 *C. S. P. Col.*, 19 June, 1628.
68 Manch. Pap., no. 416.

Notwithstanding his own [Elfrith's] island, which was pointed and aimed at, he hath yet reserved undiscovered to himself. So I put it only into my Lord's own hands and yours with such selected friends and companions as shall be thought worthy to be made partakers thereof. For he doth absolutely refuse and resolve the whole company [the Somers Is. Company] shall never more have to do with him, in respect of their ingratitude towards him for his pains and endeavors already past.

The name of it [the island] is Kathalina and [it] lies not above 20 or 30 leagues from the other where his men are left, but it differs much from that place both in the pleasantness and rich fertility of the soil, and, which is very material, half the charge will fortify this and make it invincible, which must go to the other where they are. Neither indeed can that possibly ever be made half so strong, but which is notwithstanding hopeful because freer from enemies and more out of harm's way and all danger.[69]

There is another island, called Fonceta,[70] which lies some 100 leagues to the eastwards of the Caribbee Islands and out of all the Spaniards roads and ways, which by the report of some Indians, which once strayed from thence and could never find it again, as also of some seamen who once touched there and Daniel Elfrith did afterwards speak withal; it is one of the bravest and most fertile islands in the world, having according to the pilot three fair rivers in it, and is likewise well fortified and encompassed with rocks and shoals for defence against all enemies. This island I have set Daniel Elfrith in resolution to discover, which may be done in sending to the other islands without any further charge or trouble worth the speaking of, being not above 80 leagues out of the way [the way from Bermuda to Santa Catalina], which in all likelihood will not be above four or five days' sail at the most, and so if he can find the island, as neither I nor himself do make any question, and if he find it answerable to report and our expectation, then he may

69 San Andreas lies further up on the great Moskito Bank than does Santa Catalina. Bell means that it lies more out of the track of ships from Cartagena.

70 Mythical, see below, pp. 132-134.

stay and settle with his men and provisions there without going further. But if either he or the place should fail of our hopes, then, without any prejudice at all, he may proceed forwards to the island which cannot fail, and which he knows as perfectly as needs to be, and than this island already known none can be more fruitful or more hopeful, but yet it lying in the heart of the Indies and the mouth of the Spaniards and the other lying far from both, it [Fonceta] is therefore much to be preferred before it, and there is neither of them but in short time [could] be made more rich and bountiful either by tobacco or any other commodities than double or treble any man's estate in all England; though they should utterly fail of any gold or silver mines, which notwithstanding is very hopeful, they may be enriched withal.

And as for this island, the strength and work of the land doth so much decrease and decay daily that in a short time it will be of very small value or profit, especially so much tobacco now being planted and being brought home of better quality and from richer climates and plantations, and I make a question whether this will shortly be worth anything at all. For my part, therefore, though I shall be willing for my credit's sake and the country's good, but also for the propagation of the Gospel and the service of my good God, to stay here yet one, two or three years longer if my Lord [Warwick] and yourself [Rich] shall think fit so to dispose and command me, yet longer than that same [I am] absolutely unwilling. For one year in one of those places will be more profitable than seven years here, and I am resolved that in which of those islands Daniel Elfrith shall settle his good liking and abode, that there will I settle my abode with him likewise, for out of his part of the land in both he hath promised a good proportion to myself as a portion with his daughter.

In the way and means of proceeding I have likewise delivered my opinion to my Lord, as first that Daniel Elfrith's own advice in everything may be followed, that he may be set out in a ship or two belonging solely to my Lord, yourself and such special friends, that things may be carried and done with all possible secrecy. That my Lord may get the patent of Fonceta, or rather of both, before they be discovered, which will be easily obtained and will take away all the claim and opposition of my Lord of Carlisle or any other. And thus having contracted and finished my matter and room together, I will conclude all and myself.

Your really affected friend and servant

PHILIP BELL.

Gov. Bell addressed this most important letter to Sir Nathaniel Rich as second in command and business head of the Warwick faction, whose connection with the Virginia and Somers Islands companies has already been noticed. Their interest in colonial affairs had been heightened during the years 1625 to 1629 by many causes, and Bell's letter arrived in England at a moment when the future government of the English race lay in the balance. What were the conditions governing this critical position, can be most properly considered if the career of the head of the Warwick party, Robert Rich, second Earl of Warwick, is examined.

Robert Rich, eldest son of the third Lord Rich and great-grandson of Richard, first Lord Rich, Chancellor of the Court of Augmentations to Henry VIII, afterwards lord chancellor, and the founder of the family fortunes, was born in 1587 and educated at Emmanuel College, the principal Puritan college at Cambridge under Elizabeth, where he was a contemporary of the celebrated Puritan, John Preston. He represented Maldon in the parliaments of 1610 and 1614, and succeeded his father as second Earl of Warwick in 1619. The anti-Spanish schemes of the Rich family rendered them distasteful to James I, but the hitch in the negotiations for the Spanish Match in 1618 was marked by the bestowal of the earldom of Warwick upon the third Lord Rich;

Robert Rich's strong Puritan leanings made court life distasteful to him and his attention was very early directed to colonial ventures, to which he was drawn by his interest in the privateering enterprises of his family. He was, as has been shown, an active member of the Virginia Company and in 1614 became one of the original members of the Somers Islands Company. In 1618 he possessed fourteen shares in the company and one of the divisions of the islands was called Warwick Tribe in his honour; in 1616 he and his father fitted out two ships and despatched them with a Savoy commission[71] on a roving voyage to the East Indies. Their seizure of a ship, worth £100,000, belonging to the Great Mogul, and its recapture by an East India Company's ship, involved Rich in a long dispute with the company, but this and other subsequent disputes did not prevent his active participation in their enterprises, and we find him a constant attendant at the company's courts and repeatedly borrowing from the stock ordnance and stores for his ships.[72]

In 1618 Warwick became one of the original members of the Guinea Company, newly incorporated to engage in the profitable traffic in African negroes. In the same year the *Treasurer,* commanded by Daniel Elfrith, was fitted out and provided with a Savoy commission as a man-of-war. She carried to Virginia the first cargo of negroes ever sold there and, as we have shown, her arrival provided Warwick's enemies in the Virginia Company with one of their sharpest weapons of attack. They accused him of piratical dealings, but it is quite possible that there is some connection between the *Treas-*

71 Obtained in return for a large money payment from Scarnafissi, the agent of Charles Emmanuel I, who was then upon a money-seeking mission in England.

72 *C. S. P. East Indies,* 19 March, 1627, March, 1628, March, 1629, etc.

urer's voyage and Warwick's venture in the Guinea Company. If this were so, the negroes might have been obtained in an entirely legitimate way, as Elfrith maintained. At any rate, it is one of the ironies of history that it should have been through the agency of one and the same man that negroes were first introduced into British America and that the charter of Massachusetts, the foremost abolition state, was obtained.

In 1619 Warwick took a prominent part in financing North's Guiana expedition, and in 1620 he was granted a seat in the council of the resuscitated Plymouth Company for New England and was frequently present at its meetings,[73] as was a neighbour of his, Sir John Bourchier, whose daughter, Elizabeth, had recently married Oliver Cromwell. Warwick, as the organiser of the Guiana Company, had for some time been in touch with Robinson's congregation of Separatists at Leyden, who were contemplating emigration to Guiana,[74] but the dissolution of the company turned their hopes to North Virginia, and thither the *Mayflower* sailed in August, 1620. As will be remembered, the accidents of the voyage compelled the Pilgrims to land at Plymouth in New England and outside the limit of the Virginia Company's patent, and Warwick's influence was again employed to secure from the Council for New England a patent for the land on which the new settlement was founded.[75] It is another striking fact in Warwick's career that he was the only person of high rank and influence connected with all the bodies with whom the Leyden pilgrims negotiated before they could secure a home for themselves in the New World. He was a member of the Guiana Company, the

[73] "Records of Council for New England." Printed in *Proceedings* of American Antiquarian Society for 1867 and 1875.

[74] Bradford, *History of Plymouth Plantation* (ed. Ford, 1912), I, 61-62.

[75] June 1, 1621.

Virginia Company, and the Council for New England, and it was he who, as president of the last of these, obtained the grant of the second Plymouth patent on January 13, 1630.[76]

The breach with Spain in 1623 threw George Villiers, Duke of Buckingham, the all-powerful favourite of James and Charles, on to the side of the anti-Spanish and Puritan party and in 1625 he became an adventurer along with Warwick for the discovery of the Northwest Passage.[77] This alliance of Buckingham with the Puritans was marked by Warwick's appointment as lord lieutenant of Essex; his brother Henry had been since 1618 in high favour at court and was one of Buckingham's most intimate friends. In 1623 Henry was created Baron Kensington, was sent with Carlisle to France in 1624 to arrange Charles's marriage with Louis XIII's sister, Henrietta Maria, and on his return was created Earl of Holland. Holland henceforward became the queen's mouthpiece in English politics and was always hostile to the Spanish party at court. Warwick's connection with the court was shortlived; he sided against Buckingham in the parliament of 1626 and in November joined with Lord Saye, the Earl of Lincoln, and other Puritan peers in refusing to pay the forced loan that was the king's expedient for financing the war. The value of the Rich navy, however, was so great that in March, 1627, a very full commission was issued to Warwick authorising him to undertake hostilities against the Spaniards, the commission[78] being

[76] Bradford (1908 edition), p. 248 and note; (Ford, ed., 1912), II, 69-70.

[77] *C. S. P. Dom.*, April, 1625.

[78] *C. S. P. Dom.*, 18 Mar., 1627. Request from Secretary Coke to Attorney General Heath to prepare for the Earl of Warwick such a commission as was granted by Queen Elizabeth to the Earl of Cumberland. For enlargement, v. *ibid.*, 17 April, 1627. The exact bearing of this and some of the other commissions of the period upon the prize law of the time is dealt

modelled on the lines of Queen Elizabeth's commission to the Earl of Cumberland. By an enlargement of the commission in April, 1627, Warwick was authorised to invade or possess any of the dominions of the king of Spain or the archdukes in Europe, Africa, or America, but the issue of this commission was not at all well received by the court party and we find Secretary Nicholas writing in the following October that Lord Warwick's commission would never have passed had it not been for the puzzle of the great preparations then in hand for the Rochelle expedition.[79]

In pursuance of this commission Warwick, with the aid of some London merchants,[80] fitted out a fleet of eight ships and put to sea in the hope of capturing the Brazil fleet. He failed in his attempt and himself narrowly escaped capture, while his financial resources were badly crippled. In 1628 and 1629 he sent out more ships and took prizes both from the Spaniards and from the Genoese, which brought him little profit but involved him in legal disputes that were unsettled for many years. Among other ships he despatched the *Earl of Warwick* and the *Somers Islands* to the West Indies on the voyage that is referred to in Capt. Bell's letter. Warwick did not stand alone in these ventures, but may be regarded as the head of a clan, composed on the one hand of his own relatives and adherents and on the other of a body of powerful London merchants. We have seen the clan in action in the disputes of the Virginia Company, and during the years that had since elapsed, the group had

with in an article on ''Early Prize Law,'' by Mr. R. G. Marsden in the *English Historical Review* for April, 1910.

79 *C. S. P. Dom.*, 25 Oct., 1627. Nicholas's Letter Book, p. 64.

80 Coke MSS., Hist. MSS. Comm., *Twelfth Report*, App'x, p. 297. Warwick to Sir John Coke, ''I agreed with Mr. Attorney and the Judge of the Admiralty upon a commission and shewed it to divers merchants, my partners, who have come in and adventured their money.''

been further cemented together by the growing unity of feeling in the Puritan party. The intimate business alliance of such members of the Upper House as Warwick, Saye, and Brooke with great London merchants is prominent throughout our pages and we must recognize that these commercial bonds are of great importance in the history of the time, as rendering it easier for great nobles and wealthy country gentlemen to unite with the city merchants and to work side by side with them in the constitutional struggle against the crown. Such a union would have been impossible at an earlier period.

CHAPTER II

PURITAN EMIGRATION AND THE FORMATION OF THE PROVIDENCE COMPANY

To appreciate justly the causes governing the course of colonial events in the momentous years 1628-1629 is impossible without some realisation of the general posture of affairs in England and Europe at the time and to this we must for a moment turn our attention. The high hopes with which the nation had welcomed the accession of the debonair young king and had taken up arms once more against the hated Spaniards, had crumbled under disaster after disaster. The Cadiz expedition had ended in demoralisation and disgrace, the vaunted French alliance had been frittered away in ignoble squabbles and had resulted in naught but the use of English ships against Protestant Rochelle; nothing had been done to aid the King of Denmark in delivering the persecuted churches of Bohemia and the Palatinate, while the expeditions for the relief of those Rochellois whom England had encouraged in their resistance to their king, had returned each a more broken, more diseased, and more disgraceful failure than the last though Rochelle was slowly starving to death with a shuddering dread of the vengeance of Richelieu in a final sack. Nor were home affairs in a more hopeful condition; the incompetence of the government was flagrant, but its demands for money were unceasing and those who refused its forced loans were imprisoned without trial or banished from their homes. The countryside swarmed with unpaid and mutinous soldiery, torn from their parishes by the press-gang and billeted on all below the rank of gentleman. Robbery and outrage afflicted their unwilling hosts, and no redress could be obtained; yet while the poor were thus oppressed and the rich were fleeced without warrant of law, the religious feelings of some of the most upright members of the community were wounded by the silencing of the Calvinistic lectures and pamphleteers; the protagonists of the Arminians received preferment to the highest dignities in the church, and the penalties against recusants remained a dead letter to please the queen and her brother, the king of France, though the countries were at open war. Never in English history had the government faced so united an opposition as when Charles I's third parliament opened in March, 1628, but never did a monarch fail so to realise his position. For two months the debate of grievances went on behind the closed doors of parliament, while to common men the outlook was becoming ever blacker.

It was during these months of gloom that there were passed from hand to hand the suggestions of one of the most respected Puritan divines, John White of Dorchester, for the founding of a refuge in another land for God's oppressed people, where a bulwark might be raised "against the kingdom of Anti-Christ which the Jesuits labour to rear up in all quarters of the world." White had been connected before with a colonising effort in New England of some Dorchester merchants and the treasurer of this defunct company, John Humphry, brother-in-law of the Earl of Lincoln, determined to obtain from the Earl of Warwick, who was now beginning to be looked up to as the head of the Puritans, a grant of land in New England whereon he and others interested in carrying out White's new project might found their settlement. In June, 1623, the Council for New England, finding it impossible to secure capital or settlers for their territory, had decided[1] to divide the whole region into twenty shares to be distributed by lot among those of the council who had paid in capital to the stock. On June 29, 1623, the drawing had taken place in the presence of King James, and Warwick had drawn as his share the region round Massachusetts Bay.[2] It was this tract that Warwick granted by patent to John Humphry, John Endecott, and their associates on March 19, 1628.[3] Endecott sailed on his first voyage to New England in June and the colonisation of Massachusetts began, almost unnoticed amidst the national troubles.

The great Commons' debate on grievances that ended on the twenty-eighth of May, 1628, in the presentation to the king of the Petition of Right, was marked by a crystallisation of the Puritan party in parliament into a form that had great influence upon the after course of events. It was the extreme Puritans who were responsible for the final mould in which the Petition was cast, and it is most noticeable that the men forming the inner ring of the party were closely united one with another by ties of relationship and sincere friendship. Warwick, Saye, and Lincoln were the exponents of the popular policy in the Lords; Sir John Eliot, the leader of the Commons, was united to Warwick by close bonds,[4] while Sir Nathaniel Rich, John Pym, Sir Benjamin Rudyerd, and Sir Gilbert Gerrard were all, as we shall show later,

[1] "Records of Council for New England," *Proceedings* of Amer. Antiq. Soc. for 1875, p. 49.

[2] See the map in Alexander's *Encouragement to Colonies*, 1624.

[3] *C. S. P. Col.*, 19 March, 1628. See also Massachusetts *Colonial Records*, 29 Sept., 1629.

[4] Forster's *Life of Eliot*, II, 64, 72, 642. See also Bagg's letters to the Privy Council, e.g. *C. S. P. Dom.*, 20 April, 1620.

intimately linked together and all took important parts in the struggle. For more than a week after the presentation of the Petition, the issue hung in the balance, but at last on the seventh of June the king yielded and the Petition of Right became the law of the land. To the lighter hearted it seemed as though the threatened liberties of England were safe, but the leaders realised that there was still much to be done, and, without an instant's delay, they proceeded to attack the king's Arminian religious policy, the illegal levying of tonnage and poundage, and, worst of all, the ministerial acts of Buckingham. So vehement were the remonstrances addressed to him that, in anger and disgust at what he thought their base ingratitude, Charles prorogued the parliament on the 26th with a speech of cutting severity. The hopes of early June were dashed and once more gloom settled down on Puritan hearts, saddened and revolted as they were by the king's ostentatious bestowal of preferment upon the Arminian prelates. For a moment the gloom was lightened by a somewhat untimely rejoicing at Felton's murder of the favourite, but the news from Germany was not encouraging, as Wallenstein drove Christian of Denmark, the champion of Protestantism, to his island fastnesses in utter rout. Rochelle at last lay prone, her walls dismantled, her merchants beggared, and her treasured Huguenot liberties gone at the bidding of the ruthless cardinal. Everywhere absolutism and Catholicism seemed triumphant and many an earnest, God-fearing man trembled as he feared that ere long the queen and Laud would bring Protestant England once more under the power of the Roman see.

The publication in December of the "Declaration touching Public Worship," was regarded by the Puritans as granting license to the Arminians for far-reaching innovations in religion, while the feelings of the merchants were outraged by the government's high-handed proceedings in the conflict over Chambers's obstinate refusals to pay the illegal tonnage and poundage. Once more, with the opening of the new year, the public gaze was fixed upon the doors that guarded the central scene in the great struggle. Parliament met again on January 20, 1629, and the Commons under Eliot's leadership at once vehemently assailed the "Declaration," and put forward in a series of resolutions against popery and Arminianism their own conception of the type of uniformity to be demanded for the church. For more than a month the debates raged round the resolutions and the religious grievances they were meant to remedy, while Charles endeavoured in vain to divert attention to the less thorny question of finance. Eliot, with even more intemperate words, refused to be turned from his chosen path and though many lesser members would have debated the threatening action of the courts against their own treasured freedom from arrest, he persisted in recalling their attention to the larger question of the national liberties, until at length the king's slender patience was at end. Never had a more moving scene been witnessed in the Commons' House than on that second of March, 1629, when Speaker Finch announced His Majesty's pleasure that the House should then adjourn. On all sides rose angry murmurs against the order; in flat defiance of it the doors were locked and, though Finch did his courtly best to obey his royal master's commands, the leaders were resolved on violence rather than be baulked of their will. While the trembling speaker was held in his chair, and the weaker members cowered weeping in their seats, it was resolved that whoever should bring in innovations in religion, should introduce popery or Arminianism, or should pay tonnage or poundage, should be reputed a traitor and a capital enemy to the commonwealth. The doors were opened, the speaker released, and to all men it seemed as though the established parliamentary privileges of England were at an end; Eliot, Selden, and other leaders were committed to the Tower.

"The increasing of our sins gives us great cause to look for some heavy scourge and judgment to be coming upon us," wrote John Winthrop a few days later.[5] "My dear wife, I am verily persuaded God will bring some heavy affliction upon this land, and that speedily; but if the Lord seeth it will be good for us, he will provide a shelter and a hiding-place for us and others, as a Zoar for Lot, a Sarephthah for his prophet." What wonder that at such a time White's message of hope should find an echo in Puritan hearts, and that God's people "should turn with eyes of longing to the free and open spaces of the New World, whither they might flee to be at peace.

The summer of 1629 was filled with events of the utmost importance to colonial history. Though only the leaders had been imprisoned for their share in the Commons' scene, every member of the Puritan party, both great and small, was made to feel the displeasure of the government. It was impossible to deprive Sir Benjamin Rudyerd of the lucrative office of surveyor of the Court of Wards, which had been granted him for life in his courtier days, but lesser Puritans might be attacked more easily. John Humphry had long been an attorney of the Court of Wards and a noticeable Puritan and now both he and his colleague, John Winthrop, the Puritan squire of Groton in Suffolk, were deprived of their offices.[6] This apparently unimportant removal was in truth of tremendous import, for in Winthrop at last was found the man who was needed

[5] London, 15 May, 1629, *Life and Letters of Winthrop*, I, 296.

[6] June, 1629, *Life of Winthrop*, I, 298.

to convert the aspirations of the Puritans into realities. Winthrop, a man already of middle age, had been afflicted during the past year (1628) with a succession of bereavements that had disillusioned him with life in England and had turned his thoughts to the proposals for migration that were occupying the minds of his friends. The Massachusetts Bay Company had received the sanction of a royal charter in March, 1629, and in July[7] Winthrop and his brother-in-law, Emmanuel Downing, rode down to Sempringham, the Kesteven seat of the Earl of Lincoln, to talk over their plans of joining the company.

Theophilus Fiennes-Clinton, fourth Earl of Lincoln, who was descended from a distant branch of the great Fiennes family that held the ancient peerage of Saye and Sele, was the most earnest Puritan among the peers, and his seat at Sempringham was the central point where were discussed the projects for a Puritan migration. Lincoln was married to Bridget Fiennes, daughter of Viscount Saye, and his sister, Lady Susan Fiennes-Clinton, was the wife of John Humphry, who had long been interested in White's colonising projects. Humphry had succeeded in imparting this interest to Lincoln and to Isaac Johnson, who was married to another of Lincoln's sisters. Winthrop found the whole society assembled at Sempringham and, though we have no account of the discussions that ensued, it is certain that the affairs of the Massachusetts Bay Company must have been talked over. Among Lincoln's dependents was his distant kinsman, Thomas Dudley, a man of an earnest and almost fanatical Puritan temper. Together he, John Humphry, Isaac Johnson, and Winthrop came to the momentous decision to cast off the dust of Eng-

[7] July, 1629, *Life of Winthrop*, I, 304.

land from their feet and throw in their lot with the Massachusetts Bay Company. In this same critical week Matthew Cradock, the governor, had suggested to the members of the company the entire transfer of the government to America, and on the twenty-sixth of August[8] it was resolved in a full meeting at Cambridge, that this step should be taken. Twelve members of the company, including Sir Richard Saltonstall, John Humphry, and Winthrop, announced their intention of leaving England to settle on American shores, and all of them took immediate steps in preparation for their voyage. From this point onwards Winthrop began to take the lead in the company's affairs, a lead at once marked by a decision and a statesmanlike foresight in marked contrast to the timorous conservatism of Matthew Cradock.

The importance of all these happenings from the point of view of our immediate subject is that every step taken by the Massachusetts emigrants was taken in concert with and often upon the advice of those veteran colonisers, the Earl of Warwick and Sir Nathaniel Rich. It is hardly likely that the idea of migration to America can have been thoroughly shaped as early as April, 1629, when Bell's letter[9] reached Sir Nathaniel Rich, but the idea was gradually taking shape and it must have been within the critical months of June and July that that decision was reached. Two courses lay open to the emigrants. On the one hand, they might sail towards what were then regarded as the bleak and inhospitable shores of North Virginia, where so many attempts at colonisation had been made to end only in disaster, and where the Pilgrims at Plymouth were even then struggling with small success against the hardships of their

[8] *Life of Winthrop*, I, 344.

[9] *V. supra*, pp. 31-34.

lot. On the other hand, they might guide their course toward the fertile islands of the Caribbean that were described so glowingly by Capt. Bell.

Warwick had every reason to counsel the colonists towards the latter course, and, though he was willing to aid them whatever their choice should be, we cannot doubt that it was southward he wished them to sail. His ventures of late years had met with little success and there was here the prospect of retrieving loss and at the same time of providing another home for his discontented protégés in Bermuda. The colonisation of St. Christopher and Barbadoes under the protection of Lords Carlisle and Marlborough, both members of the court party and both personally hostile to the Riches,[10] can have been no more acceptable to Warwick and his friends than was the success of Sir William Courteen, Thomas Warner, and Ralph Merrifield, to his merchant associates. The knowledge that fertile islands were awaiting settlement in the heart of the West Indies, and that they could be fortified with ease, must have been welcome news to so strong a hater of Spain as was Warwick. Here at last appeared a chance of redeeming the failure of his naval enterprise of 1627 and the general ill success of the Spanish war, here was a chance of carrying on the glorious traditions of the Elizabethan age and of putting once and for all that bit in the ancient enemy's mouth, that had so long been the dream of all patriotic Englishmen. It is easy for us to commend Winthrop's

[10] A personal coolness had existed between the Rich family and James Hay, Earl of Carlisle, since his quarrel with Lord Holland while they were fellow envoys in Paris in 1624. Only with difficulty had a duel then been prevented. The statement of Clarendon that Holland and Carlisle were good friends is no contradiction of our view, as it applies to a later period and the friendship can, at best, have been only superficial. The rivalry between Warwick and the Carlisle interests was an important factor in West Indian affairs as late, at any rate, as 1648.

neglect of advice and to deride those who gave it and for ten years contended that his choice had been wrongly made, but in 1629 the colonial empires of every power, save Spain, were still to make, and all experience pointed to the shores of a summer sea as those whereon colonising success could alone be obtained.

The Stuart age witnessed many departures from the ancient ways, but the one that marks more definitely, perhaps, than any other, the period as modern, has not always received the attention it deserves. For the first time we find men of the middle class, who were neither great lawyers nor churchmen and who had had no training in the narrow circle of officialdom, printing deep the impress of their personality upon the national destinies. Just as Pym and Cromwell were sprung from that upper middle class that has done such great things for the world, so in the birth throes of the Massachusetts commonwealth the critical decision was made, and made aright, by the obscure Suffolk squire, while the great noble, skilled and cautious though he was, was hopelessly wrong. The Massachusetts migration was an event entirely without precedent in the modern world; Virginia, Newfoundland, and Guiana had attracted merely the adventurers and the needy; the *Mayflower* pilgrims, though later ages have glorified them, were too few in number, too humble in station, and too far removed from the main currents of English life to be of importance; but now sober, well-to-do men of middle age, to whom the spirit of adventure was entirely foreign, were contemplating a transfer of themselves, their families, and their goods to new homes across the seas, there to found not a colony but a commonwealth. At such a crisis the caution, the experience, and the knowledge of past failures of the man of affairs stand ranged against the fervour, the enthusiasm, and the hope in the future of the new man; Warwick and Rich well knew the difficulties to be contended with and preferred to move along the well-marked lines of policy; Winthrop and White, guided as they felt by a Higher Power, were resolved upon a course that was new. The men of the future had their way and the great human stream was directed to the New England shore.

Though we are unable to examine in detail the discussions that went on between Warwick and his associates concerning the designs suggested in Bell's letter, we find that by September, 1629, they were complete, and that it had been resolved to put the project into immediate execution.[11] The total cost of the equipment of this pioneer expedition was about two thousand pounds and this had been provided by the Earl of Warwick, Sir Nathaniel Rich (£275), Gabriel Barber (£250), John Dyke, and Gregory Gawsell. An account of these men will be given when we come to deal with the membership of the company as a whole. The arrangements for the voyage were entrusted to Dyke, who engaged artificers and mariners, purchased provisions and tools, and secured from the Admiralty letters of marque for two ships. A pinnace of eighty tons burthen was entrusted to the command of Daniel Elfrith and the bark *Warwick* to that of John Tanner. Daniel Elfrith[12] had been engaged for many years in the contraband West Indian trade; he first appears as an officer serving under Capt. Fisher on a voyage of discovery to Guiana in 1614. He was put as master into a captured Spanish caravel with a cargo of

[11] Our main authority from this point onwards is the Providence records. Though Sainsbury's calendar of them is very full in places, he makes many mistakes and entirely misapprehends certain letters. We shall refer here only to the records themselves.

[12] For the early career of Elfrith see Brown, II, 885. Brown's account of his later life is misleading owing to the confusion of Old and New Providence.

meal and brought her to Bermuda in 1615 just in time to save the colony from famine, but her coming was by no means an unmixed blessing, for she brought into the islands a plague of rats that took years to eradicate.[13] Elfrith was accused of securing the vessel in the West Indies by dishonest means and, though he stoutly maintained his innocence, he was sent home to England a prisoner.[14] He soon vindicated himself and in 1618 he again arrived in Bermuda as master of the ship *Treasurer* on his way to the West Indies. Tucker, the governor of the colony, who was on the point of departure for England, suspected that Elfrith was bound roving and warned the colonists to have nothing to do with him. No heed was paid to this warning and Elfrith was received with every kindness.[15] He reached Virginia on his return voyage in the late summer of 1619 in consort with a Flushing privateer and with a hundred negroes he is said to have captured from a Spanish vessel; some of these he disposed of to the planters and they were the first of Virginia's negro servants; the rest he carried on to Bermuda, where his ship, the *Treasurer,* was broken up as unserviceable by command of the governor, Capt. Nathaniel Butler. We have seen in a previous chapter how much commotion this voyage caused in England. Elfrith seems now to have settled in Bermuda on the Earl of Warwick's land, which he worked with the aid of the earl's negroes. From 1623 onwards he was a member of the council,[16] but he did not agree well with the governor, Henry Woodhouse. He appears to have maintained that the governor was lining his own pockets with

13 Smith's *Virginia,* p. 125.

14 *V. supra,* p. 21.

15 Smith, p. 666.

16 Sir J. H. Lefroy's *Memorials of the Bermudas* is our authority for this period.

public funds and in September, 1625, he was arraigned before the council on a charge of sedition, which was the graver as he had been suspected of complicity in a plot against Gov. Butler in 1622. He was compelled to make abject submission, but on the removal of Woodhouse from the governorship in 1626, this submission was removed from the records. During 1626 and 1627 he was acting on the council, was an officer of the principal fort or King's Castle, and was looking after the boats belonging to the colony. He returned to England late in 1627.

In February, 1628, the Earl of Warwick and his associates, in virtue of his commission of April, 1627, despatched three ships on a privateering voyage to the West Indies, making Bermuda their rendezvous. These vessels were the *Earl of Warwick* of eighty tons, master, Sussex Camock, the *Somers Islands* of about one hundred tons, master, John Rose, and the *Robert* of fifty tons, master, Daniel Elfrith.[17] The voyage was not very successful and Camock with some thirty men was left behind on the island of San Andreas. Elfrith took command of the *Earl of Warwick* for the voyage home, handing over the command of the *Robert* to John Tanner. They reached England about the end of April, 1629, armed as we have seen with Gov. Bell's commendation of the projects Elfrith had formed on the voyage.

The letters of marque for the new expedition for the occupation of Santa Catalina were issued on September 28, 1629,[18] and the ships set sail on the second week of October. It had been decided that it would be best to establish a colony firmly on Santa Catalina before undertaking the more doubtful design upon Fonseca; Elfrith therefore sailed direct to Bermuda and after a

[17] P. R. O. Register Book of Letters of Marque, 1628.
[18] *Ibid.*, 1629.

few days' stay, thence to the Caribbean, which was entered by the Windward Passage. The ships called first at San Andreas, where it was found that the greater part of Camock's company had left the island in a Dutch ship, though a few, of whom George Needham was the chief, had remained to plant tobacco. After a day or two's stay Elfrith proceeded on his voyage and reached Santa Catalina about Christmas, 1629. A start was at once made on the preparations for the reception of the main body of colonists, who were expected from Bermuda early in the spring of 1630. The harbour of Santa Catalina lies to the northwest of the island and is approached by two narrow entrances well-guarded by rocks; on the north it is sheltered by a peninsula joined to the main island in 1630 by a narrow neck of land.[19] The point of this peninsula is a flat-topped bluff, some forty feet above sea-level, and on this bluff it was decided to erect the first fort, called in honour of the expedition's patron, Warwick Fort. The hills make a bold sweep round the eastern and southern sides of the harbour, ascending into three noticeable peaks, now called respectively Split Hill (550 feet), Fairway Hill, and the Mound (700 feet); the central peak of the island lies to the southward and reaches a height of one thousand one hundred and sixty feet. Between the hills and the harbour there is a flat plain and this was chosen as the site of the first settlement; houses were first erected on the neck of land close to the water's edge, the infant town being called in honour of the company, New Westminster. On the arrival of the expedition the island was found to be uninhabited save for a few Dutchmen, who were received as comrades and in their turn aided the settlers in their

[19] This neck of land was not pierced by the buccaneers till about 1670, though Capt. Rudyerd had advised the step as early as 1634 in order to make the peninsula into a kind of citadel.

preparations; under Elfrith's directions the planters chose such plots of ground in the immediate vicinity of the harbour as they fancied, and at once started clearing them and planting tobacco. No difficulties were encountered in this work, for the dry season in the island lasts from January to May and there is almost always an abundance of fresh water to be obtained. The work of building the fort was entrusted to the direction of Samuel Axe, a soldier who had seen service in the English contingents in the Netherlands and had there learned some of the principles of fortification. The spot he had selected for the fort was well chosen, as it commanded the main entrance to the harbour, and timber for its construction could be obtained close at hand. Its disadvantage lay in its distance from a supply of fresh water, but as the only attack was to be expected from the sea, this was not much of a drawback.

Elfrith and Tanner set sail again from Providence about the end of February, 1630, leaving Axe as deputy governor of the island; a direct course was steered for Bermuda, where Bell during their absence had been making arrangements with his adherents for the migration. He had retired from the governorship in December and was succeeded by Capt. Roger Wood, the late secretary, but he still retained his seat upon the council, as did Elfrith. The new colony must have been an engrossing topic in Bermuda throughout the winter, and Bell was spoken hardly of for his desertion; these strictures he was by no means ready to submit to and at a council on February 9, 1630, we find him bringing forward what he called the scandalous statements of a Mr. Ewer, who was compelled to apologize humbly for them. According to the bad precedent set in the case of previous governors, attempts were made to bring Bell to book for acts done during his governorship. He pleaded the precedent of immunity that had been established when he succeeded Woodhouse in 1626, this having been sanctioned by an order of the Somers Islands Company bearing date of November 28, 1627. The majority of the council maintained that this precedent did not apply as Woodhouse in 1627 had left the islands for England, whereas Bell was going to Santa Catalina and would be out of the company's jurisdiction; he was therefore compelled to give security to answer all such things as should be brought against him either by the inhabitants of the Somers Islands or by the company in England. Elfrith also was compelled to give account to his successor, Capt. Saile, of the things that had been under his charge in the King's Castle and was closely examined concerning the disposal of a cargo of tobacco jointly owned by several planters, that he had taken with him on his last voyage to England.

It had been decided that only men should be taken to Santa Catalina in the first instance and some difficulties were placed in the way of those who wished to leave their dependents behind in Bermuda. "Miles Port being desirous to go to St. Catulina, it was thought fit to be considered whether or no he should go without his wife and being put to question at the Council table, the Governor and all the Council did consider, (excepting Capt. Bell and Capt. Elfrith) that he should not go without her." Miles Port had therefore to abandon the voyage. The men accompanying the expedition mainly belonged to the planting class with only a few servants; they arranged with the planters remaining in Bermuda to send over a further supply of servants later. It is impossible to say whether Bell married Elfrith's daughter before his departure from Bermuda or after, but he is spoken of as Elfrith's son-in-law in letters from England in February, 1631, so that the marriage must have taken place before August, 1630. Bell and Elfrith took their seats at the Bermuda council table for the last time on April 13, 1630, and sailed for Santa Catalina before the next council meeting in May. A few days after their departure there arrived fresh supplies of provisions, etc., for the new colony, which Elfrith had arranged before leaving England; these were too late and had to be left in the Somers Islands till the following year.

While these events were taking place oversea, the organisers of the enterprise in England had not been idle. Rumours that the Earl of Warwick was engaged in some new venture in the West Indies had begun to spread abroad and the diarist, John Rous, records under date August 24, 1629, "News of an island, 20 miles long and 10 broad, discovered by a captain sent out by the Earl of Warwick."[20] On 16 February, 1630, he notes, "The ships be set to sea for New England and for a plantation near Mexico, *ut dicitur.*"[21] Although the news that something was afoot had thus to some extent leaked out, nothing definite was known outside Warwick's immediate circle, for it had been determined to fall in with Bell's suggestion and to keep the new enterprise entirely in the hands of the Earl and his usual financial associates together with a few members of the inner circle of the Puritan party. Subscriptions were invited privately during the summer of 1630 and by the early autumn the company was practically complete. It was impossible to hold any meetings of the adventurers as a whole until

[20] Camden Soc., *Diary of John Rous*, p. 43. Rous was rector of Stanton Downham in Suffolk and was in a position to learn the gossip of the Earl of Warwick's tenantry as we may find from the entry of 13 October, 1629. "The news was brought to Lees by the Earl of Warwick's coachman, who returned from the Earl at London that day, that the Earl was like to have a great prize of 6 ships of the silver fleet."

[21] This was the *second* supply, sent to Bermuda and missed by Elfrith.

November, for London and the country generally were suffering from one of those periodical visitations of the plague[22] that were so frequent down to the middle of the seventeenth century. The plague had been raging in the north of France and in Holland throughout the summer of 1629[23] and many precautions were taken to preserve England from infection but in vain. The first cases in London were reported early in April[24] and before the end of the month the capital was so infected that all those able to do so were taking steps to leave it for the country.[25] Pym, for instance, had been intending to take Barrington Hall for the summer, but Sir Thomas Barrington wrote to his mother in May, "My wife, out of her provident care of yourself and us, thinks that fear of the sickness dispersing is cause enough to keep that house free for a refuge."[26] So much had the ravages of the plague dislocated affairs that the christening of the infant Prince Charles in June was announced throughout the country by proclamation instead of by heralds, as was the custom in such cases,[27] while the festivities themselves were hastened through as much as possible. In August Saint Bartholomew Fair and Southwark Fair were prohibited by proclamation for fear of infection, while London was practically deserted by people of rank, and business was at a standstill. By the end of October, however, the worst was over in London, and November saw the usual current of life resumed, though in many counties, where infection still existed

22 For this visitation of the plague and its destructive effects at Cambridge, v. Masson's *Milton,* II.

23 *C. S. P. Dom.,* 16 Oct., 1629.

24 *Ibid.,* 10 April, 1630.

25 *Ibid.*

26 Hist. MSS. Comm., *Seventh Report,* App'x, Sir T. B. to Lady Joan B. May, 1630.

27 *C. S. P. Dom.,* 15 June, 1630.

as late as Christmas, the usual autumn musters were abandoned.

As soon as it was possible to assemble in London with any reasonable safety, Warwick took steps to gather his friends together and the first meeting of adventurers in the new company took place at Brooke House in Holborn[28] on the 19th of November; definite and immediate action was decided upon and on the 4th of December the patent was sealed granting formal incorporation to the company by the style of "The Governor and Company of Adventurers of the City of Westminster for the plantation of the Islands of Providence, Henrietta, and the adjacent islands lying upon the coast of America."

The propositions for the formation of the company that had been circulated during the summer of 1630,[29] had mentioned £200 as the amount of the first adventure and some portion of this had been paid in before November by most of the adventurers. The amount necessary to complete this adventure money of £200 in each case is given against the name of each adventurer on the first page of the company's journal and we are thus provided with a complete list of the original members:

[28] Brooke House, the usual meeting place of the company, lay in what was then a fashionable quarter, at the corner of Gray's Inn Lane and Holborn and immediately opposite the still-existing Staple's Inn; Brooke Street and Greville Street were built upon its site before the beginning of the eighteenth century. The locality is curiously identified by an entry in *C. S. P. Dom.*, 1633, p. 164. A spy who had been set to watch Lords Saye and Brooke, suspected of too great familiarity with the Dutch ambassador, sat in the gateway of Staple's Inn for some time to watch the ambassador come out from Brooke House. Other meeting places of the company were Warwick House, a little further west along Holborn, and Sir Gilbert Gerrard's or Mr. Pym's lodgings, both of which were then in Gray's Inn Lane. Jessop, the secretary, was a member of and had chambers in Gray's Inn itself.

[29] None of these letters have been discovered, but it has been possible to arrive at their import from references in the records.

19 November, 1630	ALREADY PAID £	TO BE PAID £
Earl of Warwick	100	100
Earl of Holland	—	200
Lord Saye and Sele	100	100
Lord Brooke	—	200
Jno. Robartes, Esq.	—	200
Sir Benjamin Rudyerd, Knt.	125	75
Sir Gilbert Gerrard, Bart.	100	100
Sir Edward Harwood, Knt.	100	100
Sir Nathaniel Rich, Knt.	125	75
Sir Edmond Moundeford, Knt.	100	100
Jno. Pym, Esq.	125	75
Richard Knightley, Esq.	125	75
Jno. Gurdon, Esq.	100	100
Gregory Gawsell	125	75
Jno. Dyke, merchant	125	75
Jno. Graunt	125	75
Mr. St. John's of Lincoln's Inn	—	200
Chr. Sherland, Esq.	—	200
Gabriel Barber	100	100
Original venture	£1575	£2225
New total venture		£3800

Sir Thomas Barrington, Bart., was admitted an adventurer on January 21, 1631, and paid in £200. This completed the full number of twenty whole shares. The adventurers present at the first meeting[30] before the patent was sealed and the company formally incorporated, decided to increase the first adventure from £200 to £500, of which £200 was to be made up at once, £100 paid at Michaelmas, 1631, and the remaining £200 as and when required. The officers for the first year were provisionally elected, the Earl of Holland being chosen

[30] Saye, Brooke, Rudyerd, Gerrard, N. Rich, Moundeford, Pym, Gurdon, Gawsell, Dyke, Graunt.

governor, John Dyke, deputy governor, John Pym, treasurer, and William Jessop, secretary.

In examining the list of adventurers it is to be noted that they fall into four classes according to the nature of the inducement that led them to take shares in the company. With one exception, Dyke, all of the members were strong Puritans and though some members have been classed as induced to join the company by their Puritanism, this is not to preclude the others from being swayed by the same motive. The first group of members includes those who were intimately connected with the Earl of Warwick and his schemes; to this class may be said to have belonged his brother, the Earl of Holland, Sir Nathaniel Rich, John Dyke, Gabriel Barber, and Sir Thomas Barrington. The second group includes members of the inner ring of the Puritan party and all, save Harwood, members of the parliament of 1628-1629. The adventurers belonging to this group were Viscount Saye and Sele, Robert, Lord Brooke, Sir Benjamin Rudyerd, Sir Gilbert Gerrard, Sir Edward Harwood, Richard Knightley, Christopher Sherland, and, most important of all, John Pym. Then come three members induced to join by Pym's personal influence, John Robartes, John Graunt, and Oliver St. John; and finally there is a little group of East Anglian squires, Gregory Gawsell, John Gurdon, and Sir Edmond Moundeford.

A full account of the members of the company would, as may be seen from the above list, involve a biographical study of nearly all the Puritan leaders and our attention must therefore be confined in the main to their connection one with another and to their interest in colonial affairs down to 1630. Sidelights will be thrown on the characters of some of them in the course of our pages, but it may here be remarked how intimately the members of the company, and, what is almost the same thing, the leaders of the Puritan party, were allied one with another, with the principal emigrants to New England, and also in some degree with the emigrants to Providence itself. This intimacy was of great moment in the events of the time and provided the link between the Puritan leaders that was needful to enable them to build up slowly during the silence of parliament an organised and powerful party of resistance to the arbitrary policy of the crown.

With the Earl of Holland, the nominal governor of the company, we need concern ourselves very little. His career is well known in the history of the period and his connection with the company was of the slightest. In none of his public employments had Holland displayed ability, but his courtly graces placed him very high in the favour of both Charles and his queen, and, at a time when court favour was the surest road to the obtaining of privileges, it was important to have so acceptable an advocate as Holland to plead one's cause. He never seems to have taken any interest in colonial ventures, but his cupidity and his family ties rendered him willing to accept the titular position of governor of the Providence Company, providing he might share in the company's dividends without expenditure of capital. He never subscribed a halfpenny to the company's funds, but in return for his interest at court was credited with a fully paid share in all distributions of profits. He attended only one meeting of the company.

Sir Nathaniel Rich (1585-1636)[31] was one of the best known and most respected of the Puritan leaders. He was the son of Richard, illegitimate son of the second Lord Rich, by his marriage with the daughter of John

31 The short life of Rich in the *Dict. Nat. Biog.* needs emendation. It quite misrepresents his share in the work of the Providence Company. Brown gives more accurate information.

Michell, sheriff of London. He was admitted to Gray's Inn in 1610 and entered parliament for Totnes in 1614. His brother Robert was wrecked on Bermuda with Sir George Somers in 1609 and was probably the author of the pamphlet, *Newes from Virginia,* published in 1610. According to Brown, Robert Rich was living in Bermuda in 1617 and died there in 1620. Sir Nathaniel Rich early took a large interest in the colonial enterprises of his family and became well known in public life; he was knighted in 1617 and served upon several royal commissions. He was an original member of the Bermuda Company, a member of the Council for New England, and managed the Warwick interests in the courts of the Virginia and East India companies; for his conduct of his party's case in the quarrel in the Virginia Company he was bitterly attacked by Sandys and his faction in the House of Commons in 1624, but he was one of the most prominent members of the Council for Virginia appointed by the crown on the dissolution of the company. In the struggles of the parliament of 1628-1629 Rich took a prominent part and his speeches in the debate on the Petition of Right have been preserved. We may regard him throughout his career as the Earl of Warwick's man of business, who had a very large share in shaping the family policy.

William Jessop, who was appointed to the secretaryship of the company, was a young student of Gray's Inn, who had already done a considerable amount of clerical work for the Rich family. He occupied the post of secretary to the company and to the patentees of Saybrook throughout their existence, and these appointments proved the opening to a prosperous career; he became later legal agent to many noble houses, was clerk to the House of Lords under Henry Elsing in the Long Parliament, clerk to the Council of State under the Commonwealth, and clerk to the House of Commons in the Long Parliament of the Restoration. He died in 1675, leaving a considerable fortune. Two London merchants took a share in financing the first voyage of exploration, and both had been actively engaged in privateering enterprises and colonial trade and sharers in Warwick's ventures. The two were men of quite different stamp, though both were typical London merchants of the time. Gabriel Barber was one of the earliest adventurers in the Virginia Company and an original member of the Bermuda Company. He was a close adherent of the Warwick party and in 1623 was deputy governor of the Somers Islands Company, while he was a heavy shareholder in the East India Company, and in 1625 we find recorded the sale of £1200 of East India stock by him.[32] That he was both wealthy and public spirited we may judge from his anonymous donation of £550 with the promise of more for the founding of the first free school in Virginia.[33] John Dyke was a member of the Fishmonger's Company in the City of London and an adventurer in the Virginia, Bermuda, Muscovy, and East India companies. His father, Thomas Dyke,[34] had come to London from Yorkshire in the reign of Queen Elizabeth and had done well as a foreign merchant. In 1612 he was one of the adventurers in Hudson's voyage to the Northwest Passage; on his death in 1617[35] his adventures in the East India, Virginia, and Bermuda companies were left to be divided among his five sons. At the request of the eldest, Robert, his share was passed on to the third son, John Dyke, who thenceforward took

32 *C. S. P. East Indies,* 4 March, 1625.

33 Barber signed himself "Dust and Ashes." See Fiske, *Old Virginia and her Neighbours,* I, 234.

34 Harl. Soc. *Visit. of London,* I, 233.

35 *C. S. P. East Indies,* 4 March, 1625.

the lead in the family affairs. His interest in colonial matters was entirely financial and we find in the registers of letters of marque[36] repeated issue of letters for ships owned by him in partnership with the Earl of Warwick and others. He was an adherent of the Warwick party in the Virginia quarrel and was one of the Council for Virginia appointed in 1624. His appointment to the deputy governorship of the Providence Company was entirely owing to his commercial experience and, it will be shown later, the company suffered severely from its connection with him. He may be taken as a type of the grasping financier who regarded West Indian adventure with a favouring eye only as long as it returned him large dividends.

It is hard to say whether his attachment to the Rich family or his ardent Puritanism was the more potent motive in securing Sir Thomas Barrington's adhesion to the company. The Barrington family was one of the most important Puritan families of the second rank and was allied with practically all the leaders in the constitutional struggle. The priories of Leighs and Hatfield in the parish of Hatfield Broad Oak, near Felsted in Essex, had been granted to Chancellor Rich upon the Dissolution and from him the Barringtons had purchased the priory of Hatfield in 1564.[37] Here, henceforth, the family resided on terms of close intimacy with the Riches, whose principal seat was at Leighs Priory. Sir Francis Barrington, the first baronet, married Joan, daughter of Sir Henry Cromwell, the "Golden Knight" of Hinchingbrook, and aunt of John Hampden and Oliver Cromwell, the future Protector. Lady Joan Barrington was one of the most remarkable women of her time, who kept up to her very latest years a voluminous correspondence

36 *C. S. P. Dom.*, 1625-1630.
37 Wright's *Essex*, II, 310.

with her numerous family and whose advice was repeatedly sought by the leaders of the Puritan party, both clerical and lay. She took an intimate interest in New England and kept up a correspondence with many of the Massachusetts emigrants. Roger Williams, the founder of the colony of Rhode Island, often corresponded with Lady Barrington and married one of her nieces.[38] Many letters from the Eliot family are preserved among the Barrington correspondence and there are some reasons for believing that Oliver Cromwell met his future wife, Elizabeth Bourchier, at Lady Joan's house, for she and Sir John Bourchier were near neighbours. Sir Francis Barrington represented Essex in all parliaments from 1601 to his death in 1628 and was one of the earliest members of the Virginia Company. Thomas (c. 1590-1644) was knighted in his father's lifetime and succeeded to the baronetcy in 1628; he represented various boroughs in the Rich interest in the parliaments from 1621 to 1628, when he succeeded his father as knight of the shire for Essex. During the struggles over the Petition of Right he was one of the inner circle of Puritan leaders, and was a fellow member with Pym and with his brother-in-law, Gerrard, of many important committees. He married as his second wife, Judith Litton, who was connected with the family of St. John of Bletsho and hence with the Russells, Earls of Bedford. As one of the deputy-lieutenants of Essex, Barrington carried out the directions of the lord lieutenant, the Earl of Warwick, and was a person of great importance in the county. Many of the extant letters from Providence are addressed to him as deputy-governor of the company for 1633-1634.

William Fiennes (1582-1662), first Viscount Saye and

[38] Brit. Mus., Eg., 2643, fo. 1, Williams to Lady Joan Barrington, 2 May, 1629.

Sele, has been largely forgotten by succeeding generations, but down to the opening of the Civil War he was regarded by all as the typical Puritan and as one of the most intractable opponents of arbitrary government in church and state. Educated at Oxford a little earlier than Pym, he succeeded his father in the revived barony of Saye and Sele in 1613. His Puritanism was of the strongest and he was, from 1621 onwards, one of the most prominent of the anti-court and anti-Spanish party; to the breaking-off of the Spanish Match Saye owed his promotion in the peerage, but this did not modify his uncompromising hostility to arbitrary power and during the parliament of 1628-1629 he was the king's most implacable opponent in the House of Lords, and was the most skilful tactician among the Puritan leaders. His daughter, Bridget, was married to Theophilus Fiennes-Clinton, Earl of Lincoln, and through this connection and his intimacy with Warwick, he began about 1629 to take an interest in colonisation. He shared in the work of the Providence Company and in New England affairs from this time and we shall have a good deal to say concerning his schemes. Many of the Puritan emigrants to Providence came from the neighbourhood of his seat at Broughton near Banbury. Saye's fortune was hardly equal to his rank and some part of his interest in colonisation was probably to be attributed to his hopes of profit from his ventures. He purchased in 1633 a share in the Providence Company for his eldest son, James Fiennes, but the latter took no part in the company's affairs.

Robert Greville, second Lord Brooke (1608-1643), was the adopted son of his great uncle, Sir Fulke Greville, first Baron.[39] He sat in the parliament of 1628-1629 for the family borough of Warwick and succeeded to the

[39] Harl. Soc. *Lincolnshire Pedigrees,* II, 431.

barony soon after attaining his majority. The inclination towards Puritanism that he had imbibed during his education in Holland, threw him under the influence of Warwick and Saye, and it was they who led him to take a share in the Providence Company's enterprise and later interested him in the colonisation of New England and especially of Saybrook.[40] The large fortune he had inherited enabled him to be of much financial assistance to the company, and, as he grew older, he became more and more interested in its work and ready to carry on some portion of it at his own charge. He married Katherine Russell, daughter of Francis, fourth Earl of Bedford; this connection and his talents, wealth, and position caused him to fill a very prominent place in the Puritan struggle.

Sir Benjamin Rudyerd (1572-1658), son of James Rudyerd of Rudyerd in Staffordshire,[41] came to court to try his fortune at the height of Queen Elizabeth's reign, and his brother, James, started his career in the City of London about the same time. He played a prominent part in the literary world under James I, and was granted through his patron, the Earl of Pembroke, the lucrative position of surveyor to the Court of Wards for life. He was knighted in 1618, entered the House of Commons in 1620 as member for Portsmouth, and sat in every subsequent parliament down to his death. Although the anti-Spanish views he had imbibed in early manhood under Elizabeth placed him, like Pembroke, in opposition at first to King James's foreign policy, the breaking-off of the Spanish Match allowed him to take up a more moderate position, and in the parliament of

40 Fulke Greville, the first Lord Brooke, had been an intimate friend of Raleigh's and had taken great interest in his schemes of colonisation. v. Brown, I, 15.

41 Harl. Soc., *Visit. of London*, II, 215.

1623 he acted as spokesman for the government. But his zeal for church reform threw him on to the side of the opposition and in the parliament of 1628-1629 he definitely took his stand with the Puritan leaders and became one of the chief members of the party. He was an intimate friend of the Earl of Warwick and Sir Nathaniel Rich[42] and it was this friendship that led him to join the Providence Company. He was a regular attendant at its meetings for some years, though later his interest somewhat cooled.

Sir Gilbert Gerrard, Bart., of Harrow-on-the-Hill, Middlesex, succeeded his father in 1583 and was admitted to Gray's Inn in 1592. He married in 1620, Mary, daughter of Sir Francis and Lady Joan Barrington, and was thus more strongly confirmed in his sympathies with Puritanism. He entered parliament as member for Middlesex in 1621 and thenceforth, except in 1626, when he was pricked for sheriff of the county, he sat in every parliament down to the Long Parliament, as one of the inner circle of the Puritan party. The Gerrard family had been connected with colonial ventures since the early part of Elizabeth's reign, but Sir Gilbert does not appear to have taken any personal interest in colonisation prior to the founding of the Providence Company in which he was led to take a share by his friendship with the Earl of Warwick, Sir Nathaniel Rich, and Pym. He was an active member of the company and served as deputy-governor in 1634-1635; the company's meetings were occasionally held at his house in Holborn.

Sir Edward Harwood (1586-1632),[43] one of the four

[42] For the intimacy of the families see Brit. Mus., Eg., 2646, fo. 54.

[43] Brown calls Edward Harwood the son of Leonard Harwood, member of the Virginia Company. This is shown to be incorrect by Harl. Soc., *Lincs. Pedigrees,* II. 458, where William Harwood of Thurlby, father of Edward, is given as dying in 1600.

standing colonels of the English contingent in the Low Countries, had long had an interest in colonisation. He was for many years a member of the Virginia Company and possessed four shares in the Somers Islands Company. He was bound by ties of close intimacy with the family of the Earl of Lincoln and his family seat of Thurlby was not far from Sempringham. His brother, George Harwood,[44] one of the feoffees for impropriations in 1627, was the first treasurer of the Massachusetts Bay Company[45] and may have had something to do with interesting the Clinton family in the project. Sir Edward Harwood's sympathies were very strongly Puritan and there is some reason to suppose that he was of assistance to the Pilgrim Fathers during their sojourn in Leyden and may have aided them to secure their patent from the Earl of Warwick. During the education of Lord Brooke in Holland, Harwood was in close touch with the latter, and as his residence abroad precluded his attendance at the Providence meetings save on one or two occasions, Lord Brooke acted as his proxy. Harwood was killed in action at the siege of Maestricht in 1632.

Richard Knightley (1593-1639) succeeded to the family domain of Fawsley in Northamptonshire on the death of his cousin, Sir Valentine Knightley, in 1618. He was one of the most respected members of the Puritan party and represented Northants in the parliaments of 1621-1622, 1624-1625, 1625 and 1628-1629. He was prevented from sitting in that of 1626 by being pricked sheriff of his county. Sir Valentine Knightley had been a member of the Virginia Company and Richard Knightley succeeded to his interest in colonial affairs, which interest may have been augmented by his marriage with Anne,

[44] *Lincs. Pedigrees,* II, 458. S. P. Dom., Car. I, cclv, ii.

[45] Elected 28 February, 1628-1629, Massachusetts *Colonial Records,* I.

daughter of Sir William Courteen. His house at Fawsley was often a meeting place for the opposition leaders and the Providence Company occasionally met there at the same time. The Knightleys were close friends of the Hampdens, and Richard Knightley's son married one of John Hampden's daughters, while his brother, Nathaniel,[46] a merchant tailor of London, was married to a daughter of Alderman Johnson of the Virginia Company. The adhesion of the Knightley family to Puritanism was traditional, for at the time of the "Marprelate" controversy in Elizabeth's reign many of the tracts were printed upon a secret press at Fawsley in the house of Sir Richard Knightley.

Christopher Sherland of Gray's Inn, recorder of Northampton, represented the borough in the parliaments of 1623-1624, 1625, 1626 and 1628-1629. He held a high position in the counsels of the Puritan party and was the reporter of several committees of the House of Commons. He came under the unfavourable notice of the government along with George Harwood as one of the feoffees for the impropriations of the tithes of Dunstable, Cirencester, and Hertford in 1627.[47] His strong Puritanism led him to take frequent part in the debates on religious questions in parliament. He died early in 1632.

The most important executive office in the Providence Company, as in the Virginia and Somers Islands companies, was the treasurership. To this office his strik-

[46] Harl. Soc., *Visit. of London,* II, 35.

[47] Neal in his *History of the Puritans* gives his name as Sherman, but a reference to the original list among the Domestic State Papers proves that this should really be Sherland. S. P. Dom., Car. I, cclv, ii. The Feoffees were a prominent group of Puritans, in whom were vested the impropriate tithes of certain benefices. These tithes they administered for the support of Puritan lecturers, and they therefore fell under Laud's displeasure and were dissolved. See *Publications,* Mass. Col. Soc. XI, pp. 263-277.

ing financial ability and experience secured the election of John Pym. Of those who have exercised a commanding influence on English history there is perhaps no one whose career has been less studied than has Pym's. His only modern biographers, Forster, Gardiner, and Goldwin Smith,[48] concern themselves almost entirely with his public life in parliament and are in great part devoted to the last three years of his life, when his name was on every lip. The whole ordered development of his career, however, marked him out to his colleagues in the inner circle of the Puritan party during the intermission of parliaments as the natural successor of Eliot in the leadership in the struggle against arbitrary power, and the commanding position he at once took up on the opening of the Long Parliament, must have seemed entirely natural to the men whose schemes he had advised and directed ever since the prison doors closed upon Eliot in 1629. The master-mind that governed the whole course of the Providence Company was Pym's, and it is necessary therefore to deal with his earlier career at some length.

John Pym (1584-1643) was the son of Alexander Pym of Brymore, Somerset; his father died when he was very young and his mother, Philippa Coles, married within a year or two Sir Anthony Rous of Halton St. Dominick, Cornwall, with whose family Pym was brought up. Sir Anthony's second son by his first wife married Pym's sister Jane, born in 1581, while his fourth son was Francis Rous, the celebrated provost of Eton, who played an important part in the Puritan struggle. We shall find several members of the Rous family mentioned in the Providence records. Pym matriculated at Broadgates Hall (now Pembroke College), Oxford, in 1599, his step-

[48] A popular biography of Pym has recently appeared, but to this the same criticism applies.

brother, Francis, having graduated from the same college three years before; in 1602 he became a student of the Middle Temple but was never called to the bar.

Sir Anthony Rous was the representative of the interests of the great Russell family on the Devon and Cornish border. The parish of Halton St. Dominick lies under ten miles from Tavistock, the spoils of whose abbey had fallen to the Russells at the Dissolution;[49] the region is rich in lead and copper mines and from these mines the family then drew a large share of their wealth. The interest of the third Earl of Bedford was sufficient to secure for young Pym a lucrative appointment in the Exchequer and on June 11, 1605, an order[50] was issued to draw a grant to John Pym in reversion after Henry Audley of the receivership of the counties of Hants, Wilts, and Gloucestershire. How long he waited for his office does not appear, but from 1613 we find occasional references to his work in the financial business of the counties. The monetary difficulties that beset James I must have added considerably to the work of Pym's post and in 1618 he is found writing to the Lords of the Treasury that it was impossible to raise a sum of £2000, which he had been directed to procure by the sale of some crown rents.[51] Pym entered parliament for the first time for the borough of Tavistock in 1620,[52] the borough being entirely devoted to the Russell interest. He at once began to take an active part in the committee work of the Commons, and showed even thus early a strong interest in religious questions. He was naturally urged towards Puritanism by his serious temper; and

49 See *Dict. Nat. Biog.* art. William Russell, first Earl of Bedford, XLIX, 446.

50 *C. S. P. Dom.,* 1 June, 1605.

51 *C. S. P. Dom.,* 28 Sept., 1618.

52 The statement that he sat in the parliament of 1614 for Calne has been shown to be incorrect.

the influence of his step-brother, Francis Rous, and of his friend, Charles Fitz-Geffry, put him definitely upon the Puritan side. The death of his wife, Anna Hooke,[53] in 1620, increased his devotion to religion. He was a member of the Commons' committee of 1620-1621 upon religious grievances and his work, while it brought him into notice with the Puritan party, led to his detention along with other prominent Puritan members at the end of the parliament. From his confinement in his own house he had to be released early in 1622 by Cranfield's influence to carry out some important financial work for the Exchequer,[54] but he was compelled to return to confinement when the work was complete. Cranfield found his assistance in the Exchequer so useful, however, that he secured from the king Pym's full release about the end of the year.

In the first parliament of Charles I, Pym began to take a really prominent part, especially in committee work; an experience in financial affairs, so uncommon outside the official members of the house, made him reporter of the committee on the lord treasurer's financial statement, while his mastery of detail caused his repeated choice as reporter of the numerous other committees upon which he sat. It is most noticeable in the Commons' journals of this period how frequently the names of a small knot of members occur upon the important committees that then did so large a share of the work of the House; Sir N. Rich, Sir B. Rudyerd, Sir G. Gerrard, Sir T. Barrington, Christopher Sherland, and Pym himself, were repeatedly serving together in this way, and one of them was in most cases chosen reporter of the committee. The intimate personal friendship unit-

53 Capt. Hooke, a relative, was in the years 1634-1635 a principal leader of the malcontents in Providence.

54 Hist. MSS. Comm., *Fourth Report,* App'x, De la Warr MSS., p. 305, etc.

ing them and this common experience in public work made the group the most powerful body in England outside the official hierarchies.

Pym continued deeply interested in religious and financial matters and was entrusted with the management of the financial articles of the impeachment of Buckingham, May, 1626. He conducted the impeachment of Mainwaring in the parliament of 1628, but in the riotous scene that closed the session of 1629 he took no part. With the dissolution of parliament and the arrest of Eliot, his public career must have seemed closed and he therefore turned, in the practical way that characterised him, to the new interest of colonisation that had lately begun to occupy his mind. Opportunities for the exercise of statecraft in the early seventeenth century were denied to any Englishman outside the ranks of the high nobility or the narrow circle of permanent officials; to a man like Pym, who had had for ten years a share, though a small one, in the government of his country, who had sat in every parliament since 1620 and had slowly built up for himself a reputation for capacity, the closing of all hope of further influence on his country's life with the closing of parliament, must have been a hard blow to his ambition. But the schemes for Puritan colonisation presented themselves to him with their vistas of opportunity and Pym seized upon them with avidity and devoted wholeheartedly to the Providence Company's affairs his time, his thought, and his fortune. For eight years the company absorbed him until the events of 1638-1639 again encouraged a hope that the great struggle still remained to be won, and he felt that a part upon the great stage once more was calling him.

Pym seems first to have come into contact with colonial affairs in 1628, when he was appointed reporter of the Commons' committee upon the petition of the Somers

Islands planters. The committee's investigation much interested him in the affairs of the islands and the report, which was drawn up by him, Sir Nathaniel Rich, and two others, strongly represented to the king the planters' claim for relief. The Bermuda charter had been granted to the company on June 29, 1615, but now after an interval of thirteen years it was submitted to parliament for confirmation. It is difficult to account for its presentation after so long a delay, but it may have been due to a desire on the part of the crown to show the Commons, who had been attacking so many royal grants to companies, that some of them were quite unexceptionable. The bill of confirmation was sent to a select committee comprising among others Sir Nathaniel Rich (reporter), Pym, Barrington, and Rudyerd.[55] The interest in Bermuda thus excited in Pym's mind caused him to purchase several shares of land in the islands; on the formation of the Providence Company his new interest in colonisation further expanded and he was prepared to accept the treasurership, which was offered to him by a unanimous vote. Although Pym for the next eight years devoted so much time to the Providence Company, he still found enough energy to do other work. He retained his post in the Exchequer, and that he still hankered after governmental work which did not commit him to approval of arbitrary power, is shown by his willingness to serve in 1632 as a commissioner for Gloucestershire to enquire into the causes of depopulation and of the conversion of arable land to pasture.

John Robartes (1606-1685)[56] was led to invest money in the Providence Company either by his friendship with

55 For the information concerning these committees refer to *Commons' Journal*.

56 Succeeded his father as Lord Robartes of Truro in 1634, and was created at the Restoration Earl of Radnor.

Pym or by his connection with the Rich family. He belonged to a Cornish family that had attained to great wealth by dealings in tin and wool. His father, Richard Robartes, had for years suffered from governmental extortion and one of the charges in the impeachment of Buckingham, which it fell to Pym to prove, was that he had compelled Robartes to purchase his barony in 1625 at a cost of £10,000. The family was closely allied with Pym and the Rous family by marriage, William Rous, eldest grandson of Sir Anthony Rous, having married Maria, sister of John Robartes, in 1617, while John Robartes himself married Lucy Rich, second daughter of the Earl of Warwick. He was educated at Exeter College, Oxford, where, according to Wood, he "sucked in evil principles both as to Church and State."[57] In 1630 he was just beginning to take an interest in public affairs and his intimacy with the promoters induced him to take a share in the Providence Company, but he was never a regular attendant at its meetings though he could be depended on to follow the lead of the older members.

It was certainly Pym's influence that led Oliver St. John to take an interest for the first time in colonisation and to invest in the Providence Company. A cadet of the house of St. John of Bletsho, Oliver St. John was in 1630 beginning to acquire a practice as a pleader under the ægis of the Russell family. He had married Lady Joan Barrington's favourite niece Joan, daughter of her brother, Henry Cromwell, and was the old lady's constant correspondent on business matters. He had been called to the bar at Lincoln's Inn in 1626 and was at this period earning a reputation among his friends as an acute lawyer. He had been sent to the Tower in November, 1629, for communicating to his patron, the Earl of Bedford, Dudley's tract on *Bridling Parliaments,* but

[57] Wood's *Athenæ Oxonienses,* III, 271, IV, 178.

was released on the birth of Prince Charles in June, 1630. His services were always called into requisition by the Providence and Saybrook patentees in legal matters, and to the reputation for legal acumen he acquired among the Puritan leaders we may attribute his selection as Hampden's counsel in the Ship-Money case, when he was quite unknown to the nation at large. It was through Pym also that John Graunt came to join the company. He had for years been an employé of the government in various posts under the Exchequer[58] and was therefore in all probability an old personal friend of Pym's. He was, at the time of which we are writing, clerk of the cheque in the Exchequer and in charge of all the king's messengers. His financial abilities were made use of by the Providence Company, who employed him as auditor of their accounts.

The last group of adventurers owe their connection with the company to the interest in Puritan colonisation that they had acquired from their neighbours. Gregory Gawsell was lord of the manor of Watlington, John Gurdon was the eldest son of old Brampton Gurdon of Assington, Suffolk, and Letton, Norfolk, while Sir Edmond Moundeford was lord of the manor of Feltwell. All these places lie within a radius of twenty miles from John Winthrop's home of Groton, Suffolk, and all three men were friends of the Winthrops and their relations. Puritanism and the desire for emigration were particularly strong in this corner of East Anglia, and it was this fact that led them to invest in the Providence Company. Gregory Gawsell was probably entrusted by the Earl of Warwick with the oversight of the estates of the Rich family in Norfolk and Suffolk. He was a man of considerable importance in the county, as is shown by his position as treasurer for the Eastern Counties' Asso-

[58] *C. S. P. Dom.*, 12 July, 1619, 23 July, 1620; 1635-1636, p. 182.

ciation in the Civil War.[59] His sister was married to one of the Saltonstall family, but he himself was never married; his tomb, with a long Latin inscription narrating his virtues, is in Watlington Church.[60] John Gurdon was an intimate friend of John Winthrop[61] and his sister married Richard, eldest son of Sir Richard Saltonstall;[62] he was also well known to Sir Nathaniel Rich. He came to the front during the Civil War, was a member of the Eastern Counties' Association and one of the king's judges. His name is spelt in the Providence records *Gourden,* but he must not be confused with John *Gauden,* chaplain to the Earl of Warwick and after the Restoration Bishop of Worcester, who is said to have been the author of the *Eikon Basilike.* Sir Edmond Moundeford represented Thetford in the parliament of 1628-1629 and the county of Norfolk in the Short and Long Parliaments. He took as active a part in the affairs of the Providence Company as his residence so far from London would allow, and a letter from him to his friend Sir Simonds d'Ewes concerning the company is extant.[63]

The intimate bonds uniting the members of the company, and in a wider circle the leaders of the Puritan party, cannot fail to be remarked in these brief notices of their careers, but there is a second fact about them, that is, perhaps, not so obvious. It is remarkable what a preponderant part East Anglia played in the great Puritan emigration and in the Puritan revolution ten years later, and here we find that, outside London, the Providence Company was mainly of interest to men from the eastern shires. It would be a study of great

59 S. P. Dom., Car. I, Vol. 539, no. 291, 30 May, 1645, Gawsell's signature.

60 Blomefield's *Norfolk,* VII, 480. For Gawsell's pedigree see Harl. Soc., *Visit. of Norfolk.*

61 Mass. Hist. Soc. *Coll.,* 4th series, VII, 632.

62 *Ibid.,* p. 251.

63 Brit. Mus., Harl. MSS., 207, fo. 211.

interest, but one that lies beyond the scope of our present subject, to examine the causes that, between the years 1630 and 1640, specially predisposed the men of eastern England to emigration. The tendency seems to have affected most strongly those living in an area that is spread out in a great horseshoe around the low-lying fen country that drains into the Wash. Puritanism was certainly stronger in this part of England than in any other, but this would hardly be sufficient to account for the phenomenon, and it is probable that a minute enquiry would reveal the workings of some deep-seated economic cause, a probability that is strengthened when we recall that throughout the early Stuart period there was in the area in question constant agitation of an economic and agrarian character, as is evidenced by the Domestic State Papers.

CHAPTER III

THE SAYBROOK PROJECT AND THE SETTLEMENT OF PROVIDENCE

While Bell and Elfrith were getting their colonists together in Bermuda and establishing the foundations of a colony in Santa Catalina, matters were moving apace with the emigrants to Massachusetts. Endecott on his second voyage in 1629 had established the settlements of Salem and Charlestown, and the main expedition under Winthrop's leadership left Southampton Water on March 23, 1630. The more important members of the company, such as Dudley and Johnson, accompanied Winthrop, but John Humphry, the first deputy-governor, was left behind to look after the company's affairs in England,[1] and Winthrop's eldest son, John, remained to sell off the family estates and refresh his knowledge of fortification for use if necessary in defence against the Indians. The intimate connection of the Providence Company's leaders with the Massachusetts enterprise at this time was most marked and they were constantly rendering services to the emigrants. Just before sailing, for instance, we find Isaac Johnson writing to Winthrop concerning his son John's studies in fortification:[2] "We have writ a letter to Sir N. Rich to get a letter from him to Capt. Gosnall that your son may by his means take a view and plot of Harwich Fort for us; for which I pray you will let him have time. . . .

[1] Massachusetts *Colonial Records,* 23 March, 1629-1630.

[2] Mass. Hist. Soc. *Coll.,* 4th series, VI, 31.

Warwick, as lord lieutenant of Essex, was in command of all the fortifications in the country.

P. S. I have sent Sir N. Rich his letter for your son, which, I hope, is sufficient.'' On December 9, 1630, John Humphry writes to Isaac Johnson at Charlestown:[3] ''We are all much bound to my Lord Say for his cordial advice and true affections. As also to my Lord of Warwick. Sir Natha: Rich deserves much acknowledgment of his wise handling. . . . My Lord of Warwick will take a Patent of that place you writ of for himself, and so we may be bold to do there as if it were our own. Write letters abundantly to him and others, though they deserve them not as he doth. My Lord Say told me he had writ a letter to you, but I cannot learn where he hath left it.''

This patent that Humphry mentions is of great interest as it shows us the beginnings of the movement that resulted a few years later in the foundation of the Saybrook settlement. It will be remembered that in a previous chapter we spoke of the division by lot in 1623 of the lands of New England between the subscribing members of the Council for New England owing to the great parliamentary opposition that the council had encountered as a monopoly. From 1623 to 1628 the Council for New England was in a moribund condition and appears to have done little or nothing. About the beginning of 1629, however, the Earl of Warwick began to take a renewed interest in its affairs and in concert with Sir Ferdinando Gorges began to resuscitate its activities. It has been the custom of writers to represent Gorges as in a state of perennial hostility to the Puritan colonists of New England and, if we only considered the period from 1632 onwards, this does correctly represent his attitude, but in the period 1629-1632 all the contemporary accounts of his action are consistent with his own version of what occurred. His attitude towards the Puritan colonies was entirely benevolent providing the

[3] *Ibid.*, VI, 15.

interests of his own family were not injured, and he was quite willing to join Warwick in smoothing matters for the colonists as much as possible. In his *Briefe Narration* he puts the matter thus:[4] "The King, not pleased with divers the passages of some particular persons, who in their speeches seemed to trench further on his royal prerogative than stood with his safety and honour to give way unto, suddenly brake off the Parliament. Whereby divers were so fearful what would follow so unaccustomed an action, some of the principal of those liberal speakers being committed to the Tower, others to other prisons—which took all hope of reformation of Church government from many not affecting Episcopal jurisdiction, nor the usual practice of the common prayers of the Church, whereof there were several sorts, though not agreeing among themselves, yet all of dislike of those particulars. Some of the discreeter sort, to avoid what they found themselves subject unto, made use of their friends to procure from the Council for the affairs of New England to settle a colony within their limits; to which it pleased the thrice-honoured Lord of Warwick to write to me then at Plymouth to condescend[5] that a patent might be granted to such as then sued for it. Whereupon I gave my approbation, so far forth as it might not be prejudicial to my son, Robert Gorges', interests whereof he had a patent under the seal of the Council. Hereupon there was a grant passed[6] as was thought reasonable, but the same was afterwards enlarged by his Majesty and confirmed under the great seal of England."[7]

[4] *Archæol. Amer.*, III, xlv.

[5] A word implying in the seventeenth century not the attitude of a superior towards an inferior, but mere acquiescence.

[6] Warwick's Patent of 19 March, 1628.

[7] The Massachusetts Charter of 4 March, 1629.

The Council for New England was in a state of revived activity under Warwick's presidency from 1628 onwards, and it was by his direction that the draft of a grant was prepared late in 1630. A printed version of the deed that was subsequently based on this draft has come down to us through Trumbull, the historian of Connecticut,[8] but neither of the original documents nor any record of their official enrolment has ever been discovered, and a large amount of controversy has raged round the question of their validity. The subject need not detain us here, but it may be suggested that in promising a further patent to the Massachusetts settlers, Warwick was relying on his control of the New England Council and his temporary agreement with the Gorges. The so-called patent that is printed by Trumbull is not at all usual in form and may have been the informal draft, which, before it could be sealed, would have had to undergo revision at the hands of the lawyers. The grantor of a territory must himself have a legal title before he can validly transfer it to others, and it certainly cannot be said that Warwick, even though he was president of the New England Council, had either a clear or an undisputed right to make grants of the territory that was nominally vested in the council.

Warwick and his friends, however, undoubtedly acted on the assumption that they could dispose of the desired territory, and it appears safe to take Trumbull's version of the grant as correct in the main. On March 19, 1632, Robert, Earl of Warwick, regranted the land for a distance of forty leagues from the Narragansett River to the following peers and gentlemen: "the right honourable William, Viscount Saye and Sele, the right honourable Robert, Lord Brooke, the right honourable Lord Rich, and the honourable Charles Fiennes, Esq., Sir

[8] Trumbull's *History of Connecticut,* I, 495.

Nathaniel Rich, Knt., Sir Richard Saltonstall, Knt., Richard Knightley, Esq., John Pym, Esq., John Hampden, Esq., John Humphry, Esq., and Herbert Pelham, Esq.'"[9] With the exception of the last named, we can identify each of these gentlemen as intimately interested in the Puritan migration to Massachusetts, and six out of eleven as members of the newly founded Providence Company. No action to enforce the grant was taken as yet, but from the surrounding circumstances we may be certain that the preliminary steps now taken were not without aim, but were in pursuance of a settled policy. The project for a great migration was seizing more and more upon the minds of Puritan men, Massachusetts had just been founded as one home for the refugees, Providence, it was hoped, would soon become another; many attempts were being made by godless men, such as Oldham or Mason, and by Arminians, such as the Brownes, to found settlements along the New England coasts. It would be well to secure a further large part of New England for the expansion of the new Puritan community and for a refuge for the Puritan settlers from Providence if Puritan hopes in the West Indies should be disappointed. We shall see how some of these anticipations were verified four years later, but in a way entirely unexpected to the first patentees.

Before we gather up the scattered threads we have collected and attempt to weave with them the story of the Providence Company, let us pause for a moment and regard the changes that had taken place along the American seaboard since we surveyed it as it was in 1600. The infant French colony around Quebec and along the banks of the St. Lawrence was beginning to be called Canada and was in 1631 for the moment in the

[9] The Clinton family were allied with the Pelhams and this man was probably a relative of the Earl of Lincoln.

hands of the Franco-Scottish brothers Kirke; in Nova Scotia the French Acadians at Port Royal and Sir William Alexander's rival Scottish colony had begun their century-long conflict. Along the shores of Maine a few scattered fishing settlements were all that yet existed, but the rise of Massachusetts as a stable community had begun, and Plymouth had already quite a respectable history of struggle behind it. Neither Dutch nor English had yet entered the valley of the Connecticut, though at the mouth of the Hudson River Manhattan had commenced a precarious existence as the Cinderella of the Dutch colonies. It was not till 1632 that George Calvert, the first Lord Baltimore, abandoning his attempts at colonisation in Newfoundland and Virginia, secured from Charles I the proprietorship of Maryland, though already William Claiborne had established a plantation on Kent Island in the Chesapeake and settled there about a hundred men from Virginia.[10] Virginia had in 1631 long since passed the struggling stage and was on the high road to prosperity; Bermuda, as we have seen, had disappointed the hopes of its colonisers, and Sir Robert Heath's attempted colonisation of "Carolana" had proved entirely abortive.

Matters in the West Indies had as yet changed little; St. Christopher and Nevis had just been cleared by Spain of their English and French settlers, but these had almost immediately returned. St. Martin's, Saba, and St. Eustatius were each held by a few Dutchmen, and others were attempting a colony on Tobago; Martinique already had a few French settlers and Barbadoes was definitely showing signs of becoming a prosperous English colony. The rest of the Lesser Antilles were still abandoned to the cannibal Caribs; off the shores of

[10] *J. H. U. Studies,* XIII, Latané, "Early Relations between Maryland and Virginia," p. 11.

Tierra Firme the Dutch had already made Curaçao into a place of arms and thence were maintaining the profitable clandestine trade with the Spanish colonies. In Guiana they were the only nation achieving anything like success, though English and French were still making attempts at trade and settlement. It was in Brazil that the Dutch West India Company were achieving great things at the expense of Spain and were making the most successful attempt to maintain an empire in tropical America that has ever been made by a non-Iberian nation. The Iberian monopoly of the New World had in thirty years been utterly destroyed, all the great colonising nations had taken their first steps westward and already the lists were being prepared for the struggle for colonial power that was to rage through the next two centuries with ever-varying fortunes.

There does not appear to have been in 1630 any invariable method of securing from the crown the right of planting a colony, grants being issued both under the sign manual and under the great seal, while some colonies were commenced without any direct license from the crown. The most formal, but at the same time the most costly method, was to obtain the issue of letters patent under the great seal, and this was the method chosen by the Providence Company. The letters patent were prepared upon the direction of a secretary of state by the attorney-general in consultation with the legal representative of the company, Oliver St. John, and were engrossed upon the patent roll[11] on December 4, 1630. The total cost of the patent including the necessary fees amounted to some £60, but in this total the numerous douceurs paid to the clerks of the Privy Council, etc., were not included. The company was incorporated under the title of "The Governor and Company of Adventurers

[11] 7 Car., I, Part 14.

of the City of Westminster for the Plantation of the Islands of Providence or Catalina, Henrietta or Andrea, and the adjacent islands lying upon the coast of America,'' and the limits within which the company's activities were confined were the tenth and twentieth degrees ''from the Equinoctial line towards the Tropic of Cancer,'' and the two hundred and ninetieth and three hundred and tenth degrees of longitude. The area thus marked out for the company's enterprise is some six hundred geographical miles from north to south by one thousand two hundred miles from west to east. The longitude was measured eastward from Ferro in the Canaries and the two hundred and ninetieth meridian (88° W. of Greenwich) passes through Cape Catoche and the head of the Gulf of Honduras, while the three hundred and tenth meridian (68° W.) runs through the Mona Passage between Hispaniola and Porto Rico. The parallel of 10° N. lat. passes to the north of the Isthmus of Darien and the northern limit of the patent just included the northern shore of Hispaniola.

The patent follows the general lines of the colonial patents of the period, and, as copied into the company's entry book, fills its first twenty pages. The Earl of Holland was named as first governor of the company and his deputy was to be elected annually in every Easter term. A general court was to be held upon the last Thursday of every term to ordain forms of government and appoint officers for the company and colony, while ordinary courts might be held at any time. Men, women, and children might be transported to the colony as the company desired unless the king should ''expressly forbid any particular person or persons to the contrary''; the company was to administer the oaths of allegiance and supremacy to all persons passing to the colony. These provisions as to the government's veto and the oath of allegiance were quite usual and had been inserted in all grants since Gilbert's patent of 1579, but they are of special interest when we remember that between 1630 and 1640, contrary to earlier usage, they were often put into effect, and many ships conveying emigrants to America were stopped by order of the crown. The sole right of trade within the prescribed limits was granted to the company upon the customary conditions of paying a royalty to the crown of one-fifth of all precious metals found. All persons resident or born within the limits of the patent were to be free denizens,[12] the company might give their officers the right to execute martial law, and the ordained magistrates and judges were to have full jurisdiction of life and death. The company might fit ships and furnish them with arms and ammunition and were granted in case of attack power of reprisal upon their assailants or any others of the same nation, after permission to obtain satisfaction had been granted by the crown. This is a clause not met with in earlier patents, but it was inserted here in view of the colony's position in the heart of the Spanish Indies and the likelihood of attack. The commission from the Earl of Warwick under which the first expedition had sailed, having been issued in time of war, gave fuller powers of hostile action, but the powers granted to the company and its servants were quite wide enough to cover a good deal of warlike activity.

In view of the English political situation in 1630, perhaps the most interesting provision of the patent is the last: "The privileges of the Company shall be confirmed by an Act of Parliament, if Parliament shall think fit to agree to the same, and the King promises to

[12] No mention is made of negroes, but it seems to be understood that "person" means "person of European descent."

give his assent to the confirming Act when passed." A similar clause had been added to the Guiana patent of 1627,[13] issued to the Earl of Warwick and others, but it was an unusual provision and may have been inserted because so many of the adventurers of the company had been members of parliament. It is at any rate noticeable that such a clause should have been inserted in an official document at a time when Charles I and his ministers were building up a system designed to render the crown independent of parliamentary subsidies and the accompanying parliamentary interference with the executive which they had learned to expect and which they so detested.

Even before the issue of the patent active preparations were being made by the company through the deputy-governor for the despatch of a strong expedition to Providence. The arrangements for arming the expedition were entrusted to the Earl of Warwick, who on January 10, 1631, was given permission by the Privy Council[14] to purchase from the crown and to ship to the colony twenty pieces of ordnance with their carriages and appurtenances and one last of powder. Each member of the company was urged at an early court to seek out as many men and boys as were fit to be sent, the numbers of which were to be reported to the deputy, who would give them directions when and where to assemble.

The emigrants were divided into three classes:

1. *Labourers,* or, as we shall afterwards call them, *planters,* who were to cultivate the ground, sharing the profits of their toil equally with the company.

2. *Artificers,* also to share their profits equally with

[13] Raleigh's patent of 1584 received parliamentary confirmation. Brown, I, 13.

[14] *Acts of Privy Council, Colonial,* I, p. 265.

the company, or else to work solely for the company and be allowed meat and drink and £5 a year wages.

3. *Apprentices,* usually called *servants,* above fourteen years of age, who entered into indentures for a term of years and were furnished meat, drink, and clothes during their apprenticeship. If any apprentice had any special faculty, he was to be allowed a reasonable recompense for its exercise. For the better encouragement of the planters and artificers, apprentices were to be allotted to them, their transportation and provisions being paid for by the company; this allotment of servants was the usual method adopted by the company to discharge their obligations to their officers.

The vessel chartered for the voyage was the *Seaflower* of two hundred tons burthen, of which John Dyke was part owner and John Tanner, Elfrith's fellow commander of the first voyage, was appointed master. Dyke had purchased a large magazine of commodities and laded the *Seaflower* with them from his warehouses in Billiter Lane.[15] His conduct in the matter was by no means irreproachable and, when the accounts for the voyage came to be made up on the return of the vessel early in 1632, it was found that very high prices had been charged. The quality of the provisions for use on the voyage and of the commodities to stock the company's store in the island, was very inferior and the many aspersions cast upon Dyke in the matter, impugning either his good faith or his judgment, caused a complete breach between him and the company from which he was paid out in 1632.

[15] Pym paid Dyke various sums on account as the furnishing went along. A sheet of accounts in Pym's own handwriting, giving particulars of various amounts disbursed, is among the Bouverie MSS. (Hist. MSS. Comm., *Tenth Report,* App'x, p. 85.) A copy of Purchas's *Pilgrims* cost £2-14-6, and six dozen catechisms for the plantation cost 12s.

The command of the passengers in the *Seaflower* was given to Capt. William Rudyerd,[16] younger brother of Sir Benjamin Rudyerd, who had seen some service in the Low Countries and whose military experience therefore recommended him to the company for strengthening the defences of the colony. The ninety passengers were solely men and boys; a barber surgeon was engaged to look after their health on the voyage and to remain in the island on arrival. It had been found impossible to secure the services as minister of the Mr. Ward who had been asked for by the emigrants from the Somers Islands, the company giving as their reason that they did not wish the Somers Islands Company to think their men were being drawn away. Grave, experienced ministers, it was found, were reluctant to leave their wives and children and therefore a young Welshman, Lewis Morgan, was sent to care for the spiritual welfare of the colonists. The company recommended him as a very sufficient scholar for his time and a studious and sober man, but their expectations of him were woefully disappointed and he proved a complete failure. The emigrants in general came from localities where the personal influence of the adventurers was strong, especially from Essex, recruited by the Riches and Sir Thomas Barrington, from Northants, recruited by Mr. Knightley, and from Oxfordshire by Lord Saye; there were also several Cornish and Devon men recruited by Pym. In addition a good many Welshmen went out among the earlier emigrants and it may be conjectured that some of these had been among the earliest sufferers from Laud's repressive ecclesiastical policy.[17]

16 For Rudyerd Pedigree see Harl. Soc., *Visit. of London*, II, 215. For some unexplained reason Rudyerd did not sail in the *Seaflower*, but went out in the *Little Hopewell*, in July, 1631.

17 Laud was Bishop of St. David's from 1621 to 1628, when he was translated to Bath and Wells.

Discussions went on through December and January, 1631, as to the form of government to be established and the lines to be laid down for the development of the colony. The conclusions come to were embodied in a series of instructions in thirty-five articles forwarded to the governor and council, and in a very long letter addressed to Gov. Bell personally. The government of the island was entrusted to the governor and a council of six members nominated by the company. The governor was to take serious measures only in consultation with the council, save in cases where explicit instructions had been received from England. The council had power to initiate measures, but over these the governor possessed an absolute power of veto, though in all cases of such veto he was to notify the company in England of the facts of the case at the first opportunity. This constitution was similar to that in force in Virginia during the later years of corporate control and was regarded as the most suitable form of government for an infant colony. Sir Nathaniel Rich and Warwick had vivid recollections of the early difficulties of Virginia under her first charter, when it was only by chance that Capt. John Smith had been able to make himself supreme and save the colony in spite of the members of his council.[18] The elective element was probably considered unsuitable in the council for the first few years, in view of the continual discord that existed in the elected Bermuda assembly, but that there was no general objection to the elective principle in colonial government is plain from the company's resort to it in Tortuga in 1635.

The governor and council were constituted the supreme judicial tribunal in all cases, civil and criminal, but all cases of importance were to be proceeded in by way of jury empanelled from the planters. Oaths were pre-

18 If one view of a much-debated case is to be trusted.

scribed to be taken by the governor, the council, and every planter over the age of sixteen; the governor's oath fills thirty closely written lines in the journal and abounds in scriptural quotations and phrases; extreme hostility to the Roman Church is expressed, but no mention whatever is made of the Church of England, which is also tacitly ignored in the planter's oath, another form of great length. The question as to the appointment of the first governor had much exercised the minds of the company at one of their earliest meetings; it had been suggested that the government should be vested jointly in Elfrith and Bell, but as it was feared that this might lead to friction, the decision was reached that Elfrith should be sole governor till his return from the colony. On hearing of this decision, the Earl of Warwick, who had been absent from the meeting, intimated that Elfrith had expressed his content if the government were conferred on his son-in-law Bell, solely, as better qualified by his experience in the government of the Somers Islands, and as he (Elfrith) might often be absent from the island on the company's business. This of course clinched the matter and Bell's commission was signed and sealed on February 7, 1631.

Capt. Philip Bell was the younger brother of Robert Bell, a prominent London merchant and member of the common council for Lime Street Ward. Robert Bell was deeply interested in colonial enterprise and had been one of the most successful factors of the East India Company; he was a member of the Northwest Passage Company and one of the commissioners for regulating the affairs of Virginia in 1624. Philip Bell became a member of the Somers Islands Company in 1624[19] and his acquaintance with Dyke, then deputy-governor of the company, recommended him for the governorship of the

[19] Lefroy, *Mem. of Bermudas*, I, 375.

islands in 1626 when Woodhouse had to be superseded. He left England for Bermuda in September, 1626, and took his seat as governor at the council table for the first time on February 16, 1627,[20] being then about thirty years of age.[21] Bell's governorship of Bermuda was unmarked by any special incident, but he had considerable difficulty in quelling a dispute between rival ministers and only succeeded in procuring peace by prohibiting all vestry meetings in the islands.[22] That his stay in Bermuda was not entirely happy, we have noted in an earlier chapter, but Bell must have acquired a large amount of experience in dealing with cantankerous councillors and discontented planters.

Capt. Daniel Elfrith was appointed admiral of the island and next in precedence to the governor, while the members of the first council were Capt. Samuel Axe and Lieut. Hugh Price, resident in the island, and Capt. William Rudyerd, William Rous, and John Hunt, who were to go out in the *Seaflower*.[23] William Rous owed his appointment to his kinship with Pym, being the eldest grandson of Sir Anthony Rous of Halton St. Dominick. He had married Maria, elder sister of John Robartes,[24] and we shall find him playing an important part in the island's affairs. John Hunt was appointed secretary of the council, Roger Floud, sheriff, and Thomas Fitch and Thomas Jenks, clerks of the company's stores. The dignity of the governor and council was jealously

20 *Ibid.*, I, 409.

21 Ligon (*Hist. of Barbadoes*, p. 24) visited Bell as governor of Barbadoes in 1647 and describes him then as a feeble old man. His will and that of his wife have been found by Mr. N. Darnall Davis, the author of *Cavaliers and Roundheads in Barbadoes,* who believes that the Philip Bell mentioned in 1669 (*Acts of Privy Council, Col.*, I, 506) was a nephew.

22 Lefroy, *Mem. of Bermudas,* I, 469.

23 Went out in *Little Hopewell* in July, 1631.

24 Harl. Soc., *Visit. of Cornwall,* p. 195.

regarded by the company, who forwarded a tipstaff or mace to be the ensign of government and thus described it: "On the one end upon a plate of silver is a portrayment of the seal of the Company, viz. three islands and the words written about it, '*Legem ejus expectabunt,*' taken out of Isaiah, 42., 4, 'The islands shall wait for his law,' which prophecy we hope may in some sort be fulfilled by planting the Gospel in those islands. On the end of the staff upon a plate likewise of silver are engrossed these words '*Innocens liberabit insulam,*' taken out of Job, 22, 30, 'The innocent shall deliver or preserve the island,' a good memento at all times when we go to God's house or to places of counsel and judicature."

Minute directions were given as to the ecclesiastical arrangements of the island. Two parsonage houses were built, one near the harbour and the other on the southwest shore; the minister, while he continued single, was to be lodged and dieted in the governor's house in order to make the governor's family an example to the rest of the island. He was to administer the sacrament monthly, and the company, with the state of religious affairs in England in their minds, summed up their desires for his success by saying: "We pray you to give him all the encouragement you can, for our sincere aim and desire above all things is to plant the true and sincere Religion and worship of God, which in the Christian world is now very much opposed."

The peace with Spain, concluded at Madrid on November 5, 1630, had been proclaimed in England on the fifth of December,[25] and its particulars were conveyed by the company to the governor and council. They added, however: "It seems there is no peace between us [and

25 *Howe's Continuation of Stowe's Annals,* p. 1046. John Humphry to John Winthrop, Mass. Hist. Soc. *Coll.,* 4th series, VI, 15.

the Spaniards] in the latitude where you are, and therefore you must be careful and vigilant to prevent their attempts, as ever.'' Even at the present day the great body of rules and understandings, that we call international law, has at times of crisis very little force to restrain the proceedings of belligerent nations and it is still hard to determine exactly when a state of war begins and when it ends. In the seventeenth century outside the limits of western Europe even the rudimentary international law of the time did not exist, and it was almost a recognized maxim that there was ''No peace beyond the line.'' The Providence Company were quite right in assuming that the treaty would do little to bring to an end the chronic state of war in the Indies, and more than forty years were to elapse before it was possible for England and Spain to agree upon a treaty of peace for their American possessions which should outlaw the disturbers of it and brand as pirates those who undertook belligerent acts in the western seas. To preserve the semblance of peace as long as possible the colonists were cautioned against taking the offensive against the Spaniards, but in order to be prepared to repel attack, the greatest efforts were to be devoted to fortification. Capt. Axe was to be maintained in command of Warwick Fort, already built, and a new fort, called Fort Henry, was to be erected to command the watering place in the southwest of the island and the approach to the southern entrance of the harbour; of this fort Capt. Rudyerd was appointed commander and he was also to act as muster master general of the island. Another fort, afterwards called Darley's Fort, was to be built upon the peninsula upon which Warwick Fort stood, but more to the eastward, so that the enemy's approach to the harbour might be further barred. These directions were improved upon by Bell and his council and a fourth important fort, called Black Rock Fort, was built on Black Point and completely guarded the harbour's southern entrance. A private signal was to be arranged to guard against dangerous admittances; when the approach of any unknown ship was signalled from the lookout station on The Mound, the forts were to be manned and all precautions taken. With regard to the Dutchmen in the island the company advised caution. Although the English and Dutch in the West Indies were still closely allied in their common hostility to Spain, there were signs that their ways were beginning to diverge, and the English were becoming jealous of the greater success of the Dutch, who, it must be remembered, had recently captured the great prize of the Plate Fleet[26] and were engaged in building up an empire in Brazil. "We desire," wrote the company, "that the Dutchmen that are with you, may be very well respected that they may have no cause of complaint to us or their friends. We give you power to yield them such contentment as you, yourself, shall think reasonable: yet be careful that you give them no interest in any land whatsoever, otherwise than as occupiers and manurers. And, being of another nation, you will do well to have a care what letters they send out of the island."

Full directions as to the social organisation of the plantation were given by the company. The freemen without servants were to be distributed into families of at least six or seven persons; of these one was to be chief and was to take special care "that he with his whole family, besides public duties, do daily, morning and evening, pray together unto God that his blessing may be upon them and the whole island." Freemen were to be allowed to choose their own partners, but stores were only to be delivered out of the company's

[26] Under Admiral Piet Hein, 8 September, 1628.

magazine to the chief of the family, who must give security to pay for them out of the produce of his and his fellows' plantations. The members of the family were to be responsible for one another's good behaviour, a device that was a favourite one with the colonial organisers of the early seventeenth century; it had been tried without much success in the early years of Virginia[27] and had been prescribed by the Massachusetts Company to Endecott for adoption by the servants sent out by the company under his charge.[28] Neither in Massachusetts nor in Providence did the prescribed system meet with any measure of success. Within a couple of years in Providence it had fallen into comparative disuse and had been superseded by the ordinary plantation system. The first planters, who had chosen their own ground and had been tilling it for a year past, were not to be dispossessed, but the company would not allow them the whole profit of the tobacco they had raised. The system of half-profits that had caused so much discontent among the Bermuda planters was still retained, and the company divided their share of the first year's tobacco that was to be returned by the *Seaflower* between Elfrith, who received three-fifths of it, and Axe who had two-fifths, an arrangement that produced considerable bickering and left a lasting breach between the two men. The planters were specially cautioned against falling into the error that had so nearly brought Virginia to ruin in its early years, and every family was directed to plant twice as much corn as would feed its members. Excess of tobacco planting was strictly prohibited and liberal rewards were promised to any who would introduce a staple commodity suitable for growth in the island. Elfrith was directed to sail in his pinnace to other West

[27] Bruce, *Economic History of Virginia.*
[28] Doyle, *Puritan Colonies,* I, 95.

Indian islands, Spanish, English, or Dutch, in search of such a commodity, and of sugar-canes, figs, oranges, and other fruit trees for the island's benefit. Unfortunately Elfrith's partiality for roving did not permit him so peaceful a voyage and his journey developed into a mere piratical cruise, for which he had to be severely reprimanded by the company.

The apprentices or servants sent out to Providence were of quite a different class to the criminals sent to Maryland and Virginia and the youths decoyed and deported to Barbadoes in later years. Many of them were young men of a fairly good social class, who looked forward to making a career for themselves and had emigrated in hopes of receiving at the end of their two or three years' indentures servants of their own. Many of the men sent were specially recommended to the officers and notably one, Pearsall, kinsman and late servant to Sir Edmond Moundeford, and Ralph Walcott, a near relative of Lord Brooke, who, during his indentures, was to serve the minister. The system in its inception, therefore, was by no means the oppressive one that it afterwards became in the colonies; a servant's lot in Providence was by no means easy, but if it were, as unfortunately it often was, but a form of slavery, this was not the intention of its organisers, who had simply modelled it upon the apprenticeship system then universally in use in England, but who had not yet learned the impossibility for white men of hard field labour in a tropical climate.

The total number of passengers in the *Seaflower,* the vessel that was to convey the first emigrants from England to Providence, was ninety and the vessel set sail from the Thames in the third week of February, 1631. Her voyage must have been a terrible one for her passengers; the provisions supplied by Dyke proved very bad, the bread was mouldy and the beer sour, and not merely was the quality poor, but the master, John Tanner, who owned a share in the ship, refused the passengers sufficient rations and kept a large quantity of provisions for private sale on reaching the island. On her voyage the vessel touched at Bermuda and took on board a few of Elfrith's adherents, who had been left behind in 1630. Providence was reached about the end of May, 1631, the governor's instructions were delivered, the surviving passengers landed, and the full life of the colony definitely opened.

CHAPTER IV

THE PLANTING OF TORTUGA (ASSOCIATION) AND TROUBLES IN PROVIDENCE

In our preliminary survey of West Indian history we showed that St. Christopher was planted by Capt. Thomas Warner in 1623, and that after a few initial difficulties a stable colony had been established, which from 1626 onwards was taken under the protection of James Hay, Earl of Carlisle. In the spring of 1623 a young shipmaster, Anthony Hilton by name,[1] born and brought up in the bishopric of Durham, was employed by certain merchants of Barnstaple in a voyage to North Virginia for the fur trade and for the exploration of the Hudson River[2] in the hope of discovering the Northwest Passage before the Dutch, who were just beginning to undertake the settlement of Manhattan in earnest. Sailing by the usual outward course via the West Indies, which had not yet been abandoned in favour of Argall's more northerly route, Hilton touched at St. Christopher

[1] The account here given is based upon that given in 1675 of the settling of St. Christopher and Nevis by John Hilton, the aged store-keeper of Nevis, younger brother of Anthony Hilton. The account was despatched to England to be used in the negotiations with France concerning the islands and thus came into the possession of Thomas Povey, among whose papers it is preserved in the British Museum (Eg., 2395, fo. 503). It agrees with the account published by Capt. John Smith in 1629 (*Works,* p. 903), and, where capable of verification, with the extant letters from the islands. It seems right, therefore, that credence should be attached to Hilton's statements, but his chronology needs some slight emendation.

[2] We learn this from a letter written by Hilton to his mother from on board ship at the commencement of the voyage, May 4, 1623. The letter is extant among the Manchester Papers. Hist. MSS. Comm., *Eighth Report,* p. 47, No. 364.

and there made the acquaintance of Capt. Warner. He was much struck with the possibilities of the island for tobacco growing and, on his return from America after the failure of the Hudson River project, imparted his design for planting there to certain Irish gentlemen, who proved willing to finance him. Resigning his employment with the Barnstaple merchants, he again set sail for St. Christopher with a few followers and, arriving safe, was granted by Warner a plantation on the windward side of the island, where he was the first to settle. St. Christopher was not yet free from Carib raids and Hilton's first plantation was soon destroyed. He managed to escape, however, and, clearing another plantation on the leeward side, raised there a good crop of tobacco and returned with it in the autumn of 1627 to Ireland, where it was disposed of to good advantage.

The experience Hilton had had, determined him that he would do better to plant another island rather than remain in St. Christopher; he obtained financial aid, therefore, from a London merchant, Thomas Littleton, and having procured a patent from the Earl of Carlisle, attempted to settle upon the island of Barbuda,[3] but as he and his associates found that island very barren and were also dissatisfied with Antigua and Montserrat, they ultimately decided to plant the small island of Nevis, where they landed on July 22, 1628. Other planters were attracted from St. Christopher and by the end of the year nearly a hundred and fifty persons were assembled in the island under the governorship of Anthony Hilton. Warner returned to England from St. Christopher towards the end of 1628, leaving as his deputy in the island one Aston, a personal enemy of Hilton's; matters did not long remain on a peaceful footing and on an accusation that Aston had attempted

[3] Smith, p. 910.

to suborn one of his servants to murder him while on a visit to St. Christopher, Hilton took up arms in his defence. Before open hostilities took place, however, a great English ship coming into the harbour, Hilton took refuge on board and returned to Nevis. The news of the tumult reaching England, Lord Carlisle determined that Hilton was an unsuitable person for governor and that it would be well to remove him and replace him by one of his own kinsmen. Before the design could be carried out by the earl's commissioners despatched from England, Hilton got wind of it and fled in a small west country ship then loading tobacco in Nevis harbour.[4] Arrived in England, Hilton attempted to make his peace with Carlisle, but within a very short time news arrived that both St. Christopher and Nevis had been taken by a Spanish fleet on September 7, 1629, and the inhabitants, both French and English, expelled, though some had escaped to the mountains and others had taken refuge on adjacent uninhabited islands. On the retirement of the Spanish armada, these fugitives returned and a provisional government was again established in the islands.

Sir Thomas Warner, now knighted for his services, returned to St. Christopher early in 1630 with further colonists, but Hilton had got into difficulties with Littleton over financial matters and only returned to Nevis to gather round him a few personal adherents of both nationalities and to migrate from the island to a fresh home. There are reasons to suppose that Hilton's acquaintance among the rovers of all nationalities was more extensive and peculiar than was fitting even in those days of laxity. His knowledge of the rovers' resorts led him to fix for his new place of settlement upon the island of Tortuga off the north coast of Hispaniola and only a

[4] August, 1629.

few miles away from the opening of the Windward Passage.

This island was far removed from any of the Spanish settlements in Hispaniola and had long been used by rovers of all nationalities as a resort where they might replenish their victuals and refit their ships. It was especially a resort for French rovers and since the mountains in the centre of the island abounded in wild hogs, fresh meat could always be obtained. According to De Laët,[5] the French and Dutch obtained large supplies there and were accustomed to call Tortuga "L'Isle des Porceaux." Only a narrow strait, some two miles wide, separates Tortuga from Hispaniola, in the forests covering the northern shore of which great herds of cattle then ran wild. Upon the shores of Cape San Nicolas, some forty miles away, a few Dutchmen had established themselves and were engaged in making salt and curing the flesh of the cattle they slew in the forests.[6]

Hilton's colonists, finding Tortuga much to their liking, resolved to make it their permanent home and despatched some of their number to England to secure financial assistance and supplies. They succeeded in interesting in their case Dr. Samuel Rand,[7] a doctor of physic well known in the City of London, and John Hart, a colonial merchant of the second rank; finding, however, that more powerful assistance would be needed before they could obtain from the crown the loan of the ordnance they required, in the middle of May, 1631, they got into touch with the Providence Company and suggested that an arrangement should be come to for mutual benefit. The idea was well received by the company, and

5 De Laet, J., *Novus Orbis,* French translation, 1640, p. 13.

6 Hence according to the accepted explanation derived from Du Tertre, 1654 (III, 141), the term "buccaneers" from boucan—dried meat.

7 Harl Soc., *Visit. of London,* II, 184.

a committee, consisting of Sir Nathaniel Rich, Pym, Dyke, Barber, and Graunt, was appointed to carry on the negotiations; by the end of May, 1631, terms satisfactory to both sides had been agreed upon and the planters were taken under the protection of the Providence Company. The Tortuga adventurers,—Capt. Anthony Hilton, Capt. Christopher Wormeley, and Capt. Richard Bragg, resident in Tortuga, Robert Wormeley, who was going there, Dr. Samuel Rand, and John Hart,—were to be permitted to join the Providence Company so far as it concerned itself in Tortuga; the fee-simple of the island was vested in the company, who were to receive twenty per cent of all future commodities raised by the Tortuga planters, but who took no responsibility for past expenses. Each member of the Providence Company contributed £70 and each Tortuga adventurer £40, towards the cost of a first magazine for the island, and it was resolved to send six pieces of ordnance with the necessary ammunition for purposes of fortification.

The northern limits of the first patent of the Providence Company, 20° N. lat., were such as just to exclude Tortuga, which lies in lat. 20° 4′ N. A petition was, therefore, prepared and presented to the king by the Earl of Holland, praying for the enlargement of the company's grant to include Tortuga and all other unoccupied islands lying within three or four degrees of their former grant. On June 17, 1631, a grant[8] was accordingly issued extending the limits of the company's rights to all islands lying between six and twenty-four degrees from the equinoctial line in north latitude and between the degrees of longitude of the earlier grant (290°-310°) so that these islands were not in the actual

[8] *C. S. P. Dom.*, 17 June, 1631. A copy of the enlarged grant in Jessop's writing is extant among the Sloane MSS. (Brit. Mus., Sloane, 973.)

possession of any other Christian prince nor were formerly granted to any of his Majesty's subjects. This enlarged grant immensely extended the company's opportunities, for the parallel of 24° N. passes through the Florida Channel and the Bahamas, while 6° N. runs well to the southward of the Isthmus of Panama, and the whole of the central portion of the West Indies was, therefore, claimed as a field for English colonisation after the light-hearted manner of the time.

A large amount of discussion took place concerning the despatch of the required supplies, and it was strongly suggested that it would be well to undertake nothing until the spring of 1632, when the prevalence of the "norths"[9] would keep the Spanish fleets in port and the company's vessel might reach Tortuga in safety. In the end, however, the urgent need of the colonists for an immediate supply prevailed and directions were given to Hart, who had been engaged as the company's factor or "husband," to charter a small vessel for a voyage of seven or eight months. He secured the *Little Hopewell,* a small vessel of some sixty tons with seven guns, at the rate of £32 a month, the owners being also allowed the free freight of twelve cwt. of tobacco. Matthew Harbottle, who had already served the company in the first voyage, was appointed master at the rate of £4 per month, a rate of pay somewhat higher than that usual in the royal navy of the period.[10] It was decided, owing to the difficulty that would be experienced in raising any considerable number of servants in such a time of good employment,[11] that it would be better to

[9] Storms and north winds prevailing during the months of December, January, and February. The large Spanish war vessels were very unseaworthy and remained in port during the winter.

[10] Clowes, *The Royal Navy,* II, 13.

[11] 1630 had been a year of plague and scarcity; 1631, as we see from this entry in the records, was, on the contrary, prosperous.

postpone the sending of many men from England and to trust to recruiting men for the colony in the West Indies. Many of the English plantations in the Caribbees and notably Nevis, the company heard, were in a bad way and were likely to dissolve, so that the new plantation if it offered good prospects would probably attract those who deserted, and by this means its strength might be rapidly increased.

The government of the island was placed in the hands of Capt. Anthony Hilton, who was to be succeeded in case of death by Capt. Christopher Wormeley; a council of six persons was nominated, and Anthony Roberts was sent out from England as clerk of stores in charge of the magazine. Careful directions were drawn up for the fortification of the harbour, which lay on the shore nearest Hispaniola, and, to mark the change in the status of the island, it was resolved that its name should be changed and that it should henceforward be called the "Island of Association." It was not expected that the prosperity of the new colony would depend mainly upon the planting of such commodities as tobacco and cotton, which were looked to in Providence, but it was hoped that a large revenue would be derived from the export of the dye-woods growing in the forests that covered the island. The introduction into Europe of new dyeing materials had been a noticeable result of the opening-up of the West Indian trade during the latter half of the sixteenth century. Among the most important of these dyes were the red dyes derived from various woods, known as logwood, Brazil or braziletta wood, and Campeachy wood, the best qualities of which grew on the shores of Yucatan, but which were also plentiful in many of the Caribbees. Perhaps one of the most potent inducements to the Providence Company to aid the Tortuga adventurers, was the fact that large quantities of these valuable woods might be cut and exported from the island, and one of the cardinal provisions of the original agreement was that no merchantable wood was to be cut in the island but under license from the company, who were to receive one-fifth of the proceeds. Unfortunately, however, stringent legal enactments[12] were in force in England against the importation of these woods, which had been fraudulently used by dyers and did not in their hands produce fast colours. It was necessary, therefore, to carry the wood to France or Holland, where the use was permitted, and this rendered the restriction of cutting to the company's licensees incapable of enforcement, and the difficulties with which the colony of Association had to contend from the beginning were due to the cutting of wood by interlopers with the connivance of the company's officers.

The *Little Hopewell* was got ready for sea by the middle of July, 1631, and, after embarking her passengers and goods, sailed from the Thames on July 23. Her master had received directions that, after landing the magazine and ordnance at Association, he was to proceed to Providence, there to deliver a letter for the governor and council and to land Rudyerd and Rous, who had not sailed in the *Seaflower* as originally intended. The master was to carry from Association to Providence any surplus corn that was available and on his return voyage was to lade with tobacco and wood at Association, which cargo he was to bring to Europe. The voyage was successfully prosecuted along these lines and the *Little Hopewell* returned to England on April 20, 1632. What happened to her cargo of wood does not appear, but the presumption is that by the connivance

[12] 23 Eliz., cap. 9. Continual attempts to smuggle the prohibited dyes into England were being made, and the lucrative patent place of searcher for prohibited dye-stuff was much sought after. See *C. S. P. Dom.*

of the Earl of Ancram, who was then patentee for logwood, it was quietly smuggled into England and disposed of.

Further emigrants to Association were despatched by the *Charity* in May, 1632, under the lead of Samuel Filby,[13] who took out his wife and several servants. He had been a planter in St. Christopher and was thus experienced in West Indian planting and looked forward to a prosperous career in the island. The accord between the company and the Tortuga planters was not long uninterrupted, for before the close of 1631 it was learned by a "stranger" English ship, the *Whale,* touching at Association on her way home from Providence, that it had been found impossible to recruit wood-cutters at Nevis and St. Christopher as expected, and that much wood was being cut in the island by French and Dutch with the connivance of Capt. Hilton, who was pocketing the proceeds for himself and exporting the wood in French and Dutch ships. Many objections were, therefore, made by the adventurers to subscribing towards a second magazine that had been promised for 1632. They felt that they had no assurances as to the future intentions of the planters and that, if the prohibition of trading with interlopers was incapable of enforcement, there was no guarantee whatever of a return for their expenditure. Pym, however, maintained that Association ought to be looked upon in connection with Providence and as providing a second string to the company's bow. When responsibility for the island was assumed, a magazine had been promised for October, 1632, and Pym held that the promise having once been given, it should be adhered to. He agreed that Englishmen were unsuited to the labour of wood-cutting in tropical forests, where "there

13 A letter from him is extant among the Barrington MSS.

was an abundance of offensive flies,'' but he pointed to the fact that the Dutch ships carrying negroes to the Spaniards passed close by the island on their voyage, and suggested that it would be possible to obtain from them a supply of labour well suited to the work. Pym finally carried his point and a magazine was despatched to the island according to promise about the end of July, 1632. A minister, Mr. Key, was engaged to care for the spiritual welfare of the colonists and sailed by the same ship; he must have found a very arid field for his labours, for the class of colonists in Association was very different from that in Providence. The more adventurous spirits from St. Christopher and Nevis, augmented by rough woodsmen of at least three nationalities, many of whom had spent years roving the Indies for plunder, were not promising disciples for a young minister chosen by the straitest of English Puritans. Mr. Key's stay in the island was by no means happy, and within a couple of years we find him obtaining permission from the company to proceed to Providence, where he found employment with Capt. Camock's expedition to the mainland of Central America.

Pym's suggestion of the possibility of employing negroes for wood-cutting must have been based upon private information received from Hilton, for by February, 1633, Hilton had already purchased forty negroes and was employing them in the island. So profitable did the new departure appear that the company were desirous of entering into an arrangement with him, whereby twenty of these negroes were to become their property and were to be employed under his direction and along with his men in the wood-cutting, the charge of supervision and the profits to be equally divided. They directed him to procure more negroes on their account from the Dutch, and if it were found that there were more than could be profitably employed in Association, the extra hands were to be sent to Providence.

The first intelligence of the safe arrival of the *Seaflower* at Providence reached England in December, 1631, letters from the island being brought by an English ship, the *Whale,* that had touched there on her voyage through the West Indies.[14] She had also touched at Association and brought thence some sixty cwt. of tobacco, the produce of the plantation, which proved to be of good quality and was disposed of to advantage. By the same or some other "stranger" ship came George Needham, who in 1629 had been left behind by Capt. Camock to plant tobacco in Henrietta. Needham brought with him a good supply of tobacco, which was purchased from him by the company, but his carriage and behaviour were so offensive to them that they refused him any further assistance. He apparently felt it as a grievance that no steps were to be taken for the carrying on of the plantation he had begun in Henrietta, and was incautious enough to express his dissatisfaction openly. However, being summoned before the treasurer, Pym, and expressing his contrition, some assistance was granted to him for his more pressing needs and, on promising never to repeat his harsh words against the company and Capt. Elfrith, he was told that he should be employed in the next ship to Providence and have servants allotted to him. The company was the readier to pardon Needham as he had had long experience as a planter in the West Indies, both in Bermuda and in St. Christopher, and such experience was a valuable asset in a new colony.

[14] From letters of about this date from New England it would appear that the *Whale* had sailed to Massachusetts with emigrants in 1630 and thence to the West Indies in the hopes of picking up a cargo. Many ships did this in later years.

The *Seaflower* arrived in England on her return voyage from Providence on April 2, 1632, and for the first time the company were placed in possession of full information concerning the happenings in the colony and the steps necessary to place matters on a satisfactory footing. The misusage of the *Seaflower's* passengers on the outward voyage and the bad and insufficient provisions supplied to them have already been mentioned; not only the provisions but also the magazine she took out for the supply of the planters proved very bad. Dyke had supplied articles of the very poorest quality and had charged the company full prices. They, expecting to be recouped by the planters and ignorant of the facts, had fixed their retail prices accordingly, and in consequence bitter murmurings resulted. To overcharge for worthless goods was by no means a novel proceeding on the part of Dyke, and many of the old Bermuda planters must have remembered with disgust that such malpractices had characterised his proceedings towards the earlier colony,[15] while he was the bitterest opponent of the policy of allowing freedom of trade to the planters. As has been shown, the complaints of the company resulted in Dyke's practical dismissal and from thenceforward Pym, as treasurer, took the oversight of the provisions and supplies sent to the island, being assisted by the company's husband, John Hart.

The *Seaflower* had left Providence on her homeward voyage on December 21, 1631, and steered direct for home by the usual course through the Florida Channel. On her way between Cuba and Florida she was attacked by a Spanish man-of-war from Havana and compelled to fight her way clear. The attack must have been a fierce one, for she was three times boarded, but the

[15] See the full account of the proceedings relative to the attempts of Delbridge of Barnstaple. Lefroy, *Mem. of Bermudas,* I.

Spaniards were finally repulsed with great loss. Six or eight men were wounded and four Englishmen killed, including Mr. Essex, a planter who had gone out in the first voyage but was now returning to England without the company's permission. Capt. Tanner, who had lost an eye in the fight, was warmly commended for his prowess, but the company now began to realise more clearly the risks they ran in establishing a colony in the heart of the Indies, and it was resolved that even more stringent precautions than before must be taken for the immediate arming and fortification of the colony.

Under Bell's careful guidance the immigrants from the Somers Islands, after clearing the two acres of ground allotted to each of them of the timber and undergrowth that covered it, had begun by planting corn.[16] When their future subsistence was thus assured, the rest of their ground was planted with tobacco, the crop they had always been accustomed to raise in Bermuda. Indian corn and pease were found to grow very rapidly and bear excellently, so that when the *Seaflower* arrived, there was ample store of provisions to maintain both the old planters and the new arrivals. These also were at once set to plant corn and by October, 1631, they had provided sufficient to maintain themselves, for it was found that two or three crops of corn a year might be raised in the tropical climate of the island. The second and third crops were hardly as abundant as the first, and were more subject to attacks of blight, but the fertility of the soil astonished the newcomers. A large proportion of the servants sent out in the *Seaflower* were set to finish the work on Warwick Fort under Axe's

[16] Many of these details are derived from a private letter written from Providence to Pym by Wm. Rudyerd and Wm. Rous in October, 1633. The letter is now among the Bouverie MSS. at Brymore, Somerset. Hist. MSS. Comm., *Tenth Report*, App'x, p. 87.

directions and the company's half-share of all provisions raised was allotted to their maintenance. In October, 1631, some eighty more Bermudians arrived and set to work with a will in clearing their ground. By the end of November they had planted their corn, but the dry season was coming on, the crop did not flourish, they found that the excess of stores the earlier immigrants had accumulated was insufficient to fill so many extra mouths, and the last comers were the first to feel the dearth. As was so often the case in the early days of a new colony, it was found that the immigrants were of very unequal capabilities, and that some of them showed a strong distaste for hard work. Those who had by their efforts provided for their subsistence, were unwilling to deprive themselves for the benefit of newcomers, especially when those newcomers were as alien in sympathy to them as were many of the Bermudians. The religious difficulties that were agitating England were reproduced in little in the Somers Islands and although those who accompanied Bell to Providence mainly belonged to the Puritan party, there was an admixture of others, and the eighty arrivals in October, 1631, were men who had been gladly spared from the Somers Islands as undesirable members of a hard-working society. The immigrants from England were practically all strict Puritans of the same type as those who were leaving England for Massachusetts Bay and, being by far the stronger party in the island at this time (1632), aimed at a strictness of religion and discipline that their fellows were ill suited to observe.

Gov. Bell, although Puritan in sympathy, had shown during his government of Bermuda that he would not sacrifice the well-being of a colony to religious differences, and he attempted to preserve a balance between the parties and to insist upon hard and unremitting work by all for the strengthening and fortification of the island. Lewis Morgan, the young Welsh minister of the settlement, was not prepared to submit to the governor's control and, aided by a planter, Mr. Essex, fomented and focused the discontent of the planters against both Bell and the company. It may be that Morgan and some of his adherents were sincere in basing their discontent on religious grounds, but from their complaints we may guess that, while Morgan's bitterness was occasioned by disillusionment and by finding that his work was a great deal more difficult and uncongenial than he had anticipated, many of the planters were actuated in the main by their hostility to the company's insistence upon the same system of profit sharing that had been so much objected to in the Somers Islands.

Morgan voiced his own complaints in a private letter despatched by the *Seaflower* to Sir Nathaniel Rich, while the general objections of the planters were embodied by him in a petition from them to the company and entrusted to Mr. Essex, who secured his passage by pretending to have received permission from the company to return home when he desired. As we have seen, Essex was slain in the *Seaflower's* fight off Florida and the whole of his papers, showing the genesis of the petition, fell into the company's hands when the vessel reached England. Morgan's letter to Sir Nathaniel Rich was "so stuffed with bitter expressions" and so avowed "a spirit inclined to sedition and mutiny," that the company at once resolved that he must be sent home without delay. They saw in him the author or at least the fomenter of so much seeming discontent among the planters that he might cause a revolt in the island from the company's government. Preparations for the despatch of reinforcements to the island by the new ship, the *Charity,* were far advanced when the *Seaflower* arrived, and in order to avoid delay at this critical juncture, the sailing was expedited as much as possible and full directions for dealing with the crisis were sent out to the governor. Bell was directed to suspend Morgan at once from the ministry without vouchsafing him any explanation. A day or two before the vessel was to sail on her return, he was to cause Morgan's arrest, sending him at once on board ship and allowing him no intercourse with those on shore. He was to be brought home in strict confinement and the company promised to deal severely with him when he reached England. The governor carried out these directions with promptitude, and the culprit came before the court on the *Charity's* return, March 15, 1633. His long confinement had already induced a contrite spirit and, after a very severe rating by Pym and Sir Nathaniel Rich, he humbly begged the pardon of the company. They did not desire to carry matters to an extreme against the person of a minister, however unworthy, and permitted him to make a humble acknowledgment in writing of his mutinous, unworthy, and uncharitable conduct as sufficient amends. Payment of his salary was refused, but to maintain him until he could secure further employment, a gratuity of £5 was bestowed on him through the treasurer, and the company agreed to allow him a small sum for the books he had left behind him in the island.

Though Morgan was thus easily dealt with, to settle the complaints in the planters' petition was a much more difficult task. What, perhaps, galled the company most was Morgan's insinuation to the planters that the adventurers were solely and covetously desirous of profit for themselves and that they put on a hypocritical show of godliness for the encompassing of ungodly ends. To answer this most unjust and unworthy accusation, the company devoted three closely written folio pages of their letter to the governor and some extracts from this letter give us an indication of their aims in founding the colony. The planters' "bitter insultings and infamous libels are such as it behooves not one Christian man to write to another," and the company wonder how men can so much forget their duty to God and their respect to those "who have sought their good safety and welfare both for soul and body not [the adventurers'] own profit as some . . . have published there and sent home written." Each adventurer has expended £600 at least;[17] while in other plantations £25 or £50 was the usual share and if a man laid out £100 before return of profit, "he was accounted a great Patriot, but scarce a wise Adventurer." The planters gain a comfortable subsistence abroad, which they never do at home, "and have likewise means to do God and their countrymen great service in spreading Religion and advancing the honour of the English name in those, till of late, almost unknown parts of the world." The planters are like the Israelites for their murmurings. "It is nothing to them to have been the first men that have laid that foundation of so great a work, to raise an eternal monument to their never-dying Glory in propagating God's true religion and spreading the English empire. Oh, no! but the Planters must be presently rich, the Adventurers poor and, as much as in you lies, discouraged wholly from proceeding in that noble work of providing a refuge for those oppressed for righteousness sake." The company are glad to learn that there are still some godly and discreet persons left, who are steadfast like Joshua. Let them admonish the guilty and threaten their return home with shame and dishonour; for the sake of the righteous and for their sake only, the Adven-

[17] That is, up to the date when this letter was written, May 10, 1632.

turers hope God will send his blessing upon the colony and multiply it exceedingly.

Treasurer Pym's hand is visible in many of the phrases of this lengthy reproof, but his practical mind could not be contented with mere admonition without an attempt to remove any real causes of discontent that might exist. The elements hostile to the Puritan atmosphere of the colony must be at once removed and directions to this end were given: "Whereas complaint is made of the superstitious and evil disposition of some of those that came by the *Seaflower* and other ships from the Somers Islands, we would have you to send them back by this ship [the *Charity*] to their former habitations if the season of the year shall be convenient so that the voyage may not be prevented thereby." Strict instructions were given to the master that he was to land these passengers at Bermuda and nowhere else. That the company did not mean to be respecters of persons in their dispensation of justice was shown by their original intention to order the trial of Capt. William Rudyerd on charges of drunkenness, swearing, ill-carriage towards the governor, and other misdemeanours since he had been in the island, but on the appeal of his brother, Sir Benjamin, and the Earl of Holland, himself, it was finally resolved that if he were a reformed man and no longer likely to breed division or hinder the progress of religion, he should not be brought to trial but merely admonished. His drunkenness caused the company to write: "That by the taking away the cause of some abuses we may in some measure prevent their increase, we do order that all the strong waters out of our magazine that come in this ship or that shall hereafter come in any other ship from us, shall be taken into our store and be issued thence by our officers according to directions from you [the governor], excepting such private supplies as shall be sent from particular friends to persons well-qualified with temperance." It was learned that some in the island had sent to England for cards, dice, and tables. Bell was directed that if any of these baubles should arrive, he was to have them publicly burned and strictly to prohibit the use of such ungodly things under severe penalties. Lawful recreations, however, such as chess and shooting, might be permitted and even encouraged as long as they did not conflict with work.

That the planters might have encouragement to piety and the furtherance of the true religion, three ministers were sent, Arthur Rous as lecturer, Hope Sherrard[18] as minister of New Westminster, and Mr. Ditloff as minister of the southwest part of the island. Arthur Rous[19] was the fifth son of Sir Anthony Rous by his first wife and was thus the younger brother of Francis Rous, and Pym's step-brother. He had married a daughter of Nicholas Roope, a shipowner of Dartmouth, who had many ships engaged in the privateering trade, and by her Rous had a large family who accompanied him to Providence; it was therefore considered convenient that a house should be built for him near New Westminster and that he should preach a lecture there on some week-day. Hope Sherrard's early history cannot be traced; he played a very important part in the island's story and some letters from him have been preserved. Ditloff seems to have been one of those poor Palatine ministers, dispossessed by the Spaniards, on whose behalf many collections were made in English churches about this time. The company enjoined respect and attention to

18 His name is spelt Sherhard in the records and in some contemporary accounts he is called Sherwood. His extant letters are always signed as above.

19 Harl. Soc., *Visit. of Cornwall* (1620), p. 195.

the ministers as an aid to piety. "We advise you all therefore as to an humble and sincere obedience to their message and a devout and respective carriage towards their persons. At the Council Table they shall sit covered, but at such times as they deliver their opinion, we require that they stand uncovered. . . . That they may have much encouragement to spend their times and pains in the service of your souls and that God may make their endeavours effectual to the confining of those that stand, to the increase of Grace and the conversion of those who are yet strangers from God to the knowledge of his Grace, wherein our prayers shall not be wanting, and to the attainment whereof our charge of their entertainment shall not seem burdensome, we would have you presently assign unto them all proportionable quantities of land and to take some course that their servants may be provided for with diet, lodging and washing till they shall be able so to dispose of themselves that they may make convenient provision for their maintenance."

The company's care for the providing of the island with worthier ministers than Morgan, was blessed in the case of Sherrard, but Rous only lived a few months after landing, being carried off by fever in 1634. Ditloff proved faint-hearted and returned to England in disgrace in May, 1634, leaving Sherrard as the only minister of the colony. Ditloff was accused in letters to the company of a levity of conduct unbecoming in a minister and was called upon to exculpate himself before receiving his salary. A vivid little glimpse of the time is afforded in his answers to the charge; in reply to Pym's enquiry whether it was true that he and others used to sing on the Sabbath Day songs that were not divine, he answered that "Mr. Rous taught him songs, called *catches,* the meaning of which word he understood not, the matter of which was the motion of creatures as the nightingale and the like." Rous and Sherrard sang with him, but never on the Lord's Day. Ditloff was not content to bear the attacks made upon him without retaliation, and told Pym that he was informed that many of the planters who went out with him thought Rous insufficient, "not being able to pray extemporary and would soldier-like beat his men." "If these things were so," he wrote, "Mr. Rous was fitter for a buff-coat than a cassock, and he did not think himself to have been at fault in the opinion." The company apparently did not think so either, for in the end Ditloff was paid the money owing to him, and departed into his own country.

These trivial details have their importance in our enquiry as showing the type of society the company and some of the colonists were aiming to establish in the island, and as suggesting the similarity of the colony in its inception to Massachusetts. The founders of both wished to provide a refuge for the oppressed victims of Laud's ecclesiastical régime, each was to be a sanctuary where the Puritans might worship God after their own fashion, each was to be a society ordered according to the dictates of religion and governed with justice and equity, but upon the strictest Puritan pattern. In each colony there was a section of the community hostile to Puritanism; in Massachusetts the earlier settlers, such as Morton, Gardiner, and Oldham, were for a time a real danger to the fruition of the ideals of its rulers and had to be suppressed or driven out; in Providence the "superstitious" Bermudians had to be got rid of. But, whereas their conditions of comparative isolation enabled the rulers of Massachusetts to found a pure theocracy that lasted unchanged for forty years, the situation of Providence, the enervating effects of its tropical climate, and the ever-present temptation to prey upon the neighbouring Spaniards, proved fatal to the Puritan ideal, and before it had been settled five years converted the island into a mere fortified base, whence privateering warfare might be waged against the Spanish Indies.

CHAPTER V

ENLARGEMENT OF THE ACTIVITIES OF THE COMPANY

That the foundation of an ideal community and the pursuit of a profitable investment for trading capital are incompatible aims has been so often demonstrated that the proposition may nowadays be regarded as a truism; but even in the seventeenth century experience had shown that it is impossible to combine business with sentiment, however noble. The Pilgrim Fathers of 1620 had been financed for their voyage across the Atlantic by London merchants interested in fishing and the fur trade, but the arrangement led to so much friction that in 1627 the settlers bought up the whole of the stock by instalments and became entirely independent of outside control. John White's company of Dorchester adventurers at Cape Ann in 1623 found it impossible to satisfy the demands for profits of their backers in England and within a year or two were abandoned to support themselves as best they could. The only attempt at Puritan colonisation that succeeded, the colonisation of Massachusetts, succeeded because of the inherent difference between it and other attempts. Except in the early venture at Salem, Massachusetts was never a plantation financed in the main by adventurers remaining at home in England and bound down by their English ties and interests; it was a migration of settlers almost after the pattern of a Greek colonisation, a migration of men depending solely upon their own resources and expecting no return for the capital they had invested save what they aided in acquiring by their own personal efforts and privations.

The Providence Company from the start attempted to combine two divergent aims, and although its members subscribed largely and generously to the enterprise at first, yet the capital they contributed was an investment and not a gift. From the first even the more strongly Puritan members of the company, such as Saye and Pym, expected to receive some return upon their expenditure, though they desired at the same time to found a community upon the strictest Puritan pattern; the merchants, however, to whom the financing of schemes of exploration and colonisation was a regular matter of business, looked upon the colony merely as a likely speculation and had little sympathy with the aspirations of their fellow members. A very short time convinced them that there was little profit to be obtained and, as we have seen, Dyke, who had attempted to make a profit out of the scheme at the expense of his fellow adventurers, abandoned the company in 1632, his share being purchased by Saye, Rudyerd, Pym, and Graunt. Gabriel Barber, a man of finer fibre, if of less business capacity, also left the company in 1632; his enterprises had for some years been succeeding ill[1] and he now found the necessity of realising his investments in order to stave off bankruptcy. In return for the reimbursement by the company of his out-of-pocket expenses upon his share, viz., £500, he assigned to them his five allotments of land in the Somers Islands and these were henceforward the joint property of the Providence Company and were leased and worked by the well-known merchant, Humphrey Slany. For the expenses he had been put to for the first voyage, the company reimbursed Barber by

[1] *C. S. P. East Indies*, 4 March, 1625. Sale by Barber of £1200 of East India Stock. Other similar entries.

the payment of £200 cash, a composition that was also offered to Dyke, but at first refused. Sir Nathaniel Rich was reimbursed for his expenditure by the assignment of one-quarter of Dyke's share in the company without payment. Barber did not long survive his financial shipwreck and died some time in 1633.

It had been resolved in the first six months of the company's existence that, in order to keep the control in the hands of the original members, not more than twenty whole shares should ever be created, but it was found impracticable to refuse absolutely to admit new members, and the difficulty was got over by allowing members, while increasing the total sum invested, to let some portion of the new capital be provided by their friends, portions of the whole share being assigned to them and the voting power of an entire share being wielded by a majority of those owning it. It is unnecessary to enter into details as to the way in which these fractions of shares changed hands, though it is possible to trace them all in the records. A list of the new members, however, will show that the company after Dyke's retirement was entirely confined to members of the Puritan party and that the merchant element had abandoned the enterprise. Henry Darley, who joined the company in November, 1632, was a personal friend of Pym's and a strong Puritan; he and his younger brother, Richard, were sons of Sir Richard Darley[2] of Buttercrambe in Yorkshire and Elizabeth, daughter of Edward Gates, possibly a relative of Sir Thomas Gates, the governor of Virginia. Darley played an important part among the English Puritans and both he and his brother were prominent members of the ruling oligarchy under the Long Parliament and the Commonwealth. Darley took great interest in the projects for Puritan emigration and subscribed

[2] Harl. Soc., *Visit. of London*, I, 216.

£50 to the funds of the Massachusetts Bay Company before May, 1628.[3] He and his brother offered to the Rev. Thomas Shepard, when silenced for Nonconformity by Archbishop Laud, £20 a year towards his support.[4] Sir Thomas Cheeke of Pirgo, Essex,[5] was married to Essex Rich, sister of the Earl of Warwick, and had been a member of the Council for Virginia, 1612-1620. He sat in all parliaments from 1624 to the Long Parliament, for various Essex seats, and was a strong Puritan. His daughter, Essex Cheeke, married as her second husband, Edward Montagu, Viscount Mandeville, about whose connection with the company we shall have much to say later. James Fiennes was the eldest son of Lord Saye and became later second viscount. His younger brother was the celebrated Colonel Nathaniel Fiennes of the Civil War. John Michell, who bought a quarter of Sir Nathaniel Rich's share in May, 1633, was probably a cousin of Rich, whose mother was a daughter of John Michell, sheriff of London.[6] William Ball, who bought half of Sherland's share on his death, may have been the William Ball who in 1634 was attorney of the office of pleas in the Exchequer[7] and must have been known to Pym and Graunt. John Upton of Lucton, Devon,[8] who purchased a quarter of Pym's share in November, 1632, and thenceforward acted as the company's agent in the west of England, had married Pym's half-sister, Dorothy Rous. He did a good deal of work for the company and subscribed several sums to their capital.

By May, 1633, £1025 had been paid upon each whole share, of which Lord Brooke held two, but when fresh

3 *Archæologia Americana,* III, lxxx.
4 Autobiography of Shepard, p. 36.
5 Brown, *Genesis,* II, 883.
6 Brown, II, 978.
7 Harl. Soc., *Visit. of London,* II, 40.
8 *Visit. of Devon,* p. 293. *Visit. of Cornwall,* p. 195.

capital had to be raised in June, 1634, it was decided to introduce an arrangement somewhat similar to the modern device of preference shares. The sums now paid in as multiples of a quarter-share (£256 5s.) were to be reimbursed and receive dividends from the profits gained before anything was paid on the original shares. Practically all the adventurers subscribed to this new stock, and three new adventurers, William Woodcock, Thomas Barnardiston, and William Boswell, also joined. John Hart, the first "husband" of the company, died in 1633, leaving his affairs in a somewhat involved condition. The arrangement of giving full power to the "husband" to act in the company's name had been found to lead to abuse and it was determined by Pym that a new system of management was necessary. His interest in the company and its projects had been steadily growing and he was now prepared to place his business capacity entirely at the service of the scheme. The new husband, William Woodcock, who was engaged on the recommendation of Lord Brooke, was to be merely the company's executive agent to carry out the plans drawn up by the treasurer. The details of all arrangements were to be submitted to and decided upon by Pym, and no orders were to be valid unless they were signed by him and by Secretary Jessop. Woodcock, however, was allowed to have a share in the business and subscribed to the preference stock.

Thomas Barnardiston,[9] a London merchant, engaged in the East India Company's trade, was a near relative of Richard Knightley of Fawsley and brother of Sir Nathaniel Barnardiston, M. P. for Suffolk in 1628-1629 and an intimate friend of John Winthrop.[10] He was an important member of the Puritan party in the City of

[9] *Visit. of London,* II, 51.
[10] *Life of Winthrop,* I, 393.

London, but, like the other merchants, he did not long remain connected with the Providence Company, probably being dissatisfied with the profits and finding a far more fertile field for the employment of his capital in the East Indian trade. William Boswell, at one time secretary to the Earl of Carlisle, was deeply engaged in 1629-1630 in the attempts to settle "Carolana" with Huguenots. His slight connection with the Providence Company owes its importance to this fact.

The fullest details for a treatment of the company's financial history are contained in the records but they hardly appear to afford sufficient matter of interest to detain us. It must suffice here to say that a large part of the company's business was carried on in very modern fashion by means of short-dated loans, largely from wealthy Puritans such as the Earl of Lincoln and Lord Grey of Groby, but also from other capitalists such as Edward Cecil, Viscount Wimbledon, and from London merchants in the ordinary way of business. Pym managed all these transactions and must have been kept very busy, for he was continually reminding the members of the company of the debts that remained to be paid off and suggesting to them means of raising money for the purpose. The general total indebtedness of the company was a continually increasing amount and great complexity was introduced into the accounts by attempting to keep the finances of each voyage distinct and by paying out the profits upon each voyage in dividends without accumulating any reserve fund. Although the company was a rudimentary joint stock concern, it was a very inefficient one and the contrast between it and a modern enterprise is very great.

While the desire of the founders of the company to keep its shares entirely in the hands of Puritans was easily fulfilled, their scheme for attracting Puritan emigrants to the colony met with only a very slight measure of success, though they made every endeavour to carry it through. In order to avoid the ill-usage of which the passengers in the *Seaflower* had been the victims, it was decided to charter a ship which should be entirely officered by the company's men, and the *Charity,* a vessel of two hundred tons, was got ready to sail in the early part of 1632 under the mastership of Thomas Punt. The engagement of three ministers for the island has already been mentioned and all three sailed in this ship, the command of the passengers in which was entrusted to Henry Halhead and Samuel Rishworth, Puritans of the true New England type. Henry Halhead was a native of the town of Banbury and a dependent of Lord Saye; like his patron, he was always to the fore in defence of ancient rights, and in 1632 he had made himself so obnoxious to the authorities that he was compelled to emigrate. In March, 1628, forty soldiers, billeted in Banbury, had engaged in rioting and had set fire to the houses of some of those opposed to them. The parish constable, in trying to prevent further outrage, had been maltreated by the soldiers and failed to obtain redress from the justices, who, from fear of the government, considered that they had no power to punish the soldiers without consent of their captains. The constable appealed to the House of Lords[11] then sitting and brought forward Halhead to prove the truth of his statements. The lords sent for the justices and admonished them, while the offending soldiers were punished with stripes. To the end of his life Halhead maintained the interest in opposing enclosures that he had imbibed under Lord Saye in

[11] "House of Lords MSS." (Hist. MSS. Comm., *Fourth Report,* App'x, p. 13), 26 March, 1628, Petition of George Philips, constable of Banbury; see also *Lords' Journal,* III, 700, 708.

1617.[12] In 1650, after his return from the West Indies, there appeared from his pen a small work against enclosures under the title of *Inclosure Thrown Open*, showing the practice to be wicked by quotations from Scripture and many other sources.[13]

One hundred and fifty passengers in all were gathered together for the voyage to Providence under Halhead's leadership and these were of a more strongly Puritan type than any other emigrants to Providence. Those coming from Essex were directed to come to a rendezvous in London and boarded the *Charity* there; those from Devon and Warwickshire, together with Lord Saye's party from Oxfordshire, assembled at Plymouth and were lodged at the company's charge in the houses of Puritan sympathisers while waiting for the ship. The cost of transportation, £6 per head including victuals, was borne by the emigrants themselves in most cases, but when poverty prevented their paying before leaving England, the company arranged that the emigrants might repay the passage money out of their first year's profits in the island. No servants were sent out to the planters in this voyage, the emigrants being all freemen and many of them taking with them their wives and families. The majority were agriculturists, but a good many mechanics also went out, such as carpenters, sawyers, coopers, smiths, and brickmakers.

Although great care had been taken in the preparation of the instructions for the voyage, they were almost entirely disregarded by the master, and the passengers suffered even more cruelly than had those in the *Sea-*

[12] Privy Council Register, James I, Vol. III, pp. 111-115. Quoted by Prof. E. C. K. Gonner in *Eng. Hist. Rev.*, 1908, p. 482.

[13] *Inclosure Thrown Open or Depopulation Depopulated Not by Spades and Mattocks but by the Word of God, the Laws of the Land, and Solid Arguments. And the most material Pleas that can be brought for it considered and answered.* By Henry Halhead. London, 1650.

flower. The *Charity* had not long left Plymouth when a dangerous sickness broke out on board and the surgeon appealed to the master for the issue of stores for relief of the sick. Not only did Punt refuse this reasonable demand, but he stinted the passengers and seamen of the poor food allowed them; one-third of their allowance of biscuit, one-half of their beer, and a proportion of their pease were abated, while only three stock-fish and a half were allowed each week between forty persons. That this niggardliness was solely due to Punt's desire for illicit gain was shown by the fact that he privately disposed of twenty-eight butts of beer on reaching Providence and of a large amount of biscuit on his return to England. The despotic power of a master on shipboard was even greater in the seventeenth century than it is to-day and Punt's reply to all complaints was an order for a flogging for the complainant. One seaman who grumbled was first flogged and then tied to the capstan for two hours with fifteen heavy cannon shot about his neck. Though Halhead was in command of the passengers, Punt threatened him with the "bilboes" or heavy leg-irons for mutiny, because he had directed one of his own body servants to go ashore without the master's express permission. The company did their best to bring Punt to book for his misdeeds on his return to England and he was examined before certain masters of Trinity House concerning the allegations against him. After the case had dragged on two or three months, it was found that no satisfaction was obtainable through Trinity House and it was decided to pay Punt and his accomplice, the purser, the wages owing to them and to abandon any further proceedings. It can hardly be wondered at that the emigrants who had voyaged to the island under such painful conditions, sent back most doleful accounts to their friends in England, and the company found great difficulty in consequence of these reports in securing further emigrants.

In the original proposals from Elfrith to Gov. Bell, that ultimately led to the formation of the Providence Company, he pointed out as the most likely place for a colony an island, which he called Fonseca, and which, he said, lay "some one hundred leagues to the eastwards of the Caribbees out of all the Spaniards' roads and ways."[14] At the end of 1632 Pym's energy felt the need for some fresh outlet and his thoughts turned to Fonseca as the most suitable scene for further activity of the company, for it was said to be of considerable size and great fertility. The existence of such an island had been confidently believed in by the Spaniards throughout the sixteenth century and the growth of the myth is an interesting subject of enquiry.[15] The name "San Bernaldo" was in use by the Spaniards quite early in the century for one of the Caribbee Islands, which were then only very roughly and vaguely marked upon the maps. By 1544 the name had become definitely applied to a fair-sized island marked as lying well out of the chain of the Lesser Antilles and bearing about E. N. E. of Tobago. The Sebastian Cabot map of 1544 gives it in this position and this is repeated in several other maps of somewhat later date; in some of these it bears also the name of "Fonsequa" or "Fonseca," and is given a very noticeable cross-like outline, probably thus indicating that it had been scrupulously copied from earlier maps; in other and more accurate maps it is marked definitely as lying in the position which Elfrith described. In the "Ruttier for the West Indies," printed

[14] *V. supra*, p. 39.

[15] For some of these references the writer is indebted to the courtesy of Mr. E. Heawood, librarian of the Royal Geographical Society, and of Mr. W. R. Kettle, editor of Finlay's *Directory of the North Atlantic*.

by Hakluyt,[16] there is a list of all the more important West Indian islands and their latitudes, where we find: "The island of Fonzeca standeth in Degrees of latitude 11¼." One of the most reliable maps of the American coast and islands in the early seventeenth century is that of Sebastian de Ruesta, cosmographer to the Contratacion House of Seville, and on this map Fonseca is marked as bearing due north of what is now French Guiana.[17] In letters from the Indies to Spain in 1630, the corsairs are said frequently to take refuge in the island of Fonseca, while on February 28, 1628, Charles I granted[18] to Philip, Earl of Montgomery, "the islands lying between 8 and 13 degrees of north latitude, called Trinidado, Tabago, Barbudos, and Fonseca."

Both in Spain and England, then, the island was assumed to have a real existence and it was only towards the end of the seventeenth century that it disappeared from the maps. In the excellent atlas of N. Visscher (1650)[19] there is no mention of the island, but it is occasionally met with as late as 1866, when Keith Johnston's *Royal Atlas* definitely marks it and in the accompanying Index Geographicus its exact position is given as 12° 27′ N., 54° 48′ W. Upon an admiralty chart of 1848 no island appears in this position, but a rock termed "La Gallissonnière Rock" is marked. The non-existence of both island and rock was finally ascertained by the officers of the United States government brig *Dolphin,* who in 1852 obtained a sounding of two thousand five hundred and seventy fathoms near the reputed position. The lengthy period through which the existence of an

16 Hakluyt's *Voyages* (Everyman Library), VII, 267.

17 Brit. Mus., Add. MSS., 5027a.

18 Sign Man., Car. I, Vol. V, no. 22, *C. S. P. Col.,* 1574-1660, p. 87. In Brit. Mus., Sloane, 3662, fo. 46, the version of this patent calls the island "San Bernaldo."

19 *Atlas Contractus Orbis Terrarum.* N. Visscher, Amsterdam, 1650.

island lying far out of the chain of the Antilles was assumed as certain, gives to Fonseca or San Bernaldo a rather more tangible position than such an entirely vague and mythical island as "St. Brendan's Isle," though even this in 1628 was granted by patent as a field for colonisation. In the rudimentary state of the science of navigation in the sixteenth century, the accurate determination of longitude was impossible and mariners worked entirely by means of latitude and dead reckoning. It is quite possible that an early navigator, taking a course more southerly than usual, should have failed to allow for the westerly drift of the great equatorial current and should have made his first land fall two or three days before he expected it upon Tobago, or even Barbadoes. Hakluyt gives the latitude of Tobago as eleven degrees, which differs very little from the eleven and one-fourth degrees of Fonseca. The existence of the island having once been assumed, it was very difficult to prove it mythical and the mistake, like many another, was copied by writer after writer for two hundred years.

At a meeting of the Providence Company on November 26, 1632, in John Pym's house,[20] it was definitely decided to extend the area of the company's activities and it was resolved that £25 should be paid in on each entire share of adventure towards the expenses of a voyage of discovery to Fonseca. As the lord chamberlain, the Earl of Pembroke and Montgomery, possessed some pretensions to the island, it was resolved to invite him to join as a private adventurer in the enterprise, but Pembroke, whose West Indian ventures had not been graced with much success and who had been involved in a long contest with the Earl of Carlisle concerning the right to

[20] Pym's house was at this period on the eastern side of Gray's Inn Lane, only a few doors away from Brooke House. Nugent's *Mems. of Hampden*, I, 296. *C. S. P. Dom.*, 16 Jan. 1637-1638, Return of Justices of the Peace.

Barbadoes, declined to have anything to do with the enterprise and tacitly renounced his rights in favour of the company. A pinnace, the *Elizabeth,* was hired at the rate of £4 per month, and Matthew Harbottle, lately master of the *Little Hopewell,* was appointed to the command. The pinnace was to call at Association and take on board Capt. Hilton, who would direct the voyage. During the winter the subscriptions were all collected and Pym made enquiries of those experienced in West Indian navigation as to the proper course to pursue. These enquiries were evidently unsatisfactory and were sufficient to cast doubts not only upon the feasibility of the enterprise, but even upon the existence of such an island as Fonseca. Pym's native caution was far too strong to allow him to throw away his own and his partner's money in the chase of a will-o'-the-wisp, and in March, 1633, he came to the conclusion that the Fonseca design should be abandoned in favour of a project more likely to offer success.

Hilton had laid before the company in his letters two schemes for the outlay of capital in Indian trade. The first of these schemes involved the seizure of islands in the Florida Channel, either the cays where Key West now stands, or some of the western Bahamas; this was far too bold a plan for the company to sanction, for it really courted failure. The Spaniards' brutal massacre of Ribault and Laudonnière's Florida colonists some seventy years before[21] was still vividly remembered, and that the governor of Havana would do what he could to maintain Spain's exclusive policy in Florida waters had been clearly brought home to the Providence Company by the narrow escape of their vessel, the *Seaflower,* on her homeward voyage through the Straits. Hilton's second project was for a trade with the Indians in the

[21] By Menendez, 20 Sept., 1565.

Gulf of Darien and this was far easier to carry out. Although within a few score of miles of a world's highway so much travelled as is the Isthmus of Panama, the country round the Gulf of Darien is, even to the present day, little visited, and the wild and intractable San Blas Indians inhabiting its hills and swampy shores have never bowed beneath the Spanish yoke. From Porto Bello to the head of the gulf, the coast is lined with small islands, the creeks between which had from the middle of the sixteenth century formed a favourite refuge for English corsairs, where they might mature in safety their plans against the Spanish treasure convoys.[22] The hostility of the Darien Indians against the Spaniards was intensified by their alliance with the Cimarones or negroes, who, having fled from the plantations round Panama, had taken refuge in the Darien swamps and hills; their friendliness towards the English was, however, very marked and was an important factor in the history of the Isthmus for two hundred years.[23]

In March, 1633, the Providence Company definitely decided to divert the subscriptions that had been received for the Fonseca design, to the fitting out of a trading voyage to Darien. A pinnace, the *Elizabeth,* was purchased and placed under the command of Matthew Harbottle, who, as mate of the *Charity,* had protested against Punt's malpractices, and had given evidence against him. A Dartmouth pinnace, the *Pole,* was chartered under the command of her owner, Nicholas Roope, and was fitted out to accompany the *Elizabeth.*

22 Drake, while preparing for his attack on Nombre de Dios in 1572, spent some time among the Darien Indians and the Cimarones. John Oxenham also visited them in 1575. Hakluyt, VII, 63, 64.

23 Dampier and his companions spent many months in Darien in 1679, and there is a contemporary map of the locality in his *Voyages.* In 1739 Governor Trelawny of Jamaica organized a revolt in Darien to facilitate Admiral Vernon's attack on Porto Bello and Panama.

Forty-two passengers went out with these vessels to Association and Providence, half of them being servants under bond, who had been recruited for the company by paid agents and were of an entirely different character to the earlier Puritan emigrants. From Association the vessels were directed to sail to St. Christopher or Barbadoes to obtain cotton-seed, and thence to Providence. If Hilton desired to do so, he was to take command of the expedition, but if not Richard Lane, a protégé of Lord Brooke's, was to direct the course of the traders after leaving Providence. Hilton did not care to leave the scene of his profitable duplicity and Lane therefore acted as cape-merchant or supercargo and had charge of the "cargazoon." As an evidence of the care bestowed by Pym upon the instructions issued to the company's commanders, it is worth while to examine those issued to Lane in detail.

Lane was directed on his arrival in Providence to plant carefully the madder he took out and to leave explicit directions with responsible persons for its cultivation. He was then to take on board Roger Floyd and six or eight other persons and to sail to the Bay of Darien, "which lies South-east and by South from Cape Cattina not far from Porto Bello upon the continent of the West Indies." On arrival there he was to take what steps he thought fit for finding a suitable landing place and to take care to conceal his movements from the Spaniards. "If you shall see cause to fear discovery by the Spaniards or danger by foul weather, you may give the Master direction to put into the harbour lying thereabout (as we are informed between the main and an island called Isla de Pinas)[24] where she may ride out of sight of such ships as may pass by and out of danger of

[24] A favourite place of concealment of the rovers among the Islas de San Blas. See Dampier's *Voyages*.

wind.'' He was to use all possible means to ingratiate himself with the Indians, ''taking care that [he] be not too liberal nor that they may have cause to suspect [his] own disesteem of the commodities.'' He was to use all possible means to conceal from them the object of his coming, but was to express a desire of renewing friendship with them as ''favourers of the English nation and especially of Don Francisco Draco (whose name they seem to honour).'' He was to make advantage of them by trade for gold, etc., to discover what things might be obtained from them and their value, and to labour to possess them with the natural goodness of the English nation. He was to restrain any boisterous carriage to the women and particularly ''mocking, pointing or laughing at their nakedness.'' None of the seamen were to be permitted to trade with the Indians or to have much familiarity with them. He was to keep a careful account of all the trade he did, and when he had obtained a cargo he was to return with it to Providence.

The *Elizabeth* left England in April, 1633, and attempted to carry out the programme arranged for her, but the Darien trade proved impossible for the time being, owing to circumstances which could not have been foreseen. When the *Elizabeth* arrived in the Gulf of Darien, she found there three Dutch ships that were attempting to trade. Though English and Dutch were still closely allied through their common hostility to Spain's exclusive pretensions, there were many signs that commercial rivalries were beginning to drive them asunder. In the East, the Amboyna massacre had unmistakably shown the English what consideration they might expect when Dutchmen felt that they really had the upper hand, but in western waters conditions remained more friendly and the main complaint of Englishmen as yet was that the Dutch were so brutal in their dealings with the natives as to render it difficult to carry on trade. A flagrant instance of this brutality now dashed all hopes of the Darien trade to both nations for some years. Some small parties from the Dutch ships had already got into communication with the Indians before the *Elizabeth* arrived on the coast, and they had seen sufficient gold round the natives' necks to excite all their cupidity. The Indians had informed them that they had plenty of gold in the hills and promised in six days' time to bring down some of the hill people to trade with them. Accordingly at the end of that time some two or three hundred Indians from the interior came down to the shore, and a young man, who knew something of their language, was sent among them to try their disposition to trade. His report was evidently favourable, for the Dutch vice-admiral, seeing great hopes of gain, determined to land and go among them. In order, however, to guard against surprise, he ordered his men to carry their arms with them; this was a fatal step, for the Indians, when they saw armed men beginning to land, took to flight. The Dutch were resolved that their hopes of gain should not so easily be dashed, and pursued the natives into the woods, behaving with great brutality and seizing the gold ornaments round the necks of the women and whatever else of value they could lay their hands on. The fight soon became general and in the melée the Dutch vice-admiral was slain by an Indian dart. This loss cast his men into the greatest confusion and it was only with difficulty and after the loss of several of their men that they succeeded in regaining their boats and taking refuge on shipboard. It was patent to everyone that all hopes of peaceful trade must be abandoned for the time being and after a short delay and a few unsuccessful attempts to trade on other parts of the coast, the *Elizabeth* returned with her cargo to Providence.

Other trading ventures had been directed from Providence in 1631 and 1632 and in these Daniel Elfrith had played the leading part. It will be remembered that at the first election of officers Elfrith had chosen the post of admiral in preference to that of governor, and in pursuance of the company's directions he set forth early in 1631 on a voyage to other West Indian islands and to the adjacent mainland of Central America in search of commodities suitable for raising in Providence. The first voyage and others, performed by Elfrith during 1631 and 1632, met with very little success and Elfrith had to be severely reproved by the company for his aggressive acts at the expense of the Spaniards, but the accounts he sent home gave the company such a very favourable idea of the mainland opposite to Providence that after mature consideration it was resolved to concentrate the company's greatest efforts at Indian trade rather upon Cape Gracias á Dios than in the territory round the Gulf of Darien. The idea grew further as time went on and developed into a project for settling a great colony of Englishmen in Central America, but in the first instance, when the preliminary steps were taken in 1633, it was trade that was aimed at.

The first mention of their design to Gov. Bell was made by the company in the letters sent by the *Elizabeth* (April, 1633). He was informed that the company intended to lay the foundation of a trade upon Cape Gracias á Dios and to employ there persons acquainted with the character and language of the Indians. In order to avoid any difficulty, Bell was ordered that the Main was not to be visited until full directions as to the carrying on of the trade were received. If any Indian came to Providence from the Main no pistols, knives, hooks, or iron of any kind were to be trucked with them. The company had heard that many in the island began to look towards the Main for profit. As this would conflict with their design to found a prosperous colony in Providence, Bell was to check all such tendencies and was to exhort the planters to look for profit to their plantations in the island and not elsewhere. Immediately after the business connected with the sailing of the *Elizabeth* had been completed, Pym took up the new project in earnest. It was decided that each adventurer should contribute £60 towards the voyage and that a magazine of trade goods should be provided for £600. A pinnace of ninety tons, the *Golden Falcon*, was purchased at a cost of £405 from Lord Paulet and sent round from Southampton to the Thames to be refitted for the voyage under the directions of the Earl of Warwick. The command of the expedition was entrusted to Capt. Sussex Camock, who, it will be remembered, was Elfrith's fellow-commander in the 1627-1628 voyage and who had been left planting tobacco upon Henrietta. Sussex Camock was the brother of Capt. Thomas Camock, who had married Frances, daughter of the second Lord Rich and aunt of Robert, Earl of Warwick. Thomas Camock had for some years been interested in New England and had been living on the eastern bank of Black Point River. On November 4, 1631, he obtained through the Earl of Warwick a patent[25] for one thousand five hundred acres and proposed to settle there with his wife and family; a settlement was founded on the grant and received the name of Black Point. Sussex Camock had had a good deal of experience as a commander of privateers and his name appears frequently in the registers of letters of marque as the master of ships belonging to the Earl of Warwick.

[25] ''Records of the Council for New England,'' 4 Nov., 1631, *Proc.* of Amer. Antiq. Soc. for 1867; Doyle's *Puritan Colonies,* I, 324.

He had accompanied his patron on his disastrous expedition against the Plate Fleet in 1627.

Active preparations for the voyage went on through May and June, 1633, the arms and provisions being got ready and shipped on board the *Golden Falcon* at Dartmouth. The vessel was placed under the command of Joseph Collins as master, with Sussex Camock as captain and in command of the passengers. These were of a much better class than those sent out in the *Elizabeth* and the *Pole* and many of them were strong Puritans. They were followers of a nonconformist minister, the Rev. Henry Root,[26] and were the last distinctively Puritan emigrants to reach Providence from England. The *Golden Falcon* had orders to call first at the Dutch island of St. Martin's, where she was to take on board a supply of salt for Providence; if salt could not be obtained there at a reasonable price, the master was to purchase it at Cape San Nicolas or one of the other salt pans, which the Dutch were working upon the northern shore of Hispaniola. Having called at Association to take on board three pieces of the company's ordnance that had been left there, the master was to steer for Providence and to deliver to Gov. Bell the company's letters, to land his passengers, and then to proceed under the entire command of Capt. Camock to the cape, where the *Golden Falcon* was to be placed and remain at his disposal.

It is impossible to enter into the many details of the instructions given by Treasurer Pym to Camock for the management of the new trade, as they fill six closely written folio pages of the company's letter book, and though they abound in interesting details concerning the commodities to be searched for and the procedure to

26 Calamy, *Nonconformist's Memorial,* II, 450, gives some account of Root and says that in early life he was a considerable traveller. From 1645 to 1662 he ministered at Sowerby and died there.

be adopted, we must confine our attention to the general directions given. Capt. Camock was directed to "set" with his company upon Cape Gracias á Dios, there to discover and maintain a trade with the natives; he was to search out a fit place in which to establish a permanent colony for trade and plantation. "And," say the company, "because the hope of the business most specially depends upon God's blessing, therefore we pray and require you to make it your first and principal care to carry God along with you in all places by the diligent performance of holy duties in your own person and by setting up and preserving the true worship of God in the hearts and lives of all your company, so far as you shall be able. Also to restrain and prevent to your utmost power all sins and disorders, as swearing, drunkenness, uncleanness or the like, which will render the name of Christians odious to the very heathen and be infinitely prejudicial to the business you take in hand by drawing the curse of God upon your endeavours. . . . You are to endear yourselves with the Indians and their commanders and we conjure you to be friendly and cause no jealousy." Among the many exhortations as to the proper treatment of native races that have been sent forth from England to the pioneers of her empire, it would be difficult to find a loftier yet simpler exordium than these words of Pym, and never, perhaps, has so lasting a friendship existed between Englishmen and a native race as that which, since these words were penned, has subsisted between Englishmen and the Indian tribes of the Moskito Coast.

The eastern coast of Central America lying opposite the Island of Providence has, even to this day, been very little explored and never properly mapped. It is inhabited by various Indian tribes grouped under the generic name of Moskitos,[27] but all closely allied to the Caribs of the Lesser Antilles. The first Europeans to come into contact with them were Alonzo de Ojeda and Diego de Nuesca, the conquerors of Nicaragua, whose arms were repulsed by the Moskitos and who never succeeded in establishing a footing in their territory. A deadly hatred had always subsisted between the Moskitos and the Spaniards and, even as early as Drake's voyages, we find them, as well as the Darien Indians, fraternising with and assisting the Spaniards' most implacable enemies, the English corsairs. To the relations established with the Moskitos by Bell and Camock we may attribute the close friendship that bound them to England throughout the seventeenth and eighteenth centuries, a friendship that at times during the eighteenth century had an important influence upon West Indian affairs. The protectorate exercised by England over the Moskito Territory, or Moskito Coast Reserve, was only finally relinquished as late as 1900.[28]

The Indians were accustomed to come over to Providence at certain periods of the year for fishing and Gov. Bell was directed not to interfere with this practice. A small number of them might be persuaded to stay in the island, "but," wrote Pym, "they must be free men drawn to work by reward and they must be entertained by kind usage and be at liberty to return at pleasure." Missionary efforts were to be made among them and no idolatrous worship was to be permitted in the island "that so there shall be no mixture of Paganism with

27 This name has nothing to do with the name of the familiar Anopheles or Mosquito. It is probably a corruption of a native word and should be written more accurately Miskito. *Report of Prussian Comm., on Moskito Territory.* 1845.

28 The well-known Clayton-Bulwer Treaty of 1850, abrogated by the Hay-Pauncefote Treaty of 1900, governed English relations with this part of Central America throughout the latter part of the nineteenth century.

the pure religion of Almighty God.'' Both Camock and Bell received the most explicit directions that the Moskitos were never to be furnished with the means of practising the use of gunpowder.

CHAPTER VI

PROGRESS AND CONTROVERSY IN ASSOCIATION AND PROVIDENCE

The fullness of the directions despatched by the company to the colony in reference to the raising of commodities and their preparation for the market is a noticeable feature of the records we are dealing with. Page after page of the company's letter book is devoted to comments on the method of cultivation to be adopted, the commodities to be sought for and the sources whence they might be obtained, and not merely did the company (or rather Pym) thus give counsel to the settlers, but the greatest trouble was also taken to secure for them plants and seeds, tools and appliances from all quarters, these being forwarded with the fullest directions for their use. We repeatedly find in the letters directions for the planters to communicate with Pym in cases of doubt concerning the growth or preparation of a commodity, and it seems no unwarrantable assumption to credit him with the authorship of the general directions sent to the company's servants. The details as to the various commodities tried and the success achieved form too large a subject to be entered upon here, though they provide a valuable source of information and material to be considered in connection with a study of the general early economic history of the European colonies in the West Indies.[1] We must be content to summarise the

[1] The information available is similar to that used by Bruce in his *Economic History of Virginia in the 17th Century*, 2 vols. New York, 1896. Interesting comparisons might be drawn from Weeden's *Economic and Social History of New England*, 2 vols. Boston, 1890.

main results obtained during the first five years of the colony's life, though in the end these results proved very small.

As we have seen tobacco was the first crop attempted by the planters from Bermuda and proved of very fair quality. That raised between January and August was as good as any made in the Indies if, after the Spanish method, it were kept to mature for a year before exportation. But insufficient care was devoted to the sorting and packing and in consequence only a very poor price could be obtained in England. The company had a strong objection to tobacco-growing as the staple industry of the colony, based partly upon economic grounds and partly upon religious scruples, and their language is reminiscent of that used by the Massachusetts Bay Company in their first general letter to Gov. Endecott:[2] "[The tobacco] trade is by the Company generally disavowed and utterly disclaimed by some of the greatest adventurers amongst us, who absolutely declared themselves unwilling to have any hand in this plantation, if we intend to cherish or permit the planting of the noxious weed." Circumstances in Providence, however, proved too strong for the company and tobacco was always the principal export from the island. Two sorts of cotton were found growing wild in the island, one of short and the other of long staple, and both were cultivated, as well as varieties obtained from Jamaica and Barbadoes. Here again, however, the disinclination of the planters to take trouble in preparing and packing the product prevented a fair price being obtained for it in England. The company were continually urging the colonists to search for a staple commodity suitable for growth in the island, and offered large rewards for its discovery, but without success. It was thought that a profitable staple

[2] *Archæologia Americana,* III, 82, 17 April, 1629.

commodity had been discovered in silk-grass, or as the company called it, "Camock's flax," which grew wild in the forests of the Main. This seems to have been the fibre which is now known as *henequen* or sisal hemp,[3] derived from the fleshy leaves of a species of agave growing largely in Central America. The first samples were sent home from the cape by Camock in 1634 and were submitted by Pym to several experienced tradesmen; after a careful examination it was declared by them to be fit for several manufactures and worth about four shillings a pound. Bell was informed that "experiment upon a small quantity of the silk-grass sent from the Main shows it to be a very excellent staple commodity, vendible in greater abundance than you shall be able to send it us and at a price to exceed our hopes. May God's blessing rest upon it as a merchandize abundantly sufficient to give both us and you contentment." The great difficulty concerning the fibre was the extraction of it from the rind of the leaf; experiments were carried out both in England and in Providence under Pym's direction and some success was obtained. After a few years' trial of the fibre in the European markets, the company resolved to undertake the production of it on a large scale and to obtain a patent for its manufacture. To this subject we will return in a later chapter.

Madder and indigo planting were both tried in a half-hearted sort of way, but the inability of the planters to work their land satisfactorily with the aid only of Englishmen in so warm a climate threw them back upon tobacco and cotton as their staple crops, since these required less labour than other commodities. The most valuable exports from the island were mainly dye-woods obtained in small quantities in the forests of Providence and in larger quantities by traffic with the Moskito

[3] Chisholm, *Handbook of Commercial Geography*, p. 145.

Indians. Negroes were first introduced into Providence from Association in 1633 and thenceforward the number of them in the island was a continually increasing one, and they began before long to be a real danger to the safety of the community. While the owning of negroes as slaves occasioned not the slightest misgiving to the strict Puritans in the company, the minds of some of the Puritan party in the island were by no means at rest and one of them at least, Samuel Rishworth, held such strong views against slavery that he began to play the part of "abolitionist" and to aid the negroes in escaping to liberty. His views seem to have been similar to those of Roger Williams of Rhode Island and, needless to say, were not tolerated either by the company or by the planters. "We fear that the running away of the negroes may be of very ill consequence and do utterly mislike Mr. Rishworth's behaviour in promising to treat about their liberty if it were such as you conceive and the same is represented to us in your letter, it being both indiscreet (arising as it seems from a groundless opinion that Christians may not lawfully keep such persons in a state of servitude during their strangeness from Christianity) and also injurious to ourselves, whose service he hath made them disaffected to, and to their particular masters, who should have been advised withal before any overture touching their liberty." Rishworth is to be admonished that he is to mend his behaviour and to learn that "Religion consists not so much in an outward conformity of actions as in truth of the inward parts,"—surely an odd argument in favour of slave-holding. It was only on rare occasions that the negroes could succeed in escaping from the island, but a good number of them managed to flee into the woods and there they preserved a precarious existence. The planters' life was occasionally enlivened by a hunt after these poor savages and, though very few were recaptured, their huts were discovered and burnt amid great rejoicing. Their headquarters seems to have been in a lofty valley, known as the "Palmetto Grove," in the southeast of the island, and on two or three occasions they were driven thence and forced to disperse into the adjacent forests.

The thorough exploration that the island had received showed that it contained some three or four thousand acres of very fertile land and about four thousand more acres of land suitable for planting but not as fertile; the rest of the island consisted of rocky hills and shore unfit for cultivation. The forests clothing the lower slopes of the hills contained cedars and other varieties of hard wood, but the supply in 1634 was beginning to run short and the colonists obtained better wood from Henrietta Island, where some shallops were built with the aid of Dutch shipwrights. In very dry seasons the brooks in the island ran dry and care had to be taken to husband the water from the springs. Potatoes flourished well and were a principal article of the planters' diet; cassava, plantains, pines, oranges, bananas, and melons flourished exceedingly, but figs and vines proved indifferent. Fishing was profitable and turtles were obtained in abundance on the neighbouring cays. The planters found that since their plantations were not enclosed, they had a good deal of difficulty in rearing the cattle sent from England and from Tortuga, and in 1634 they had only twelve beasts. Sheep they could not rear at all, but hogs were many, and of poultry they had great store. At the beginning of 1635 there were five hundred white men in the island, including a few Dutchmen, and some forty white women with a few children. The negroes then numbered ninety. The dwellings of the planters were dispersed upon their plantations about the island and were substantially built of timber; at

New Westminster near the harbour there was a village of some thirty well-constructed houses surrounding a commodious brick-built church and a governor's house, also of brick.

The ever-present fear of the settlers was of attack from the Spaniards and great precautions had to be taken to perfect the fortifications required to repel such attack. The island possessed forty pieces of ordnance mounted in thirteen or fourteen fortified places, and no ship or boat could approach the island but within the command of two or three forts. For the garrison of each of these forts the neighbouring planters were assigned with their servants and they were expected to muster at least once a week for drill under the command of their captain and his lieutenants, whose plantations lay close to the fort. A gunner, paid by the company £20 or £40 a year besides his land, was in charge of the ordnance at each fort and was accustomed to give the planters regular instruction in musketry. The colonists had some dozen or so shallops which they used ostensibly for fishing, but also unfortunately for less legitimate purposes.

It has been shown above that the pinnace *Elizabeth*, which had originally been intended for the discovery of Fonseca, was in April, 1633, sent to Tortuga with directions to Gov. Hilton to attempt a trade with the Indians at Darien. Such orders, however, did not suit Hilton's purpose and he preferred to remain in Tortuga and drive a profitable trade in the company's wood with French and Dutch ships. He proved utterly unscrupulous in his dealings with the company and they found it quite impossible to secure any payment for the magazines they had despatched to him, even though they attempted by legal process in Holland to arrest ships coming from Tortuga with their wood. Two or three cargoes he certainly did send to the company's agents at Middleburg and these were disposed of to the celebrated London merchant, Abraham Chamberlayne,[4] who sold the wood to dyers in Rouen. It was bought by sample and guaranteed by Hilton to be of uniform quality, but proved in reality to be nothing of the kind, and the company was involved in a long and unpleasant dispute with Chamberlayne, who practically accused them of bad faith, and the dispute had to be finally compromised at a considerable reduction on the contract price of £23 per ton. Hilton's behaviour to the colonists sent out by the company was very unsatisfactory and we find, from a letter sent by Samuel Filby from Association to Sir Thomas Barrington,[5] that he was seizing all the tobacco raised in the island and converting it to his own profit. Tortuga was very unhealthy and almost all the English emigrants had perished from fever by the middle of 1634. But not merely was Hilton in hot water with the company, he had left a large number of debts unpaid in Nevis and St. Christopher, and his creditors were talking of arresting the company's ships there in order to secure payment. Thomas Littleton, the financier of Hilton's first voyage, even went so far as to cause the arrest of Capt. Richard Bragg, one of the Tortuga adventurers, who was in Nevis in order to obtain recruits and trade goods for the company's Darien trade. Littleton also threatened to bring a suit against the company to recover Hilton's debts in the English courts, but they refused point-blank to have anything to do with the matter and, in the face of this direct refusal, Littleton took no further steps. The company's patience with Hilton was at length exhausted and in 1634 directions

[4] Brown, *Genesis,* II, 852, gives his biography; see also *Visit. of London,* I, 148.

[5] Brit. Mus., Eg., 2646, fo. 67.

were sent out for his supersession; if it were found that the conditions in Tortuga were too bad to afford any likelihood of improvement, the remaining inhabitants were to be transported to Providence and the company's ordnance removed. Before these instructions had been long despatched, the company received word of Hilton's death in the island and of the accession of Christopher Wormeley to the governorship; more of Hilton's misdoings now came to light and it was found that he had been making Tortuga into a regular rendezvous for rovers of all nationalities.

A certain ship, the *Hunter,* had been purchased in Rotterdam and victualed and armed at Dover by a Capt. Powell and Thomas Newman, financed by the brother of the latter, a London merchant, one Lionel Newman. Some part of the ordnance was supplied by John Hart, the Providence Company's husband, without authorisation. The vessel sailed from Dover late in 1632 or early in 1633 with a few passengers for Tortuga, ostensibly on a peaceable voyage to cut wood there; just before sailing, however, the leaders announced that they held letters of marque from the Prince of Orange against the Spaniards, but they did not show them to anyone. Near the Canary Islands they attacked and captured two Spanish vessels, and on reaching Tortuga they fitted out one of these as a man-of-war and set sail on a roving cruise in the Mona and Windward passages to lie in wait for Spanish ships. They returned now and again to Tortuga for fresh water, etc., and really made it a headquarters for their piratical enterprise. Gov. Hilton gave them every encouragement, as he did to other rovers, French and Dutch, that came in. On the *Hunter's* return to Europe in December, 1634, the booty was unloaded at Rotterdam, and the Spanish government, hearing of the matter, at once protested to the English authorities against their countenancing such piracy under cloak of the Providence Company. The parties were cited to appear before the Admiralty Court and there examined, so that the whole matter became public.[6]

Although rovers were not received at Providence in quite so open a fashion as at Tortuga and though Gov. Bell in one or two instances refused harbourage to Dutch ships whose credentials were not quite satisfactory, yet the fact that Dutch men-of-war (or, as we should now call them, privateers) frequently touched at the island and sometimes sold the colonists captured Spanish ordnance, was sufficient to implicate the island as a harbourage for pirates. The proceedings of some of the colonists themselves were by no means above reproach; Elfrith had been despatched on a voyage to various parts of the West Indies in 1631 and 1632 to secure plants and trees suitable to raise in the island, and although he knew that peace had been proclaimed between England and Spain in November, 1630, and though his commission and instructions explicitly forbade him to execute any hostile acts except in self-defence, he did not scruple to attack and plunder any small Spanish vessels he came across. His own vessel being unseaworthy, in 1632 he seized a Spanish frigate[7] lying in one of the Jamaican harbours, leaving his pinnace in exchange. The company got wind of this and severely rated him for running such risks and for endangering the safety of the colony by his proceedings. The reproof had little effect, but he took good care not to let the company know of his further enterprises.

The news of Elfrith's piratical proceedings and the reports brought home by the masters of the company's

6 The principal depositions are to be found in S. P. Dom., Car. I, Vol. 282, Nos. 89 and 90. Others are among the Admiralty Court Records.

7 Frigates were small decked vessels of about thirty tons burthen.

ships of the difficulty they had had in procuring a return cargo from Providence owing to the sale by the colonists of all their produce to the Dutch, caused the company much uneasiness. They had, of course, known that in settling an island in the very heart of the Indies, they were laying themselves open to Spanish attack, but they desired to avoid as much as possible any proceedings that would put them in the wrong with the English government and deprive them of the right of asking for national support in any dispute that might arise with Spain. Pym's directions to Bell, however, were very disingenuous and savoured of a desire to do as much harm as possible to Spain without running any risks. If any ordnance taken by the Dutch were offered for sale to him, he was to purchase it in exchange for commodities or victuals, but he was to destroy as far as possible any evidence of its origin. Too great a resort of ships to the island was to be deprecated, as it might endanger its safety, but if a ship came in for relief, he might grant it at a reasonable charge. The restrictions on free trade with strange ships in general were retained, "lest your measures should be discovered and a greater envy of the Spaniards drawn upon you for being a receptacle and relief to their enemies." We must remember as some palliation of this double dealing that, at the period of which we write, the savage war between the United Provinces and Spain was still being waged, a war wherein at sea quarter was hardly ever granted by either side to its adversaries, wherein every Hollander was regarded as a rebel and traitor against his lawful sovereign and every Spaniard as a sharer in the guilt of Alva and of Philip. It was perhaps a maxim of English policy that there was "No peace beyond the line," but Englishmen and Spaniards did regard one another as honourable enemies and conducted their mutual dealings with reasonable courtesy and a desire to avoid unnecessary cruelty; no measure, however, could be too atrocious for a Spaniard or a Hollander to employ against his hated foe and not for many years were the bitter memories of Haarlem and Alkmaar assuaged. Hence the company's desire that Bell should not identify himself too closely with Dutch interests was merely an evidence of statesmanlike caution and prudence.

The company's uneasiness concerning the safety of the island, in view of the constant rumours of Spanish preparations, was increased by the reports they received of dissensions in the island. Elfrith and Axe had disagreed in 1631 about the division of the company's share of the first planters' tobacco, and, instead of showing signs of healing, the estrangement had become wider as time went on. Elfrith was constantly interfering with Axe's exercise of military authority and, in virtue of his position as admiral of the island, had succeeded in making himself a nuisance to everybody. Axe had become so disgusted at the state of affairs that he took advantage of Camock's expedition to the Main to leave Providence for the time being and settle himself on the largest of the Moskito Cays, lying midway between Providence and the cape, in charge of Camock's depot of stores and provisions. This was a considerable loss to the colony, for Axe was one of its most capable officers. Constant little disagreements were arising in the council on questions of precedence and the use of heated language; even a slight knowledge of New England history would convince us that a seventeenth century Puritan was a very touchy person and the numerous discomforts of the West Indian climate did nothing to lessen this touchiness in Providence. To a modern mind, the amount of trouble the company gave themselves in clearing up some of these silly disputes seems an egregious waste of energy.

Thomas Hunt, the secretary of the island, was accused to the company at home of what were called "grave falsifications" of the records, but when we examine the charges they turn out to involve merely a small amount of carelessness and inaccuracy. He had omitted to cancel an article in the records concerning a charge of Halhead against the Rev. Mr. Rous of enticing away one of his servants; he had sent the accusation to England and had omitted the servant's name, he had entered depositions on the matter in the records after it had been remitted to the company, and so on. And yet to this puerile charge the company devoted two whole meetings and in the end administered to Hunt a reproof of portentous weight, filling two closely written folio pages of the letter book. Lieut. William Rous, in the violence of an argument, had lost his temper and had smacked the face of Forman, the principal smith in the island; he was in consequence suspended from his place at the council table until he should acknowledge his fault. Gov. Bell, however, who found Rous too useful a member of the council to be dispensed with, absolved him from his fault and restored him to his seat without the public apology, but the company, on learning of the matter, regarded this as far too lenient a way of dealing with so heinous a fault. It was ordered that Rous be suspended until he made a public acknowledgment according to the censure, and that the governor be sharply reproved for having "acted in an undue manner." The quaint proviso was added that Rous's suspension was not to involve a suspension from training his men—the company's interests must not be neglected.

But it was not always with such insignificant charges that the company had to deal; the hot West Indian sun sometimes provoked crimes of hideous cruelty and violence at the expense of a master's unfortunate servants.

Capt. William Rudyerd returned to England in the *Golden Falcon* in May, 1634, and many in the island breathed more freely at his departure, for Rudyerd, during his three years' stay in Providence, had been noted for his cruelty to his servants. One, Fload, had suffered so much that he ran away from the plantation and took refuge in the hills, but was recaptured and brought back. Though he was suffering from scurvy, Rudyerd beat him and continued to treat him cruelly. A second time Fload ran away and complained to the governor without securing redress; Rudyerd again recaptured him, had him tied to a tree and ordered three other servants to beat him with rods and then rub salt into his wounds. Poor Fload lingered in agony for six weeks and then died of the injuries he had received. Rudyerd's influence with the company was sufficient to save him from punishment for his misdeeds, but it was evident to all that he was a very unsuitable officer to wield command.

The amount of real crime in the island never appears to have been large and the majority of the offences dealt with by the council were small offences against morality or public decency. So great a part of the council's time, however, was taken up in dealing with judicial business that in 1633 the company directed that justices of the peace should be appointed to deal with petty matters of police; only grave crimes were to be tried before the governor in council. As time went on a small class of independent shopkeepers grew up in the island, who bought the stores and provisions brought by the company's or by strangers' ships, and disposed of them to the colonists at a profit. It was against this evil of engrossing rather than against the quality of goods from the company's stores that the planters complained to the company after the first two years of the colony's existence. Pym's constant care and supervision seem to have ensured that the goods sent out in the company's magazine were reasonable in price and of good quality. In order to guard against the evils of which the planters complained, careful regulations were drawn up to ensure that these goods should be sold on their arrival in a free and open market, but engrossing still occurred until the constant resort of ships to the island and the removal of restrictions on trade with strangers practically brought effective competition into play and the evils were automatically removed.

The company had to fight hard against a system that was always tending to increase, whereby a planter, having started a plantation in the island, placed in charge of it an overseer who was to work it with negroes or white servants and to forward the profits to the owner, who had returned to England. This system was evidently a bad one and the company attempted to check it by enacting that while planters were at liberty to let their plantations and the servants, who worked them, as long as they remained in the island, as soon as they departed all their interest in the plantation was to cease, and the plantation to escheat to the company. In special circumstances, permission might be granted for a planter to come home, provided he promised to return to Providence by the next ship, and in such a case he might let his plantation for the period of his absence. It was the fixed intention of the leaders that the colony should not become what Barbadoes was already fast becoming, a colony almost wholly in the hands of servants and factors and owned by absentee landlords.

It must have become evident in the course of our enquiry that many causes were tending to form Providence into something very different from the ideal Puritan community aimed at by its English founders. Not the least of these causes were the intolerance and narrowness of the Puritan ministers and their constant encroachments upon the civil power. The defect seems to have been inherent in the Puritan temper, for we may note it at work in New England, in Scotland, and in other Calvinist communities. But whereas in Massachusetts such leaders of the colony as Winthrop and Endecott, though in favour of theocracy, had yet a strong enough backing of public opinion to limit its exercise within reasonable bounds, in the tiny Providence community the outrageous claims of the ministers resulted in the formation of two factions, a small body of zealots opposed to a large party that had lost the earnestness of Puritanism and considered solely their material welfare. A quotation or two from the records will illustrate the progressive antagonising of many of the colonists by the ministers as their claims became more and more aggressive. Henry Halhead was, as we have shown, a strong Puritan and in entire sympathy with the views of the company, but Ditloff suspended him from the sacrament (1632), "first for that he did not redeliver a stone which he had received from the Apothecary, though in answer he alleged that he supposed that he had delivered it, howsoever that he knew not where it was, yet offered to make any honest satisfaction. Secondly for affirming to himself [Ditloff] that Mate Wells was a carnal man and would sometimes swear, yet to others that he was an honest and religious man, and afterwards denying to him that he used the word 'carnal.'" The disproportion between these petty charges and the punishment meted out caused the company to write: "Though Mr. Halhead did upon answer again affirm that, in conference with Mr. Ditloff, he did not use the word 'carnal,' we think it an unfitting thing that any minister should keep a man from the Communion for the foresaid causes alleged in your letter, and cannot imagine that any Minister will be so indiscreet as to do the like hereafter and therefore in such cases we do absolutely forbid it to be done." The company further decreed that censures were to be drawn up by the civil magistrates and only if they are to be made public in the congregation should the minister be consulted. Ditloff, it will be remembered, left the island in 1633, and it was only after he had relinquished entirely the company's employment that they learned of the high-handed way in which he had interfered with the governor's ordinances concerning the management of his parish. In 1634 the company wrote: "We commend Mr. Sherrard very much for his discreet and orderly carriage, but we discommend the other [Ditloff] in all the parts of those proceedings, conceiving that no authority belongs to the Ministers or Parishioners of themselves to do an act of that nature. And whereas he claimed such a power as given to him from us by word of mouth, we do utterly disclaim it. If he had not gone to his country, we would have punished him."

Bell had had a good deal of experience in dealing with cantankerous ministers in the Somers Islands and did his best to hold an even balance between the two factions. He attempted in as far as he was able to carry out the company's desires for the preservation of a rigid decorum in the island, but he found it very difficult to prevent many of the looser sort gathering in New Westminster and refusing to do any work in the plantations. In 1634 the company wrote that those who would not work were not to have any supplies from the stores, "according to the Apostle's rule—he that will not labour, let him not eat. Let care be taken that diligence may be supplied and the sluggard clothed with rags." They very much approved of the governor's proclamation for preventing mixed dances, but "are sorry to hear that, notwithstanding your care and our direction, some have the boldness to speak against such restraints. If any shall appear to do so we wish that they may be admonished, it showing an ill-affection to piety and an opposition to authority. We forbear as yet to send more particular directions for preventing the abuse of God's creatures, but refer it to you at present to take the best course you shall be able and to advise with the ministers to second your authority with their public exhortations." But while the company were thus ready to back up the governor when his views coincided with their own, they were not in the least prepared to give him a free hand. There is an echo of the constitutional struggle in England in the reproof addressed to Bell in 1634 for his use of an independent judgment. The company supported him against the councillors who had not observed the respect due to his office, and they approved the discontinuance of his personal body-guard, of which the cost was very great, but they go on to say that in many cases he seems to have grounded his authority "upon a supposed privilege, which you call *Prerogative,* annexed to your place. Our resolution in that point will appear in the general letter, and we will only add here that we know no such thing as the Governor's Prerogative, being such that you cannot find in our Instruction, neither do we like the use of that horrid word. . . . Again for the word *absolute power,* we do utterly dislike the language and therefore would not have it once named, the same tending to the discouragement of men's stay and coming thither." Too frequent meetings of the council, they added, caused desertion of the councillors' private business and he should therefore set definite times for them and not vary them except in extraordinary circumstances. The meetings must be secret, for "it suits not with the gravity of councillors to discuss their affairs of counsel in the audience of the country especially when there shall arise any difference among them." These words have interest when we remember that they were penned by that leader of the Long Parliament whose speeches were the first parliamentary utterances to be circulated throughout the nation at large and gave an immense circulation of those gazettes and broadsheets that were the earliest forerunners of the modern newspapers.

The dissensions in the island at the end of 1634 were beginning to make Bell's position of mediator an impracticable one, for, while on the one hand the planters were writing home to the company accusing him of caring rather for his own interests than those of the company and of favouring the views of the impracticable ministers in restraint of freedom of enterprise, on the other the ministers were accusing him of impiety and despotism for attempting to curb their pretensions. Hope Sherrard had been imprisoned in his own house by Bell for persistently flouting the authority of the governor and council, and by stirring up his more fanatical followers to attack those planters who did not at once make implicit submission to his ecclesiastical censures.[8]

As we have shown, the *Golden Falcon* carried out to Providence in July, 1633, the last distinctively Puritan emigrants from England, under the command of a minister, Henry Root. The conditions Root found prevailing in the island were so little like those of a strictly Puritan community that he refused to remain, and returned to England in the same ship in May, 1634, to voice the views of the Puritan faction in the island and to open the eyes of the company to the impiety and

[8] *Cf.* Sherrard's letter of February 25, 1635, to his patron, Sir Thomas Barrington. Brit. Mus., Eg., 2646, fo. 76.

laxity that, he said, were rampant and with which Sherrard was left to deal single-handed. Root's story was supplemented by that of the protagonist of the other side, William Rudyerd, who stated that the island was not in itself worth the keeping, but could easily be fortified and held by six hundred men against any force sent to attack it, while a hundred ships might ride safely at anchor in its harbour under the command of the ordnance in the forts. These stories must have been a hard blow to Pym and the more strongly Puritan adventurers, who had aimed at founding an ideal Puritan community for the refuge of the oppressed, and had found that they had sunk their money in a colony that appeared good for nothing but a privateer's stronghold. Root proposed to return to the island with a large party of Puritans, if the company would give him a free hand in expelling those whose life and conduct did not conform to the most rigid Puritan standard. Such expulsions had already been frequent in Massachusetts Bay, as was of course well known to the company. Root's proposals were fully and carefully considered, but before a conclusion could be arrived at, many events had taken place that forced the hand of the company, and these we must now consider.

The coast of the province of Honduras, which at first runs practically due east from the head of the Golfo Dolce, takes a sharp turn to the southward at the cape which has been known ever since Columbus's discovery of it in his third voyage as Cape Gracias á Dios[9] (or Gratia de Dios), "Thanks to God," for the promise vouchsafed by this change in direction that the search for a strait into the Sea of Cathay might not be a fruitless one. The whole of the coast near the cape in either direction is low-lying and is fringed with many small

[9] Herrera, *Decadas,* 6, fo. 13.

cays. A large river empties into the sea near the cape through a many-mouthed delta, and this river has been called by many names; most maps now give its name as the Wanks or Segovia River, but it always appears to have been known to the English frequenters of the coast simply as the Cape River. The coast is fairly well peopled by tribes of the Moskito Indians and near the cape itself there are several of their villages surrounding a harbour of large size.

It was upon the shores of this harbour that Capt. Sussex Camock established his first trading post surrounded by a palisade, and it was up the course of the Cape River that he attempted to penetrate into the interior and get into touch with the Indian tribes. He did not think it safe to commit the whole of his trading truck to the chances of Indian hostility upon the mainland, so a depot was established upon the largest of the Moskito Cays lying some eight or ten miles off shore, and this was committed to the care of his second in command, Capt. Samuel Axe. The trade was undertaken in a very systematic fashion, small parties being sent out to all Indian villages within reach. The goods issued out of the store to each of the parties were entered in a register; to every party a man was assigned who could write and read, and he was provided with pens, paper, and ink, so that he might keep an exact journal in writing of the events that happened every day amongst his company, and on return to the rendezvous these journals were carefully copied into a ledger. Anyone who had strayed from his party and had not committed his observations to writing, was to be examined on his return and his statements recorded. Great care was taken to prevent private trade, especially by mariners, and the company on several occasions had up before them on return to England the mariners who were accused of breach of this rule; they even attempted to put a stop to the trade in parrots and monkeys by charging the sailors ten shillings apiece for their freight. Full directions had been given to Camock regarding the commodities he was to search out and send home, and he had a fair measure of success in the quest, but some elusive rarities baffled him. He could find "silk-grass, gum of pine trees, lignum vitæ, and other gums, annatto, tomarin, skins of all beasts that have any fur or seem vendible, cassia fistula, sarsaparilla, guiacum, mecoachan or wild potatoes, red oil and contra yerba, which is antidote against poison of serpents and arrows," but we never hear of his success as regards "the bezar stone, the manatee stone, or the stone in the alligator's head."

It was an especial fear of the company that Camock would come into contact with the Spaniards, and he was repeatedly cautioned against aggression. "We desire you," wrote the company, "to remove all occasions of jealousy or suspicion that this design should be intended for plunder rather than for the business of lawful trade. And therefore take special order that none be employed to take anything from the Spaniards or any other nation by violence or otherwise than by way of peaceful commerce. We pray you to have a special care of the fugitive Spaniard that we hear is with you lest he should escape and so make his own peace by betraying of that business. While he is amongst you let his usage be as he deserves."

By the end of 1634 the trade on the Main appeared so successful and Camock's flax promised to be so much of a commercial success, that the principal members of the company resolved that a fresh patent for the trade should be obtained and special subscriptions invited for its carrying on to the exclusion of the Hollanders who, they heard, were beginning to cast their eyes upon the

Moskito Coast. Oliver St. John and Pym were deputed to draw a patent entirely distinct from the patent of the Providence Company, and the Earl of Holland promised to move the king for a grant and to crave the assistance of the lord treasurer.[10] A good deal of discussion took place as to whether everyone in the Providence Company should be permitted to invest in the new company or whether they should not be first compelled to complete their adventures in Providence. Sir Nathaniel Rich maintained the view that no one should be permitted to enter the new company unless he had subscribed to every adventure before;[11] but Pym took the far more generous view that by subscribing at all to the Providence Company the adventurers had acquired a right to participate in any new ventures. He held that the trade at the Main was contemplated in the original design of the Providence Company, that each subscriber to the preference stock had contributed towards the expenses of exploring the Main as well as to the expenses of Providence, and that Camock's party were the employés of the whole company. He urged, therefore, that every member should have the right to subscribe if he thought fit, and even if he did not subscribe, he should have a right to a portion of the profits. Pym's views, however, were too broad for the rest of the company, and at the motion of Sir Nathaniel Rich it was resolved that everything done in the past should be neglected and only those subscribing to the stock of the new company should receive any benefit from the new trade.

[10] Weston, Earl of Portland.

[11] In the short life of Sir Nathaniel Rich in the *Dict. Nat. Biog.*, his attitude is entirely misrepresented. It is stated that he pursued a forward policy and in 1635 advocated admission of all adventurers to the trade of the Main. This is almost the contrary of his real proposal.

The new patent was issued in March, 1635,[12] to the earls of Warwick and Holland and their associates under the name of "The Governor and Company of Adventurers of the City of London for a trade upon the coasts and islands of divers parts of America." The right of sole trade with the heathen on the shores of the Caribbean was granted to the new company where they were not under the dominion of any Christian prince. The company was granted for fourteen years "the sole manufacture of all thread and stuff to be made of a kind of flagg or grass brought from those parts and not in common use in this kingdom, which is by them called Cammock's flax, and of the sole manufacture and employment of all kinds of new materials and merchandize not heretofore commonly used in this Realm, which shall by them be brought from those parts, and found to be profitable and useful here. They are to pay custom for the said Cammock's flax after the rate of the best unwrought flax now brought into this kingdom and for all other commodities after the rate of 5 per cent according to the clear value of the goods and not above." It was decided that as all the officers of the Providence Company, save the Earl of Holland, were subscribers to the stock of the new company, the same officers should serve both for the plantation and for the trade.

We have already seen that considerable difficulty was found by the company in obtaining Puritan emigrants to the colony and that only a few had gone out with Root in the *Golden Falcon* in 1633. The voyage of 1634 was planned on a more lavish scale than that of 1633, and the money obtained by the issue of the preference stock[13]

12 Docquet Book, March, 1634/5. The grant is apparently not calendared in *C. S. P. Colonial* or *Domestic.*

13 See p. 126. When this preference stock was fully subscribed the total sum paid up on each whole share of adventure was £1025. In July, 1634, the total paid-up capital of the company amounted to about £20,000.

was devoted to hiring a ship of three hundred tons, the *Long Robert,* and purchasing a pinnace and ketch to accompany her. Two well-furnished magazines were put on board and Pym gave a large amount of personal attention to seeing that everything sent was of excellent quality. It was found almost impossible to secure emigrants of decent standing, and with the exception of a few planters returning to Providence, a minister, Bartholomew Styles, going to Association, and one or two Puritan gentlemen, the passengers were bond-servants recruited by paid agents[14] and sent out to serve the officers and council. Difficulties were found in getting together even penniless servants and the company complained bitterly in their letters to the council that the discouraging information sent home in the planters' letters had prevented decent, God-fearing men of substance from emigrating to Providence. In order to make up the deficiency, the master of the *Long Robert* was directed to call at St. Christopher and attempt to recruit for the colony among the planters and servants there. He was also to call at Association and purchase thirty negroes, who were to be transported to Providence and were allotted as servants to the officers. Nothing could indicate more plainly than did these directions that the company recognised the failure of their attempt to provide in the Caribbean a second home for Puritan refugees.

The total expenditure on the voyage amounted to £3000 and the *Long Robert* and her consorts left England in September, 1634. It was expected that a full and valuable freight would be found awaiting her at Providence, but these expectations were woefully disappointed. In June, 1635, the vessel returned, bringing nothing but

[14] Eighteen shillings a head was received for servants by the recruiting agents at this period, but a couple of years later as much as 22s. was given owing to the increased difficulty of obtaining recruits.

a poor cargo of tobacco and cotton, and with many of the quondam planters of the colony on board. Their complaints of the conduct of the governor and council and their girdings at the restraints upon their conduct imposed by the minister, Sherrard, were a poor return to the company, whose orders the governor and minister had endeavoured to carry out to the best of their ability. And not merely were the Puritan members of the company hurt in the failure of their ideals of a Puritan community; their pockets also were badly hit, for the voyage of the *Long Robert,* instead of doing something to reimburse the adventurers for their previous expenditure, had added a sum of at least £1300 to the company's indebtedness. The goods brought home in the *Robert* fetched only £328-5s.-1d., and the thirteen undertakers for the voyage had to pay in £100-15s.-2¼d. each to make up the deficiency. The total amount owed by the company, not including this £1309, was £2750, and this indebtedness was a constant source of uneasiness to the treasurer, Pym. In May, 1635, he pointed out to the company that, at the departure of the *Long Robert,* the company's assets exceeded its liabilities, so that the whole of the debt had accrued in a year. He "put the Company in mind of the burden and charge of that office of Treasurer, which he had borne ever since their first incorporation, whereby he had been diverted from his own business and put upon extraordinary expense." At Sir Nathaniel Rich's motion, it was resolved to make a levy upon all members to pay off the debt. The feelings of Rich and of Pym, who had been so energetic in persuading their friends and relatives to become adventurers and to invest money in the enterprise, must have been none of the pleasantest, and from 1635 onwards we find that no more adventurers of the same class joined the company, but almost all of the additional capital raised was contributed by the wealthy men who were already adventurers, Warwick, Saye, Brooke, Rudyerd, and Pym, together with two other wealthy Puritans, Lord Mandeville and Sir William Waller.

Although the results of the *Long Robert's* voyage were not yet known, no money could be raised to send out a ship in 1635, and the needful supplies to the island to the value of £716 were forwarded by the ship *Expectation,* owned by William Woodcock, the company's husband, which was sailing for St. Christopher and was placed at the company's disposal after she had finished her unlading there. Only twenty passengers went out in her and with the exception of ten servants and of Sherrard's betrothed, who was going out to be married to him, none of them were fresh to the colony. The *Expectation* left England in April, 1635, and returned in the following December, bringing the news of the great Spanish attack on Providence, which we shall consider in a subsequent chapter. With the return of the *Expectation,* the history of Providence as a Puritan haven may be said in the main to have come to an end and consequently our interest at this point centers on different aspects of the story.

CHAPTER VII

PROJECTED EMIGRATION TO CONNECTICUT: SAYBROOK

In an earlier chapter we left the story of the Puritans of New England at the time when the great expedition set sail under John Winthrop, the elder, and the colony of Massachusetts sprang into vigorous life. From the very first there was little doubt of success, and by 1635 a flourishing and already fairly prosperous community was spread around the shores of Massachusetts Bay. Our interest now turns once more to this main stream of Puritan migration, as did the minds of the Puritan leaders in England, and it seems at last possible with the means at our disposal to supply the true version of a story that has in the past caused much controversy. After the restoration of Charles II to the English throne in 1660, it was said by the royalist writers, Dr. George Bate and Sir William Dugdale, that about 1638 the Puritan leaders, Pym, Hampden, and Cromwell, embarked on shipboard with the intention of proceeding to New England, but that they were stopped by the king's orders and compelled to remain in England, to plot rebellion. This story has been largely discredited by historians, and John Forster, the biographer of Pym, having shown that such an occurrence could not have taken place in 1638 or later, came to the conclusion that no credence could be attached to Dugdale's statement. That actual embarkation took place is certainly untrue, but our present investigation seems to make clear that the story is a fair interpretation of the plans of Pym,

Hampden, and others; and, though it is impossible to speak definitely as to the plans of Oliver Cromwell, who, down to 1642, was not regarded as a person of much importance among the Puritans, yet there is a probability that he would have followed the path of his friends had it been necessary.

The absolutist régime, that had been entered upon by Charles I after the dissolution of parliament in 1629, had by 1635 been in full activity for six years and to those who regarded externals only must have appeared to justify itself by its success. Clarendon asserts of this time that never had England enjoyed such order and prosperity and never had her material well-being been more envied by her distracted and war-ridden Continental neighbours. But in reality the mood of despair that had overwhelmed the best minds of the nation in 1629 had not been dispelled as time went on, and by 1635 it seemed as though England were destined to remain subject to a well-meaning but incapable and capricious despotism. Beneath the outward calm, deep discontent lay hid, for nearly every class in the community found itself attacked or menaced by the injudicious meddlesomeness of the government or by its unwise devices for the increase of the revenues of the crown. To the ordinary man these devices were irksome and unsettling enough, but to an earnest Puritan, whose religious feelings were at the same time being outraged by his Arminian enemies in high places, they were unbearable. The tide of migration to New England, that had begun to flow when Winthrop and his followers sailed in 1630, had moved on with ever-swelling increase, till 1635 saw the largest number of emigrants leave England's shores for Massachusetts that ever passed thither.[1] Thenceforward the tide began to slacken as the progressive

[1] Hutchinson's *History of Massachusetts Bay,* I, 41.

steps taken against the royal absolutism began to rouse men's hopes in a restoration of parliamentary government.

It will be remembered[2] that on March 19, 1632, the Earl of Warwick, then president of the New England Council, deeded a tract of land south of Massachusetts to a body of patentees including most of the members of the Providence Company. On the 21st and 26th of the following June,[3] the New England Council agreed to the rough draft of a patent to Warwick, who directed that it be made out to Lord Rich and his associates, but there is no evidence that a patent was ever actually issued. That a blank draft was drawn up is clear, but, in default of a formal confirmation by the council, the deed of March remained without validity. Warwick had for some time been getting out of touch with the rest of the New England Council, owing to his patronage of the Massachusetts settlers, and this renewed attempt to establish another Puritan settlement in New England seems to have finally brought about an open breach with Gorges, for the meeting at which it was made was the last at which the earl was present, and within a week we find the members resolving to reconstitute the council and sending to the Earl of Warwick to ask him to deliver up the council's seal. From November, 1632, the council fell entirely into the hands of the court party under the presidency, first of the Earl of Lindsey and later of Hamilton, Arundel, and Carlisle with Ferdinando Gorges as its leading and most active member. The affairs of the council became a crying scandal by 1635 and consisted mainly of quarrels over the division of lands; so serious had matters become that the king was

2 See p. 83.

3 "Records of Council for New England," at Warwick House, 21 and 26 June, 1632, *Proc.* of Amer. Antiq. Soc. for 1867, p. 100.

bound to step in, and the charter was surrendered into his hands on April 25, 1635, the last act of the council being to publish a manifesto reciting the wrongs done to its members and especially to the Gorges family by the Massachusetts settlers.

The winter of 1634-1635 was a particularly trying time for the Puritan leaders in England, who were harassed by the government at all points. At the forest court held for Waltham Forest in October, 1634, both Warwick and Barrington suffered in their estates by Sir John Finch's strict enforcement of the forest laws;[4] Saye had been attacked both on his Oxfordshire and his Gloucestershire estates, and Brooke in Warwickshire in the same way. Pym, in the winter of 1633-1634, had been twice sued by the attorney-general for remaining in London to look after the business of the Providence Company instead of returning to his house in the country. The Roman emissary, Gregorio Panzani, had been welcomed with open arms at court and conversions to the Roman Church were being announced daily; while the laws against recusants, so dear to the hearts of the Puritan leaders, were everywhere a dead letter, the archbishop's metropolitical visitation was in full swing and Puritan divines were everywhere being silenced, browbeaten, and fined. Early in 1635, Warwick had to suffer the indignity of dividing his lord lieutenancy of Essex with Lord Maynard, and on the death of Lord Treasurer Portland in March, 1635, another powerful office fell under the sway of the hated archbishop, who was placed first on the commission to exercise the lord treasurer-

[4] *C. S. P. Dom.*, 1634-1635, p. xxxiii. For Saye and the Forest of Whichwood in Oxfordshire, see Whitelocke's *Memorials*, I, 70.

Gardiner (VIII, 129) shows that there was an ever-spreading apprehension of danger at this time. The English Church might at any time fall a victim to a conspiracy carried on in the very name of the king by Laud, its prime mover.

ship. The first writ of ship-money had been levied on maritime counties in October, 1634, with a reasonable plea of urgent naval necessity, but the winter was full of rumours that the impost was to be extended over the whole country,[5] and this was quite a different matter.

The cup of bitterness for the Puritan leaders was filled to overflowing and they began to think that the time had come for them also to look across the Atlantic for fresh homes, where so many of their humble brethren had already gone. John Winthrop, the younger, had lost his wife in September, 1634, and sailed for England in October, much disillusioned with Massachusetts and desiring to begin a settlement elsewhere in New England. It was only natural that on his return to London he should enter into close communication with those who had been such good friends to Massachusetts as Lord Saye and Sir Nathaniel Rich, and should give them all the personal information he could about the new colonies. It has not been possible to trace the details of the negotiations that went on in the spring of 1635, and indeed it seems very unlikely that it will ever be possible to do so, for both Saye and Brooke were constant objects of suspicion to the government[6] and would commit as little as possible of their projects to paper.

No steps had been taken to act upon the Saybrook grant, which Warwick had drawn up, until July, 1633,[7]

[5] In June the lord keeper, Coventry, openly told the judges, ''Upon advice [the King] hath resolved that he will forthwith send out new writs for the preparation of a greater fleet next year and that not only to the maritime towns but to all the kingdom besides.'' Rushworth, II, 294.

[6] *C. S. P. Dom.*, 1635, p. 164.

[7] In the year 1633, Saye, Brooke, Saltonstall, Haselrigg, and others purchased for £2150 the interest of an association of merchants from Bristol, Shrewsbury, and other towns of western England in Piscataqua and Kennebec, and became involved with the Plymouth colony on account of the murder of Capt. Hocking. Bradford, *Hist. of Plym. Plant.* (ed. 1912, Ford), pp. 175-180, and notes.

when the Providence Company agreed to lend to Lords Saye and Brooke five pieces of ordnance, viz., two minions and three faulcons, for their use in New England, but nothing further was done until, in May, 1635, Sir Richard Saltonstall sent out twenty men—the Stiles party[8]—to the Connecticut Valley to make a beginning of a settlement under the grant, and Woodcock, the husband of the Providence Company, was directed to assemble stores for the despatch of a larger expedition. It was at last decided definitely that southern Connecticut should replace Providence as the scene of the building up of the Puritan colony planned by the patentees, and on July 7, 1635,[9] an agreement was signed with John Winthrop, jr., as leader of the pioneer expedition on their behalf. In the words of his commission, "He shall endeavour to provide able men, to the number of fifty at least, for making of fortifications and building of houses at the river Connecticut and the harbour adjoining, first for their own present accommodation, and then *such houses as may receive men of quality,* which houses we would have to be builded in the fort." The commission was signed for the rest of the patentees by Sir Richard Saltonstall, Henry Lawrence, Henry Darley, Sir Arthur Haselrigg, and George Fenwick, who had been appointed to remain in London and act as a committee in charge of the affair.[10] Large sums were being sub-

8 In July this party, composed of Saltonstall's servants led by Francis Stiles, appeared at Windsor on the Connecticut and claimed the territory by virtue of their patent. But the previous occupants from Dorchester in Massachusetts ignored the demands of these representatives of the "Lords and Gentlemen." They allowed the Stiles servants to settle on the place, but refused any recognition of the claims of the patentees.

9 Mass. Hist. Soc. *Coll.,* 5th Ser., I, 482. The agreement and commission were drawn up by William Jessop, who was acting as clerk to the Saybrook patentees. As we already know, Jessop was secretary of the Providence Company.

10 Trumbull, I, 497.

scribed to finance the expedition, for Winthrop took £2000 with him,[11] and we find Philip Nye writing to him in July, "I have sent the other £1000 by Mr. Peirce[12] to be delivered to your father for you." It was the expenditure of their capital on this design on the Connecticut River that rendered it impossible for the adventurers to secure sufficient subscriptions to send out a ship of their own to Providence in 1635. Winthrop sailed from England about the beginning of August, 1635, accompanied by the son of the comptroller of the king's household, young Henry Vane, who was deep in the Puritan counsels and upon whose judgment the leaders placed great reliance. The project was by now becoming generally known and on September 1, 1635, we find Garrard writing to the lord deputy:[13] "Mr. Comptroller Sir Henry Vane's eldest son hath left his Father, his Mother, his Country and that fortune which his father would have left him here, and is for conscience sake gone into New England, there to lead the rest of his days, being about twenty years of age. He had abstained two years from taking the Sacrament in England, because he could get nobody to administer it to him standing. He was bred up in Leyden and I hear that Sir Nathaniel Rich and Mr. Pym have done him much hurt in their persuasions this way. God forgive them for it, if they be guilty."

The interest in the north of England in the new project was very great and many of the Yorkshire gentry who

[11] This we learn with some other particulars from a letter from Philip Nye to John Winthrop, jr., 28 July, 1635 (Mass. Hist. Soc. *Coll,* 5th series, I, 210). Nye, a protégé of Lord Mandeville's, was assisting Jessop with the secretarial work. The regulations concerning residence were being very strictly enforced on the country gentlemen in 1635 and the plague was raging in London. Practically the whole work of the Providence Company was being done by a committee of Pym, Darley, and Woodcock for this reason.

[12] The celebrated New England shipmaster.

[13] *Strafford Papers,* I, 463.

had been antagonised by the harsh administration of the Council of the North, had been persuaded by Darley's influence to consider migration to the new colony. Sir Matthew Boynton of Bramston, for example, a strong Puritan and M. P. for Scarborough in the Long Parliament, wrote to Winthrop through Henry Darley:[14] "I pray you advertise me what course I shall take for providing a house against my coming over, where I may remain with my family till I can be better provided to settle myself, and let me have your best assistance, and withal, I pray you, let me receive advice from time to time what provisions are most commodious to be made there or to be sent from hence, that so I may make the best advantage of my time before I come, as also what things will be most expedient for me both for my necessary use and benefit there to bring over with me when I come." All through the autumn of 1635 preparations were going on apace, but as quietly and unostentatiously as possible. So much were the energies of the patentees immersed in the new design that Providence was entirely neglected for a time and no meetings of the company were held between the beginning of June and the end of November. On September 22, 1635, Henry Lawrence wrote to Winthrop:[15] "I shall remember you now but of two things, one is the place of our pitching, wherein (if in anything) we are peremptory for Connecticut, it being, as you know, and so continuing, the joint resolution of us all that nothing but a plain impossibility could divert us from that place, which in many respects we conceived most advantageous both for the securing of our friends at the Bay[16] and our own personal accom-

[14] Mass. Hist. Soc. *Coll.*, 4th series, VII, 164.

[15] Mass. Hist. Soc. *Coll.*, 5th series, I, 214.

[16] That is, securing the Massachusetts settlers from the encroachments of the Dutch.

modations. . . . [The other] is that fortifications and some convenient buildings for the receipt of the gentlemen may go hand in hand, for there are likely to come more over next summer, both to be witness of what you have done and to thank you for it, than you are yet aware of. Other things I shall leave to your own wisdom and the directions given you, earnestly beseeching God that He would farther suggest such things to us all as may be most for the glory of His great name and (which in this design we specially aim at) the good of His churches.'' Winthrop and Vane reached Massachusetts in October, 1635, and the first steps were at once taken to commence the new settlement. A vessel with twenty men[17] and some ordnance started in November, which reached its destination on the 24th, and formal possession of the territory was taken in the name of the patentees. Under the direction of Lyon Gardiner, an English engineer, who had seen service under the Prince of Orange, a fort and houses were built of ''a spungie kind of timber called a read oack,'' the ''pallisadoes'' being composed of whole trees set in the ground, and here, during an exceptionally cold winter, Winthrop, Gardiner, and the score of settlers made shift to live. In the spring Fenwick arrived, only to return to England in the summer for his wife, Alice Apsley, widow of Sir John Boteler of Teston, Kent, whom he brought to the colony in 1639.

Meanwhile, the Puritan leaders in England had been drawing up a suggested basis for the constitution of the colony, and this was despatched by Saye to the authorities

17 These twenty men may have been the servants of Sir Matthew Boynton, referred to in Boynton's letter of April 12, 1637, to Winthrop, releasing his servants in Connecticut from their engagements to him and giving them leave to shift for themselves. Mass. Hist. Soc. *Coll.*, 4th series, VII, 169.

in Massachusetts late in the year with a request for their suggestions upon it. This scheme[18] has always been a well-known document and has by some writers been regarded as a base attempt to foist an aristocratic constitution upon a people who had succeeded in freeing themselves from the control of absolutism. In reality the scheme was most reasonable and should be of interest to students of English history as showing in their own words what was the conception of an ideal constitution, or we might rather say what was the conception of the time-honoured English constitution, that was held by the men who, within so few years, were to sway the destinies of England for good or ill. It is of immediate interest to the student of Puritan colonisation from a narrower point of view, for from time to time, when the answers of the ruling oligarchy in Massachusetts to the patentees' demands were despatched by the pen of Cotton, is to be dated the progressive estrangement between the Eng-

18 Hutchinson's *History of Massachusetts Bay,* I, 490.

"Certain proposals made by Lord Saye, Lord Brooke, and other Persons of quality, as conditions of their removing to New England with the answers thereto:"

1. Two ranks of citizens, gentlemen and freeholders.
2. The power of making and repealing laws to lie in the two ranks assembled together.
3. Each rank to possess a negative voice.
4. The first rank to attend Parliament personally, the second by deputy.
5. The ranks to sit in two Houses.
6. Set times to be appointed for the meeting of Parliament yearly or half-yearly.
7. Parliament to have the power of calling the Governor to account and all officers to determine with a new Parliament, unless Parliament enact otherwise.
8. The governor always to be chosen out of the ranks of gentlemen.
9. The Patentees and those aiding them should belong to the first rank but afterwards appointments to it should be made with the consent of both Houses.
10. Freeholders should have a certain estate or contribute a certain amount to the public charges.

lish and the American Puritans, that will, to a certain extent, call for our attention in following chapters. To none of the patentees' demands did the Massachusetts rulers make any material objection, for these demands very closely represented the constitution under which all of the Puritans had grown up. But the Massachusetts leaders added to these demands the important and fundamental condition that civil rights should be obtainable only through church membership and, be it understood, church membership as guarded and granted or withheld by the spiritual power. The demand was impossible of acceptance by English aristocrats of the profoundly Erastian temper of Saye and of Pym, and we may already discern that two parties had sprung from the nonconforming Puritanism of King James's day; on the one hand, we have the narrow theocrats of New England, steeped in the theology and political speculations of Leyden and Dort and resolved to confine the full rights of citizenship to the orthodox adherents of their creed; on the other, we have the Erastian English squires, conservative laymen glorying in what they believed to be England's ancient constitution.

While the Saybrook grantees were contemplating an immediate removal of themselves, their families, and their fortunes to the other side of the Atlantic, the government of England was falling more and more into the hands of Laud, who, when he succeeded Weston as practical head of the Treasury in March, 1635, secured a power in the Privy Council that was thenceforth almost supreme. Colonial matters, too, began to occupy the archbishop's attention, for in 1634 he had been nominated one of twelve commissioners to supervise the colonies.[19] No objections had been found to the lines upon which New England was developing, when the

[19] Col. Pap., 28 April, 1634.

first governmental enquiry into its affairs was made in 1633, and the well-known nonconformity of the colonists was tacitly acquiesced in. But Laud's accession to power in any sphere was marked by a tightening up of administration and a legally minded supervision of details that left little room for flexibility and toleration. The quarrel over the New England Council in 1635 and Gorges's accusations against Massachusetts would have drawn the archbishop's unfavourable attention to the colony, even had he not been receiving complaints from the churchmen expelled by its rulers. For the first time, in 1635, an oath of conformity to the Prayer Book had been demanded above and beyond the usual oath of allegiance from those wishing to emigrate, and in the course of the summer the news of Roger Williams's proceedings and the views he was expounding in the colony began to reach the archbishop and roused in him the conviction that something definite must be done. When, therefore, he learned that so notable a person as Vane had gone, and that eminent opponents of the government, such as Saye and Brooke, were making preparations to go to New England, he resolved that instant steps must be taken to crush the movement and to prevent so important an accession of strength to the recalcitrant colony. For the first time the eyes of England's governors were opened to what had been going on unheeded in America; it had not seemed a very great thing that such an unimportant and dispossessed lawyer as Winthrop, such a land steward as Dudley, or such silenced ministers as Cotton and Hooker, should lead farmers and tradesmen across the Atlantic, but when men personally known and disliked at court, such as the bitter-tongued Saye or the severe and lofty-minded Brooke, began to talk of selling their estates, and when the son and heir of one so well known as Sir Henry Vane had actually sailed for Massachusetts, the matter had become serious.

Into the details of the suit of *quo warranto* against the Massachusetts Bay Company, begun in 1635, we need not enter here, but a letter[20] from Nye to John Winthrop, jr., in the same month will illustrate the way in which the government had begun to frustrate the intentions of the would-be emigrants: "We have sent you some servants, but not so many as we purposed; the reason is this. Some of the gentlemen of the north, who lay 3 or 4 months in London transacting these affairs, did think that there would have been no notice of their purposes, and therefore assumed to send us up servants, but when they came down, found the country full of the reports of their going now. Those two (being Deputy Lieutenants of the shire) did not dare to move any further in sending up of men. My lord Brooke likewise, that undertook for twenty, failed likewise and sent us not one. Our gentlemen's minds remain the same and are in a way of selling off their estates with the greatest expedition." The moment had gone by never to return; by the general trend of affairs and by the direct connivance of the government, the Puritan leaders became once more immersed in English politics, their eyes were once more turned, first to difficulties in their own counties and later to the great national struggle, and never again did they look to New England as likely to provide them with a home. In August, 1635, the second writs for the collection of ship-money were issued and, regardless of precedent, for the first time the inland counties were called upon to contribute. Special harshness was exercised in the collection from the tenants of persons of known hostility to the government, such as Saye and

[20] Philip Nye to John Winthrop, jr., 2 Sept., 1635. Mass. Hist. Soc. *Coll.*, 5th series, I, 210.

Brooke, and before the end of 1635 serious disturbances had arisen in Oxfordshire, Warwickshire, and Essex, and the Puritan leaders were soon deeply immersed in a concerted design for organising a resistance to payment that should be national in character and sufficient to tax the whole energies of the government.

The Saybrook settlement was abandoned by its promoters. Fenwick remained, burdened with heavy expenses and in daily expectation of a large accession of noblemen and gentlemen from England, but as the years passed and no results were attained, he wrote, in 1642 and 1643, to Haselrigg and Barrington, begging for information as to their plans, only to learn that Lord Brooke, Sir William Constable, and Sir Matthew Boynton had relinquished all intention of crossing the water, and that the proposed emigration had been given up, because "affairs in England had taken such a turn that persons of that character had no occasion for an asylum." Wearying of his burden and yet desirous of securing the patentees against loss, he offered their "whole interest heare and in the River" to the Connecticut towns for £3000. The towns rejecting this offer, made tender of £200 a year for ten years, payable in corn, pork, and pipe-staves, but Fenwick refused. With the failure of further negotiations, Fenwick in desperation thought of renting out the land, but soon discovered that in New England a quit-rent would not be borne. He also thought of levying a custom toll on the river traffic, but that plan also he abandoned. Realising that there was "no other way but selling out of it to the [Connecticut] towns," for the housing and fortification were in such bad repair that continued possession would cost more than could be spared, he again approached the northern colony, and on December 5, 1644, accepted their terms and transferred the title to

Saybrook to the inhabitants of Hartford, Wethersfield, and Windsor. Henceforward Saybrook was a part of the colony of Connecticut.[21]

[21] Brit. Mus., Eg., 2646, fos. 181, 182, 240; 2648, fo. 1; Mass. Hist. Soc. *Coll.*, 4th series, VII, 169, 5th series, IX, 381; Hutchinson, *Hist.*, I, 64.

CHAPTER VIII

SPANISH ATTACKS AND THE COMPANY'S CHANGE OF POLICY

Our attention has so far been directed mainly to the work of the Providence Company and its members, as far as they were involved in the great movement of Puritan migration. We must now direct our enquiry to another aspect of the subject and regard the colonies of Providence and Association in connection with the Spanish possessions that lay round about them. The Spanish dominions in America differed essentially from the settlements of other European nations in America in that the latter were either self-governing communities, such as Virginia and Massachusetts, or were under the immediate control of a commercial company, such as the Dutch West India Company, and had little direct interference to suffer from the home government. The Spanish government, on the other hand, through the Council of the Indies, exercised an all-pervading control over the colonies, and a perpetual stream of orders dealing with the smallest details of government was poured upon the governor of every kingdom in the Indies.[1] The fortunes of the Castilian monarchy, therefore, had a most potent influence upon the energy with which designs were matured and carried out, even when the designs merely concerned such small islands in the Caribbean as Providence and Tortuga. From 1628 on, the Spanish government, in addition to its constant difficulties in raising financial supplies from exhausted provinces wherewith

[1] F. A. Kirkpatrick in *Camb. Mod. Hist.*, X, 248; Bourne, *Spain in America*, 225-227.

to carry on the never-ending struggles in Flanders and Germany, had to conduct the unsuccessful Mantuan War in North Italy against Richelieu and his allies, the Pope and Venice. The task proved overwhelming and at length, in April, 1631, Olivares, the all-powerful minister of Philip IV, was compelled to sign the ignominious treaties of Cherasco, which marked another step in the downfall of Spain from her once dominant position. While the war was raging little attention could be spared for American affairs, but the short interval of peace before war with France again broke out in May, 1635, was marked by many attempts to deal with the swarms of foreigners, that since 1625 had swooped down upon the unoccupied islands of the Antilles and were rapidly strangling the remaining commerce of the Indies. Suggestions for dealing with the difficulty and for expelling the Dutch, French, and English, were invited from the governors of all the provinces surrounding the Caribbean. Many of the replies[2] afford graphic pictures of the difficulties against which the royal governors in the New World had to contend. The constant burden of complaint in the replies is that the whole of the wealth of the Indies must be despatched to Spain, though salaries are unpaid, fortresses are in need of repair, and it is impossible to find means for equipping a fleet against the corsairs. The case made out was bad enough to move even the government of Philip IV to action and strict orders were despatched that everything possible was to be done against the intruders, even though the cost reduced a little the tribute sent to Europe. The sacrifice was a great one to the Castilian monarchy, for only with the produce of the Indies could even an attempt

[2] See especially Venezuela Papers, Add. MSS., 36322, fos. 7, 69, 175, 180; Add. MSS. (Kingsborough Collection), 13992, fo. 110, 13974, fo. 71, 13977, fo. 14.

be made to satisfy the insatiable demands of Flanders and Germany upon the Spanish exchequer, and Piet Hein's capture of the Plate Fleet of 1627 had been a terrible blow to Spain's ever-dwindling credit.

St. Christopher and Nevis had been temporarily cleared of English and French in 1629, but the greatest effort was made in 1633 when Juan de Eulate, governor of Margarita, destroyed a settlement of trading Englishmen at Punta Galena, on the eastern side of Trinidad,[3] and then passed on to the capture of Tobago from the Dutch and the massacre of the unfortunate prisoners taken in that island.[4] The Windward Islands had also to suffer attack and the Dutch in St. Martin's were wiped out in the same year. St. Martin's was at this period one of the most important of the Lesser Antilles, for it was everywhere famous for its salt pans and thither collected ships of all nationalities to obtain the salt made by its Dutch colonists. After the departure of the fleet from St. Martin's and in order to avoid the return of those expelled, a Spanish garrison was left in the island[5] and there remained for some years. Curaçao was held by the Dutch in great force and owing to its defensibility succeeded in beating back the attempt of the governor of Venezuela to capture it in the same year, 1633.[6]

Needless to say, the news of this Spanish activity caused the greatest uneasiness to the Providence Company and its colonists, and some extracts from a letter of Minister Sherrard to Sir Thomas Barrington will convey an idea of their attitude towards the expected

[3] Venezuela Papers, Add. MSS., 36322, fo. 208. Juan de Eulate to King, Margarita, 20 July, 1633.

[4] *Ibid.*, 36324, fos. 89, 233.

[5] Add. MSS., 13977, fo. 509.

[6] *Ibid.*, fo. 510.

attack.[7] In January, 1634, he writes: "Blessed be God, that hath hitherto put his hook into the mouth and his bridle into the jaws of His and our enemies, that they could not so much as make any attempt upon us, and still let Him say of them as He did of Sennacherib—They shall not shoot forth an arrow here. Amen.—We have need of prayers and faith now, if ever, considering our imminent danger, having not shot for above a day's fight in case an enemy should assault us; and besides fifty of our ablest and helpfullest men are gone from us of late, some to the Main and some for England, so that we have not able men half enough to man our forts nor any power of men to speak of to repel an enemy from landing, so that we must now console ourselves as well in the want as if we had the enjoyment of means, and cast ourselves upon Him that made even the Spaniards, yea the whole universe itself. St. Martin's is taken by the Spaniard that would engross the whole world to himself, and the rest of the Islands that are inhabited in these parts by our English are threatened, and who knows how soon our turn may be if God divert not. . . . I am sorry that this island hath not better answered their honour's expense and expectation. The Lord in mercy crown their honour's noble undertakings in these parts with a glorious success that the Gospel may be planted on the Main. What glory thereby would accrue to God! How would it eternise their honour's names to posterity and how would the children yet unborn bless their honours!" Even while Sherrard wrote, the blow was preparing, but before Providence suffered, Association was attacked and its colonists scattered.

The great island of Hispaniola had been the first portion of the Indies settled by the Spaniards and had in

[7] Brit. Mus., Eg., 2646, fo. 58, Hope Sherrard to Sir T. B., Providence, 6 Jan. 163¾.

the earlier years of their domination been the seat of the principal government in the Indies. Owing to the difficulty the earliest invaders had found in subduing the Indians of the northern shore of the island, the principal Spanish settlement was founded at San Domingo in the southeastern corner of the island, and in the great savannas surrounding the city almost all of the Spanish population of Hispaniola was gathered. The native inhabitants of the island had been exterminated very early, and the wide forests covering its northern shore were in the early part of the seventeenth century inhabited only by a few bands of Cimarones or negroes escaped from the Spanish plantations. No means of communication existed through these dense tracts, and the northern shore was therefore entirely removed from Spanish influence; for this reason it was a favourite base for rovers,[8] English, French, and Dutch, who were accustomed to refit and obtain fresh victuals in its numerous harbours. No permanent settlements existed, but each nationality among the rovers had its usual gathering place. The Dutch mainly congregated at San Nicolas, the abandoned site of Spain's earliest settlement in the island, and there they carried on a considerable industry of salt-making and of curing the flesh of the cattle they killed in the forests; the French usually landed at the island now called La Gonaive, but then known to the Spaniards as El Caimito, and at a harbour on the main island of Hispaniola known as Gonaives.[9] The only settlement that up to 1635 had acquired anything of a permanent character, was that formed by Anthony Hilton round the harbour of the island of Tortuga that we know from the Providence records as Asso-

[8] An English pirate had been captured by the Spaniards at Tortuga in 1611. Brown, I, 522.

[9] Hakluyt, VII, 160, Brit. Mus., Add. MSS., 13977, fo. 509.

ciation. The depredations committed on the shores of Cuba, San Domingo, and Porto Rico by the rovers who gathered in Tortuga harbour were so frequent and so destructive that the Audiencia of San Domingo had resolved in 1633 that Tortuga must be one of the first pirate strongholds to be cleared at any cost.[10]

From the report to the Providence Company of a Dutch shipmaster, Richard Evertsen, who called at Association late in 1634, we learn that the settlement then had one hundred and fifty regular inhabitants, but there was such a large admixture of Frenchmen among these that the Spaniards took it for a French settlement. A fort furnished with the artillery supplied by the Providence Company was supposed to guard the harbour, but no proper watches were kept and no military discipline existed. The governor, elected by the planters after Hilton's death in 1634, was Christopher Wormeley, one of the original adventurers, but he had little control over the settlers and devoted his attention to making what profit he could out of incoming rovers. The Spanish expedition[11] for the surprise of the island was got ready at San Domingo during November and December, 1634, and consisted of a force of two hundred and fifty soldiers under the command of Don Ruiz Fernandez de Fuem-

10 There is no doubt that the Providence Company were quite deceived all through as to what was happening in Association. We cannot say whether Hilton ever had any intention of acting honestly and attempting to found a legitimate colony, but by 1634 his settlement was, without doubt, what the Spaniards called it, merely a pirate hold.

11 The full Spanish account of the capture of Tortuga, sent to the Council of the Indies on 12 June, 1635, is now to be found in Brit. Mus., Add. MSS., 13977, fo. 506. Du Tertre says something of the capture from the French side (I, 169 sqq.); he dates it however by error in 1638. Labat and Charlevoix, and others copy Du Tertre, while Esquemeling in his *History of the Buccaneers* with his usual untrustworthiness confuses names and dates badly. In one place he dates the capture in 1630, and in another in 1664 when D'Ogeron was governor.

ayor. The force was embarked in small frigates and in the month of January, 1635, the attack was delivered without warning. According to the Spanish account some six hundred men, women, and children had been found present in the settlement and in the ships in the harbour, but hardly a blow was struck in defence of their homes and the ordnance in the fort was found dismounted and unusable. Gov. Wormeley displayed the most utter cowardice and took instant flight in a small bark for Virginia;[12] a few of the colonists succeeded in getting away in an English ship, the *William and Anne,* that had just finished loading braziletta wood in the harbour, and among them was Mrs. Filby, the widow of Samuel Filby, who had died of fever in the previous summer. The *William and Anne,* grievously overcrowded, just managed to escape and was compelled to land a part of her passengers at Gratiosa in the Azores; ill-luck continued to dog her, for she reached Europe only to fall a wreck on the shore of Belle Isle-en-Mer (March, 1635). The first colonists who were captured by the Spaniards were ruthlessly put to the sword, while of those who fled to the woods, most were compelled by hunger to deliver themselves prisoners within a few days. No more mercy was shown to them than to their fellows and Fuemayor hanged every man. The settlement was entirely razed to the ground and, after remaining about a month, the Spanish force sailed away, leaving Association a desert.

The turn of Providence came next, but the governor of Cartagena, Don Nicolas de Judice, was not so forward

12 Wormeley became a somewhat important personage in Virginia. From *Acts of Privy Council, Colonial,* I, p. 263, we learn that in 1639 he was being accused by Mrs. Hart, the widow of the Providence Company's husband, John Hart, of repudiation of his just debts. He became captain of the fort at Point Comfort and married Frances Armistead, Mackenzie, *Colonial Families,* p. 12.

nor so secret with his preparations as had been his colleague at San Domingo. Providence lies on the flank of the course of Spanish ships sailing from Cartagena and Porto Bello to Mexico and Havana, but these vessels sailed mainly in strong fleets, and the small pinnaces from Providence left them as a rule severely alone; an easier prey passed close by the island, and to explain why Providence was such a convenient base for pirates it is necessary here to recapitulate one or two well-known facts concerning West Indian trade in the early seventeenth century. Two fleets convoyed by warships sailed annually from Seville to the Indies, the "flota" steering for Vera Cruz in Mexico and the "armada" for Cartagena. The European goods brought out by this latter fleet were exchanged for indigo, cochineal, hides, and other valuable commodities at the great fair of Cartagena, where they had been collected from all parts of Tierra Firme, or, as the English called it, the "Main." Besides the commodities reaching Cartagena from the provinces of New Biscay on the southern shore of the Caribbean, goods came mainly from the districts in the kingdom of Guatemala and from the province of Yucatan. The produce of the rich plain of Nicaragua was collected at Granada on Lake Nicaragua and despatched in small frigates down the Desaguadero, or as we now call it, the San Juan River;[13] the produce from the region round Guatemala City was sent over the mountains to be shipped in the Golfo Dolce,[14] and that from Honduras was shipped at Truxillo and Puerto Caballos. The prov-

[13] De Laet, *Novus Orbis*, p. 263: "Juan à 30 lieues de la Mer du Nord, sur l'embouchure du lac de Nicaragua, par laquelle le long d'un long et étroit canal à la façon d'une rivière, il decharge ses eaux dans la mer; elle est nommée El desaguadero des Espagnols qui transportent les marchandises de l'Europe, qu'ils ont été querir à Porto Bello, le long de ce canal à cette ville et lieux voisins."

[14] Gage, *The English American*, London 1677, p. 287.

ince of Veraguas yielded little of value, but what commodities did come from Costa Rica were mainly exchanged for European goods at the second great fair of the year, held later on at Porto Bello. The small vessels in which goods were carried to Cartagena were too frail to voyage out into the open Caribbean and kept well in towards the coast until they got into the latitude of their destination, when they steered due east across the bight at the head of which Porto Bello stood. None of the frigates were armed to any extent or capable of great resistance; all of them had to pass close under the shores of Providence and could be readily attacked in small pinnaces or even in shallops, with the prospect of a considerable booty. The temptations thus displayed were too strong for an old rover like Elfrith, and from the very beginning some of the colonists engaged in piracy. An easy market for the plunder could be obtained with the Holland ships that frequently touched at the island and it is to the facilities thus afforded for obtaining European goods at a cheap rate that we must attribute the colonists' disinclination to pay the high prices demanded for the goods in the company's magazines.

The shrewder men in the island saw the risk they must necessarily be running into by this piracy, when even the mere presence of foreigners in an island in the very heart of the Indies must be repugnant to every Spaniard. The governor and council insisted therefore on renewed energy being applied to the work of fortification, and on the taking of stringent precautions against the admission of any Spaniards or Spanish negroes into the island. The moment the company in England learned of the capture of Association, they sent warning of his danger to Gov. Bell. But the *Expectation*, by which the message was despatched, early in 1635, did not get away from her first port of call at St. Christopher before July, and at that time the warning had been long anticipated. Providence learned of the surprise of Association from some of the fugitives very soon after the event, and, needless to say, the whole island was set in alarm. Redoubled energy soon put the fortifications in good order and a constant watch was set for suspicious ships, while Samuel Axe, one of the company's best soldiers, on hearing of the likelihood of attack, left the new plantation he was engaged in developing at the Cape and returned to aid in the island's defence.

On the second of July, 1635, the Spanish fleet was espied approaching the island from the southeast and constantly sounding as it came among the encircling shoals. The force, which was under the personal command of the governor of Cartagena, Don Nicolas de Judice, consisted of three ships, four shallops, and one boat, and carried a force of about three hundred soldiers. For five days the vessels were feeling their way through the rocks and shoals only at the end of that time to come under the fire of the heavy ordnance in Warwick Fort. Again and again the soldiers attempted to force their way in to the shore in order to land, but again and again they were driven back by fierce musketry fire from the small earthworks thrown up on the beach, and at the last were compelled to retreat in disorder to their ships. A flag of truce covered a message from the Spanish commander to Gov. Bell, summoning the colonists at once to depart on pain of the penalties attaching to piracy and announcing that further reinforcements were on the way from Cartagena and that the island's defenders would be overwhelmed by force of numbers. But coming from one who had already been repulsed, these threats were of little avail, the English were quite undismayed and, a defiant answer having been returned, the battle was renewed more fiercely than before. So battered at length were the Spanish ships by the shot from the forts and so many men had they lost in their futile attempts at landing, that finally, seven days after their arrival, the Spanish vessels slipped their cables and anchors and retreated under cover of night, in haste and disorder. The attack had been repulsed and, for the time being, Providence was safe.

It was not until the return of the *Expectation* to England in December, 1635, that the company learned of the Spaniards' attempt on Providence and its gallant repulse, but the news lost nothing of its importance by the delay. We have shown how the course of affairs had been leading the company to the conclusion that perhaps, after all, Providence was not destined to be the great refuge for the oppressed Puritans that they had hoped to found, and the capture of Association and the narrow escape of their whole enterprise from overthrow were sufficient to confirm the view that Providence could never succeed as a mere plantation, but must be developed into a fortress capable of withstanding a powerful attack and, in reprisal, a base whence a profitable privateering warfare might be waged against the wealth of Spanish America. As has been shown in earlier chapters, this had been one of the aims that had led to the founding of the colony, but from 1635 onward it comes more prominently to the front, and the idea of Providence as a home for Puritans falls into the background.

The Elizabethan tradition of hatred to Spain as the common enemy still lived in the minds of Englishmen, but nowhere was it a more vital and energising force than with Warwick and his associates. No one had thrown himself more whole-heartedly into the schemes of the Providence Company than had John Pym and to no one did he yield in detesting the Spanish claims to world-wide power; in joining the company he had been primarily moved by his Puritanism and by his sympathy with John White's scheme for founding a refuge for the oppressed, but he had grown to manhood under the influence of men who had shared in the anxieties of the Elizabethan struggle, and who, under King James, believed that England had turned from her true path in foreign policy to dally with the power that was ceaselessly plotting her overthrow. For us, who know that with Philip II the Spanish power had sunk, never to rise again, it is hard to realise the intensity of fear and of hatred with which the Englishmen of that generation regarded their ancient enemy. The only right foreign policy seemed to them to lie in carrying on the traditions under which England had grown to greatness; and they wished to continue to share with the Dutch in the inexhaustible booty of the Indies, that, as they thought, had raised Holland and Zeeland from poverty to wealth. The zest with which the parliament of 1624 had turned from the humiliations of the Spanish Match to urge on the longed-for war, and the eagerness with which that of 1625 had granted supplies for the Cadiz expedition, show plainly the potency of these views, but it would be hard to express them more clearly than did Pym himself, when his voice could once more be raised within the walls of parliament:[15]

"The differences and discontents betwixt his Majesty and the people at home have, in all likelihood, diverted his royal thoughts and counsels from those great opportunities which he might have not only to weaken the House of Austria and to restore the Palatinate, but to gain himself a higher pitch of power and greatness than any of his ancestors. For it is not unknown how weak,

[15] Speech to the Short Parliament, April, 1640, Forster, *Life of Pym*, p. 117.

how distracted, how discontented the Spanish colonies are in the West Indies. There are now in those parts, in New England, Virginia and the Carib Islands and in the Barmudos, at least 60,000 able persons of this nation, many of them well-armed and their bodies seasoned to that climate, which, with a very small charge might be set down in some advantageous parts of those pleasant, rich and fruitful countries and easily make his Majesty master of all that treasure, which not only foments the war but is the great support of popery in all parts of Christendom."

Holding such views it was easy for Pym to convince himself that the Providence enterprise was worth carrying on, even though it should have to be through the agency of men who did not see eye to eye with him in matters of religion. It is this power of realising that it might be possible to secure worthy ends, though the tools employed might not conform to the most rigid standard of orthodoxy, that distinguishes the leaders of the English Puritans, and especially Pym, from the unbending rulers of New England, such as Endecott and Dudley. Pym was essentially an opportunist in the best sense of the term; while an idea seemed to him possible of fulfilment, all his energies were devoted to carrying it out, but if circumstances proved too strong for him and the idea had to be abandoned, he was always ready to modify his course and, with no abandonment of principle, to work with the means at hand for the fruition of some cognate purpose. Providence was no home for a strictly Puritan community, but it had great possibilities for the furtherance of English aggrandisement at the expense of Spain. The Dutch were carving out for themselves an empire in Brazil. Why should not England, from Providence as a base, carve out for herself another dominion in Central America and found a second Brazil upon the shores of New Spain? In so doing she would be crippling still further the enemy of God and man, and advancing her own resources at his expense. The words of a writer of the time concerning the Dutch are just as true when applied to Pym and Warwick and their partners; they "hated Spain and the Pope with a perfect hatred and firmly believed that in plundering the Spaniard they were best serving not merely their own interests but the cause of God and the true religion."[16] From 1635 onwards, therefore, this was to be the object of the Providence Company, and the putting aside of the earlier object without its abandonment can be no better summed up than in the words Pym addressed to the adventurers: "Although we cannot procure so many religious persons as we desire, yet, when the place [Providence] is safe, godly persons and families will be encouraged to transport themselves; and though God succour not our endeavours in that, yet we may make a civil commodity of it, upholding the profession of religion, moral duty, and justice, till God shall please to plant amongst us a more settled Church. . . . The planters must be heartened for the defence of the island, lest otherwise his Majesty do lose a place apt to be made of much advantage and use to this kingdom as any we know of the like bigness in the world. The strengthening thereof we must most specially regard (though in itself it never answer profit), for the better maintaining our trade upon the Main, it being so convenient for a storehouse of provision and so fit to receive and keep the goods, which shall by negotiation be procured, and for a retreat upon all occasions." Such words as these from their trusted treasurer were sufficient to clinch the determination of the active members of the company to carry on their work despite their

[16] Barlæus, *Brasilianische Geschichte,* p. 34, quoted by Edmundson in *Eng. Hist. Rev.,* 1896, p. 233.

many difficulties. They felt, however, that the task had become so dangerous and so much a matter of national concern that the government should be appealed to for help in carrying it on, and they took steps to lay their petition before the king without delay.

On learning of the capture of Association, the company had resolved that it would be necessary for them to free themselves from charges of remissness and negligence in their care of the island, and a memorandum was drawn up for presentation to Charles through the Earl of Holland, the governor of the company. In this memorandum it was shown that Association was never planted by the Providence Company of their own motion, but that in return for a promise by the planters there to pay one-twentieth of their profits, the company had agreed to supply them with ordnance and recruits. This was done in order to prevent the planters placing themselves under the protection of the Dutch, but it was pointed out that Association was always "a mixed plantation consisting of English, Dutch, and French, whereby the Spaniard was moved the rather to watch an opportunity for their displanting. This mixture was admitted by the planters without the company's direction or knowledge." While the governor appointed by the company was alive, the island was kept safe, but when he died, the planters themselves elected a governor who was neglectful of his watch and by his incompetence and cowardice left the island defenceless, and for this the company could not legitimately be held responsible.

The presentation of this memorandum was an entirely informal matter and no official notice seems to have been taken of it, but the receipt of the news of the attack upon Providence was much more seriously regarded, and a declaration concerning it, together with a demand for redress, were forthwith drawn up and presented without an instant's delay to the governor of the company for delivery to the crown. The declaration, which is written in the hand of Secretary Jessop, is still extant among the State Papers,[17] and was presented by the Earl of Holland to the king at the council board at Whitehall on Sunday, the 27th of December, 1635. After recounting the circumstances of the Spanish attack and its repulse, the declaration proceeds: "Upon this occasion it behoves us to put your Lordship in mind (being our Governor) of the extraordinary importance of the place, able to give his Majesty a great power in the West Indian Seas and a profitable interest in the trade of the richest part of America. So strong by nature as it is hardly accessible, having a large harbour with a very narrow entrance, where may ride 100 ships of good burthen under the safeguard of such forts as we have already built; being distant 40 leagues from the next continent and no sign at all that any man had ever set foot there until we took possession of it for the Crown of England. Upon this island (as y[r]. Lo[p]. knows) we have bestowed Thirty Thousand Pounds above what has been returned from thence, although his Majesty has received £1000 in one year for Custom.

"The discouragements we daily meet with both of loss and danger, do disable us to proceed in any further charge unless his Majesty will be graciously pleased to give us leave to right ourselves of this [that is, the attack] and former injuries done by the Spaniards; for y[r]. Lo[p] may remember that we had divers men slain and goods spoiled the last year,[18] and about four years since a ship of ours[19] was attempted by the Spaniards, in which fight our Captain lost one of his eyes and 10 or 12 men

[17] Col. Pap., VIII, 81.

[18] At Association, January, 1634/5.

[19] The *Seaflower*, see p. 112.

were slain and hurt without any provocation at any time on our part, we having always given strict order that none of our men should offer the least distaste unto the Spaniards.

"We do make the more speed to give yr LoP notice hereof because the Spanish commanders which thus summoned and assaulted the island, did publish an intention of their King to send greater forces to destroy that and other English plantations.

"Whereupon the inhabitants of the Island have written unto us that they must desert the place, if they be not relieved by May next, which cannot be effected unless we go presently in hand with provisions.

"All which we leave to yr LoP's consideration, that some sudden resolution may be taken to encourage other Adventurers to join with us, and so hearten the Planters for defence of the island, lest otherwise his Majesty lose a place apt to be made of much advantage and use to this kingdom as any we know of the like bigness in the world, and yr LoP with ourselves sustain a great prejudice in the loss of all the adventures which were first undertaken in the time of war betwixt his Majesty and the King of Spain, when we conceived that this design would [give] his Majesty's subjects opportunity of repairing all the losses sustained by the Dunkirkers or any other then in opposition to the Crown."[20]

From Nicholas's notes of the proceedings in Council,[21] we learn that the king referred the matter to the Council board to inform themselves of the importance of Providence and to consider whether it would be better to send venturers to hold the island or to give leave to the adventurers to offend the Spaniards there by way of reprisal.

20 [Endorsed] "Presented Sunday, 27th Dec. to the King in Council by the Earl of Holland."

21 S. P. Dom., Car. I, cccvii, no. 19. 27 Dec., 1635.

The secretaries were directed to see how far it lay with the Anglo-Spanish treaty of 1630 to suffer his Majesty's ships to defend themselves and to offend any if they be offended, being beyond the line. The investigation of the matter was entrusted to the secretary of state, Sir John Coke, and the original draft of his conclusions in his own handwriting is now preserved among the State Papers.[22] The memorial is of great interest in our enquiry as giving an unbiased survey of the company's affairs, but it is too long to be produced *in extenso* and we must confine ourselves to a few extracts from it. It begins with an account of the strategical position of the island:

"The island called St. Cathelina by the Spaniards and by our men the Island of Providence, is situated within the tropic, betwixt 12 and 13 degrees of the northerly latitude from the Equinoctial. It lieth in the high way of the Spanish fleets that come from Cartagena, from which it lieth about 100 leagues and from Porto Bello 80 leagues and about 80 leagues also from the Bay of Nicoraga,[23] at which place of the *terra firma* the Spaniards have great trade for their treasure, and all ships that come from these places must pass on the one or other side of the island within 20 leagues and may be easily discovered from thence. From Virginia it is distant about 1900 leagues, though in their course homewards they come near it. . . . [The island] will yield provision sufficient for 1000 men besides women and children. Now there are of white persons about 500, women about 30 or 40. . . . For strength the access is very difficult and a ship cannot get in without much danger of rocks and shoals. On nine parts of ten the island is compassed with rock whereof most are seen and others under water. Betwixt the rocks above and those under water there is

22 Col. Pap., VIII, 83. Many erasures and much altered by Coke in parts.

23 That is, the Nicaragua or San Juan River.

a channel so narrow that but one ship at once can well pass through it. They come in with a trade wind, which bloweth always except in part of October, in November and part of December, in all two months, when northerly winds blow, which are very boisterous. No ships can lie long about the island, nor ride at anchor safely, save only at about 3 or 4 miles from the Island and that but in fair weather and then they are also subject to fretting their cables with the rocks, and if any storm they are in great danger. The Island hath but one harbour on the [north] side, which will contain 3 or 4 score sail of ships of 300 tons, for greater ships cannot get in without much care, because they will want breadth to turn in and must come in sounding all the way. They ride within at 20 or 24 foot water, very good and safe ground and free from all danger of winds, being enclosed by a promontory that keepeth it very safe. The harbour is defended with 3 forts, one at the entrance and one on either side. In the whole island they have 13 or 14 fortified places, which have ordnance, and no ship or boat can approach but within the command of two or three of their forts. . . .

"The enemy cannot land otherwise than by shallops and therefore there should be boats to hinder their landing. The Spaniards also send treasure in shallops, which they can freight at places along the coast and by these shallops may be met with much advantage. . . . Spanish frigates, as they call them, are no better than shallops. Many are very rich. . . . Other benefit from the Island is not to be expected but what may be gotten by trade or prizes. The trade is not yet settled. . . . The planters are discouraged because many of their Adventurers are fallen off, more than half the last year [1635]. They were whole shares 18 and in all contributors in quarter shares to make 24. . . . The charge ariseth in sending men, for every man they have severally costeth them near Thirty Pounds; . . . £8000 a year will not suffice to supply it. . . . This charge cannot be raised otherwise than by war or reprisal. . . .

"The planters find not themselves able to maintain so great a charge, but may be able with the king's leave to put it off to some others to save themselves and to afford his Majesty Ten Thousand Pounds profit, whereas if it be taken out of their hands by force, they know they shall lose and can expect nothing save cruelty, as the Spaniards use to all nations that come there. . . . If his Majesty should undertake it, they expect to be reimbursed with reasonable profit. . . . The planters desire his Majesty's speedy resolution because they must before the spring desert it or supply it: which will be hard to do."

This memorial was taken into consideration by the king during the month of January, 1636, and he also viewed "the plat of the Island and Main adjacent," that had been prepared by Capt. Axe for the company and was forwarded by them, before he could determine whether to grant the company the desired assistance.

The ever-changing conditions governing Charles I's tortuous foreign policy were at the moment of presentation of the company's petition not unfavourable to the granting of the required permission to undertake reprisals. The years 1634 and 1635 had been filled with negotiations with Spain wherein Charles was prepared to offer the alliance of England against the Dutch if the Palatinate were evacuated; in August, 1635, a definite alliance against France had also been offered on the same conditions, but, when Spain showed no alacrity to close with the offer, the contrary course was considered and in November the king was prepared to listen to Queen Henrietta Maria and her adviser, the Earl of Holland, who were urging upon him hostility to Spain and an intimate alliance with France.[24] The never-ending battle in the Council went on from day to day between the pro-Spanish party, now represented by Cottington and Windebank, and their opponents, represented by Holland and Coke, who for the moment, in January, 1636, gained the upper hand. The fact that the leaders of the Providence Company, Warwick, Saye, and Brooke, were actively opposed to many points in the government's home policy, and that steps had recently been taken to frustrate their intention of emigrating to New England, would not militate against the granting of permission to engage themselves more deeply in the West Indies, for such action would entirely fall in with the government's forward naval policy. Only six months before the king had prompted the republication of Selden's *Mare Clausum,*[25] claiming for England the most exacting rights over the Narrow Seas, and the Ship-Money fleet was at this very time being equipped to enforce these rights. All things combined, therefore, to secure from the king the desired permission to undertake reprisals, and in January, 1636, this was granted.

The procedure in the matter of granting letters of reprisal does not appear to have been a fixed one, but in this particular instance no formal letters or commissions were issued. The only written record is the report of a Privy Council meeting antedated to coincide with the date when the company made formal complaint to the governor.[26] As a matter of fact, we learn from the company's records[27] that the king gave the

[24] For the whole of these bewildering changes of front, see Gardiner, VIII, 99, and authorities cited by him.

[25] August, 1635, Gardiner, VIII, 154.

[26] Col. Pap., VIII, 90.

[27] See also Col. Pap., X, 39.

desired permission only by word of mouth at the council board, but in the presence of Sir Henry Martin, judge of the Admiralty. It would seem that Martin had been specially summoned to hear the permission granted, but the whole proceeding is a commentary on the lax and shifty governmental methods of the time. It is to be wondered whether any of those who received the desired permission thought of Raleigh and his fate twenty years before for acting on a similarly loosely granted permission to wage private war, which was disavowed when he failed to succeed.

CHAPTER IX

COUNTER ATTACKS

On January 29, 1636, a full meeting of the company was summoned to Lord Saye's lodgings in Holborn under the chairmanship of Sir Nathaniel Rich, then deputy-governor, and Treasurer Pym there laid before them a full report of the story of the colony as received by the *Expectation,* and an account of what had been done by himself and the committee left in charge of the company's affairs since the last general meeting. To the declaration concerning the attack on the island, it was announced that the king had graciously replied, giving the company permission to right themselves by way of reprisal, so that whatever they should take from the Spaniard in the West Indies would be adjudged lawful prize. It was now necessary, therefore, for the company to take steps to provide an immediate supply for the planters, for their reputation required them to keep on as long as their estates would bear it. The state had a right to expect of them that they proceed with a work in which the honour of the English empire was so much bound up, or else to put it off to others that would not let it fall. Unfortunately, Pym told them, many of the company living far off found the burden too great and desired not to go on, and it was requisite, therefore, for those that were earnest in the matter to make all the greater efforts. The proportion of charge required to pay off debts accumulated in the past and to carry on the work for the future he computed at £10,000, and he desired the company to resolve at once upon means for raising this sum.

The discussion thus initiated was carried on with great vigour and all kinds of ways were proposed for managing the company's affairs more successfully than in the past. It was suggested that everything should be put in charge of one man and Pym was mentioned as the best qualified to undertake the charge; his practical spirit, however, refused to allow him to place himself in so invidious a position and he insisted most strongly that everyone subscribing to the new stock should have a vote in the carrying-on of the business. Lord Brooke was not so backward and offered to undertake the whole affair of the colony if he might have the sole management and not be bound to commit his designs to any. So sweeping a relinquishment of control did not commend itself to the adventurers and Lord Brooke's offer was declined. It was finally resolved that an entirely new stock of £10,000 to carry on the business should be raised within two years; for nine years all profits from the trade of the Main, from the islands or from reprisals, were to be paid to the new undertakers, the old adventurers having no share of the profits till after the completion of nine years. All those joining in the adventure were to have a share in the management proportional to the amount of their adventure, and Lord Brooke undertook to underwrite any portion of the £10,000 stock not taken up, in return for a corresponding voice in the direction. The whole share of adventure was put at £500, for which one vote was allotted. Those subscribing for portions of a £500 share were to decide its vote by a majority. As a result the sum of £3900 was subscribed[1] by the middle of 1636, and to this Brooke added £1000, though he could not be persuaded to fulfil

[1] Warwick £500, Saye £500, N. Rich £500, Pym £500, Woodcock £500, Barrington £500, Knightley £400, Rudyerd £250, Sir William Waller and Thomas Upton £250 jointly.

his promise to subscribe the remaining amount up to £10,000. Application was made to the lord treasurer to assist the company by the abatement of the customs duties on goods sent to the island or imported from it, and several attempts were made to secure this concession, which had been granted by King James to the Virginia and Newfoundland companies during their early years, but no success was obtained, and Pym finally moved the company to put up with the best treatment they could get from the farmers of the customs, "they being so far authorized by the book of rates, without addressing themselves therein to His Majesty."

This regeneration of the company at home occupied the whole of the winter months of 1635-1636, but immediately upon the receipt of the news of the capture of Association in March, 1635, Pym and Rich, the principal members of the committee left in charge of the business of the company during the summer, had taken steps to ensure the reoccupation of the island, and a gathering up as far as possible of the company's property there. Several names were discussed as those of persons likely to make satisfactory governors of the island and among them that of John Hilton,[2] the younger brother of Anthony Hilton, who had remained planting in Nevis. As none of these persons seemed entirely suitable, Sir Nathaniel Rich suggested that a council should be appointed to govern the island with a president to be elected by themselves, but it was finally decided that Capt. Nicholas Reskeimer[3] should be made governor, and that he should be supplied with fresh ordnance and stores sufficient to defend Association satisfactorily. The Res-

[2] The author of the account of the planting of St. Christopher and Nevis, who was then quite a young man.

[3] Or Riskinner. He had been employed in command of one of the merchant ships in the Cadiz expedition, *C. S. P. Dom.*, 1625-1626, p. 142. See also *C. S. P. Dom.*, 1619-1623, p. 557.

keimers were a family of Flemish origin, long settled at Dartmouth and deeply engaged in the clandestine West Indian trade; they were intimately allied with the celebrated privateering family of the Killigrews, and Reskeimer was probably acceptable to the company as having a large acquaintance among the rovers, who, they now realised, made Tortuga a regular place of call. He was recommended to the colonists as a soldier and a gentleman, whose military experience would serve them in repelling any further Spanish attack.[4] Mrs. Filby and the other fugitives who had reached England, were supplied with certain stores and again sent out to the island under Reskeimer's command in the *Expectation,* April, 1635. The carrying-on of the plantation was thus provided for, but it was also necessary to do something to secure the £2000 owing from Hilton's estate.

From the testimony of the fugitive planters it was evident that Hilton had been defrauding the company right and left; he had pocketed all the money paid by the planters for goods from the company's stores and had been consigning brazilwood wholesale to one Ashman, a merchant of the Dutch West India Company, at Middleburg. Over two hundred tons of wood, the worth of which must have been nearly £5000, had been despatched by Hilton during 1634, and the *William and Anne,* which had escaped from the harbour of Association during the Spanish attack, had over seventy tons on board. The wreck of the *William and Anne* at Belle Isle had placed this valuable cargo in the charge of the French government and the company had to institute suits in the French courts for its recovery and in the Zeeland courts for the recovery of damages from Ashman. The French suit

[4] Reskeimer was provided with 30 muskets, 10 pistols, 2 pieces of ordnance, 33 barrels of powder, shot and match, 30 swords, a drum and flag, a large supply of tools, and £20 cash for himself.

was successful and the company in conjunction with the insurers of the cargo managed to recover the greater portion of the goods, but no redress could be obtained at Middleburg and the suit had to be abandoned. Hilton's estate in England was sequestered by Dr. Rand for the benefit of his wife and family, but the company managed to seize all his negroes, who had escaped to the mountains in Tortuga, and these along with some women negroes[5] were sent over to Providence.

Reskeimer's appointment and the small reinforcement of the colony sent out with him, could only be regarded as a temporary means of tiding over a difficulty and it was evident that if Association was to be permanently occupied further recruits must be sent. As a matter of fact, Reskeimer turned out quite unfit to exercise the government, and died of fever almost immediately after his arrival in the West Indies; the way was therefore clear for an arrangement that had been for some time contemplated. When Rochelle capitulated on October 29, 1628, the last Protestant stronghold on the French coast was closed to the fleet of Soubise, who since 1625 had been scouring the western seas and had succeeded almost entirely in intercepting French commerce. His ships, when their home port was closed, had to take refuge in English ports and to disband their crews, who were left to fend for themselves as best they could. One of the most prominent of Soubise's captains was De Sancé, who was well known to a London merchant of Huguenot descent, Samuel Vassall, one of Sir Robert Heath's principal backers in the attempted colonisation of "Carolana."[6] A large number of De Sancé's Hugue-

5 This seems to be one of the earliest mentions of women negroes as servants in an English colony. From the company's letter we learn that they were regarded as a novelty.

6 Sainsbury, preface to *C. S. P. Col.*, 1574-1660, p. xxiv.

not followers were despatched by Vassall to Carolana, but they failed to make any satisfactory footing there and were dispersed before the end of the year 1632. Another partner of Sir Robert Heath in the Carolana project was the celebrated William Boswell, who had made many acquaintances among the Rochellois during his service as an English agent in France; in 1635 he was a regular attendant for a time at the Providence meetings, and now that Association had to be reinforced and already had a large number of French settlers, he thought it an excellent opportunity to provide for his remaining Huguenot protégés. He therefore introduced to the company a Captain Delahay, whom he recommended for the governorship and with whom the company entered into treaty. This was a very important step in the history of the Tortuga colony, for many of Soubise's followers had succeeded in making their peace with Richelieu and had been sent out as employés of the royal "Compagnie des Isles d'Amérique" to serve under de Roissey and D'Esnambuc in St. Christopher, and it is probable that some of them had been among the many Frenchmen who had already reached Tortuga.

The company were urged to come to terms with Delahay by the news they received from Association in March, 1633, by two returning planters, that they had been closely questioned by the Dutch West India Company, who had expressed an intention of taking possession of the island as having been practically abandoned by the Providence Company. After Reskeimer's death the eighty odd Englishmen in the island had formed a council among themselves for the government of the colony and to keep in subjection the one hundred and fifty negroes, twenty-seven of whom were the company's property. Several of the negroes had escaped to the woods, but the planters thought that they might be brought back into subjection if there were more white men in the island. The French were beginning to frequent Tortuga in ever greater numbers to cut the brazaletta wood and to lade with salt; they had captured some of the negroes and carried them away. These pieces of information caused the greatest possible concern to Pym and throughout the spring of 1636 we find him suggesting ways and means of furnishing Association with supplies and men, although he found it impossible to get the company to adopt any of them. All kinds of resolutions were come to and afterwards rescinded because the adventurers declined to provide more capital. It was found that a Mr. Donnington was setting up bills in London offering to transport passengers to Association, although he had had no permission from the company and the speculation was merely a private one on his own part. Pym and Saye were so strongly in favour of retaining the island as a valuable harbourage for their men-of-war, that they offered to go over themselves to carry on the plantation if the company would support them, but the rest of the active adventurers were opposed to any further dealings as a company with the island and offered to turn over their rights in it to any of their number who would undertake its supply.

It was finally settled in June, 1636, that the company's rights in Association should be vested in Brooke, Pym, and Saye, together with their merchant associate, Woodcock, who promised to provide a supply and a hundred men at a cost of £1500.[7] Delahay had sailed for Tortuga while the propositions for its arming were being debated, so the governorship of the island was conferred upon Capt. William Rudyerd, who was placed in command of

[7] Brooke £750, Pym £500 (£100 of this afterwards subscribed by Rudyerd and £100 by Waller), Saye £250. Woodcock paid the cost of the voyage.

the *James,* which after her arrival was to ply for prizes. During Rudyerd's absence on these voyages, the governorship of the island was to be placed in the charge of Capt. Henry Hunks,[8] who was to go out as Rudyerd's second in command. Everything was prepared and the *James* put to sea in August, 1636, but fate seemed to conspire against the undertakers in the matter, for after being badly buffeted by storms and never reaching her destination, the *James* returned to England in January, 1637, in a nearly sinking condition. Intelligence was received at about the same time that the English inhabitants of Association had abandoned their plantations and had removed to the main island of Hispaniola. The Association design was therefore abandoned and the subscribed capital devoted to fitting out a second ship, the *Mary Hope,* to ply for prizes from Providence under the command of Capt. Rudyerd.

The tracing of the fruitless attempts to resettle Tortuga has led us to anticipate our story somewhat, and we must now return to Providence and to the steps taken by the company to reorganise the colony as a privateering base after the Spanish attack in 1635. Capt. Philip Bell had been governor of Providence for five years, and Lord Saye and other members of the company felt that, as the colony was to be given a fresh start, it would be well for a new governor to be appointed. It was requisite that the man chosen should be an able soldier, and at the same time a godly and religious Puritan; such an one was recommended by Lord Brooke from among his dependents at Warwick in the person of Capt. Robert Hunt, who had seen some service in the Nether-

[8] Sir Henry Hunks was a connection of the family of Sir Edward Conway and had seen service under him in the Netherlands. He did not take up the Association appointment, but went to Barbadoes as governor for the Earl of Carlisle. He was succeeded in 1641 by Philip Bell.

lands and in Buckingham's expedition to Isle de Rhé. The company realised that in superseding Bell they might antagonise a party of his supporters in the island led by Elfrith and William Rous, and it was resolved, therefore, that the supersession should be carried out in the most courteous way possible in return for the mercies vouchsafed to the island under Bell's government; as all the conditions of the original contracts with Bell respecting supply of servants had certainly not been fulfilled, the company were quite prepared for "the clamours they may expect at his coming home for not making good their contracts." The private letter informing Bell of the appointment of his successor is very cool in tone and shows very little appreciation of the services he had rendered to the company; he is requested to continue cheerfully in his new place of councillor, giving assistance to the new governor publicly and privately. They trust that he will not be "transported by any jealousy" as they intend nothing towards him but what may stand with justice and honour; they will be much gladder to find him deserving of thanks and reward than any way blameworthy. After the vicious practice common to all the English colonies of the time, Bell's supersession was a signal for all those in the island who had been aggrieved by any of his acts as governor, to rise up against him and attempt to secure satisfaction from him in his private capacity. The dissensions that previously existed therefore broke out with redoubled violence and the company in their letter of 1637 had to speak very strongly in order to preserve the ex-governor from complete ruin. The judgments that had been delivered against him for acts done during his tenure of the governorship were declared null and void, and his goods and negroes that had been confiscated by the council were restored to him. He received permission to sell off his plantation and goods, and returned home in June, 1637. The company were justified in their expectation that trouble would arise over the non-fulfilment of their contracts with Bell by sending him an insufficient number of servants, and the dispute about the matter occupied the time of Treasurer Pym very much during the latter part of 1637.

Bell desired the company to compensate him by a money payment for the lack of the labours of the servants that had been promised to him as salary; he alleged that he had received some twenty-five less than had been promised and that many of those who were sent ran away or proved unfit. He had felled much ground to grow provisions for the servants he expected and was therefore involved in further loss when they did not arrive. In all he claimed £1250 from the company, but was willing to write off £400 due from him for store-goods, tobacco not paid over, and bills discharged for him in England. The company replied that they were only bound by their contract to supply men to work for him in the island, which, as it would tend to the strengthening of Providence, they were ready to do, but this answer was obviously disingenuous and it entirely failed to satisfy Bell. After six months' discussion no progress had been made in the matter, and it was decided to refer to arbitration Bell's demands and Pym's exceptions thereto. Bell nominated as his arbitrator his brother, Sir Robert Bell, while the company chose John Hampden, but refused to sign any undertaking to be bound individually by the arbitrators' award. In consequence of this and Bell's refusal to be unconditionally bound to accept the award, no conclusion could be come to by the arbitrators, and in May, 1638, the ex-governor petitioned the king, who ordered the lord keeper to give attention to the matter and decide it. The company's case was placed in the hands of Oliver St. John and in the result the lord keeper decided (November, 1638) that particular members of the company were not liable for agreements made under the common seal of the company, but no definite conclusion of the dispute had been arrived at two years later and Bell, sick of the delay, ultimately in July, 1640, accepted £50 in full settlement of his claims.

The rest of Bell's story is soon told; when he accepted the Providence Company's composition, he was contemplating a new voyage to the West Indies, and on November 29, 1640, he received permission from the Privy Council[9] to transport one hundred and forty passengers and stores to commence a plantation on the island of Santa Lucia. The plantation does not appear to have met with any success and in 1641 Bell moved with his followers to Barbadoes, where he became deputy-governor on Sir Henry Hunks's sailing for England in 1642. On Hunks's death in 1645, Bell became governor of Barbadoes,[10] and there Ligon visited him in 1647.[11] On the seizure of the island by the royalist fleet under Lord Willoughby of Parham in 1649, Bell, who was notoriously parliamentarian in his sympathies, fled to St. Christopher and there we hear of him for the last time in 1669, when he was one of the commissioners for receiving restitution of the island from the French.[12]

Capt. Robert Hunt was appointed governor of Providence by an agreement dated 1 March, 1636, and a formal commission of March 28, 1636.[13] The expenses

9 *Acts of Privy Council, Col.*, I, p. 290.

10 Bryan Edwards, *Hist. of West Indies*, I, 325.

11 Ligon, *Hist. of Barbadoes*, p. 24.

12 The Philip Bell of 1669 (*A. P. C. Col.*, I, 506) may have been a nephew. See p. 94, note.

13 Hunt was well known to many in the Puritan party, as we may learn from a letter to John Winthrop, jr., from Samuel Reade, his brother-in-law,

of the transportation of himself, his wife, three children, and two maid-servants, were to be borne by the company, who promised in case of his death to do "what should become them in honour and conscience for his wife." One hundred acres of land were allotted to him for his own benefit, together with twenty servants to work it for him; no money salary was to be paid, but he was to derive all his recompense for his pains from his land and servants. In the very full instructions issued to him, he was directed to bear himself indifferently between all the parties in the island and to endeavour to compose the acute differences that had arisen concerning Sherrard's ecclesiastical censures, many having complained that they were much aggrieved by them. The general letter from the company to the governor and council March 28, 1636, to explain the changes that the company had resolved to sanction in the island in consequence of the permission they had received from the crown to undertake reprisals against the Spaniards, is of enormous length and fills sixteen closely written folio pages in the letter book. It deals in the greatest minuteness with details of all sorts, but contains also some general declarations of a change of policy, and these are all that we can concern ourselves with. After congratulating the planters on their successful repulse of the Spanish attack, the company inform them that owing to the discouragement of many adventurers the burden of the enterprise is now cast upon very few shoulders, but they have resolved to make a further trial, and keep the island for the honour and public good of the English nation. A general amnesty for all offences up to the day of their deliverance from the Spanish attack is proclaimed, and everyone is exhorted to live in peace and

London, 5 March, 1635/6. "Mr. Hunt, I hear, is going into the Isle of Providence." Mass. Hist. Soc. *Coll.*, 5th series, I, 217.

quietness, love and amity. The permission given by the crown to undertake reprisals is confirmed to properly commissioned ships, and no man is to take prizes from the Spaniards, whether by boat or otherwise, unless specially authorised to do so. Indiscriminate attacks weaken the island until it is better fortified, and great care is to be exercised by the council to see that boats are not surreptitiously taken to prey upon the enemy; any men attempting to steal away secretly in this fashion are to be tried as traitors. To provide further for the defence of the island, the company have sent a sergeant gunner and three trained soldiers, "whom the Earl of Warwick hath taken from Landgard Fort purposely for the service of the island." The Spaniards will be more inimical to Providence than ever now that they have been repulsed, and ceaseless vigilance is to be exercised to repel their attacks. The inhabitants are to be drilled once or twice a week by the soldiers, so that they may know the use of their arms, but the soldiers are especially cautioned not to exhibit a proud and overbearing spirit, but to show mildness and justice to those under them.

Trade with Dutch ships is still much disliked by the company, because, being only for wine and sack, it has tended not to men's health but to the increase of drunkenness, disorder, and poverty. The Dutch ships have carried away almost the whole crop of the island, and, even when the company's own ship was in the harbour, the planters preferred to trade with the Dutch and run so much into debt as to mortgage the whole of their next crop. From henceforth the company will refuse to send any goods upon their own account, but they permit their husband, William Woodcock, to supply goods to the planters upon such conditions as may be agreed upon between them and his agents. Past debts to the company's stores are forgiven to those who remain and strengthen the island, but no permission will be given to planters to leave the island until they have discharged their debts in full. Four months' supply is sent with those coming over in the new ships, and by the time this is exhausted, they ought to be able to fend for themselves.

Perhaps the most important pronouncement of the letter is that in which the company definitely announce the abandonment of the system of half profits, which had been so much objected to by the planters in this and other plantations. The conditions[14] are imposed that the company shall be freed from all public charges, whether for fortification or otherwise, the crops are to be sent home by the company's ships and not sold to the Dutch, and the letter goes on to say: "That [the planters] may be more easily moved to apply themselves to building and husbandry for the improving of the land, we have resolved that all the same shall be divided into several proportions, that every man may know his own, and have a certainty of tenure and estate, some part of the land for the Governor, Captains and other officers, and the rest to be disposed into farms and tenements under such, the rent to be paid in tobacco, cotton or other staple commodities, as shall be indifferent." The estates shall be allotted in fee simple at a fee ferm rent, and time-expired servants shall be put upon plantations at this fixed charge. When the island is fully planted, they shall be transferred to the main continent and there provided for. If the servants prefer it they may remain upon the tenant's plantation and receive from him wages. The men of better quality are to have about fifty acres of land apiece, which the company think will be enough

[14] The whole of this scheme was worked out by Pym and was accepted at his suggestion.

to maintain the master and fourteen servants; men of lesser rank are to have thirty acres. The reserved rent is to be about one-fourth of the commodities produced, but the company cannot prescribe a definite rent, as they hear that the land differs much in quality. The proportions allotted are greater than the masters can conveniently manage to manure, but they are arranged so that large courts and gardens may be kept round the houses. Every planter is to be urged to enclose his own ground, and every three months or thereabouts, the governor is to inspect the plantations, to suggest improvements where necessary, and to note the proportion of ground planted with corn, with tobacco, with cotton, and so on.

In the decision of the company embodied in these directions, we have the final abandonment of the system of organisation that had been tried in so many colonies, from Raleigh's Virginia onwards, though it had never met with any measure of success. The organisation of Providence was the last collective effort of the men who had been responsible for the conduct of Virginia and the Somers Islands in their earlier years, and once more, as in those colonies, it was shown that, in order to make colonists use their best endeavours for the cultivation of the soil, it was needful to give them a proprietary interest in it, and to make their obligations fixed and certain. The constant uncertainty as to the amount due to the company under the half-profit system, and the eternal bickerings that went on concerning the quality and price of the goods supplied in the company's magazines, always tended to make the system unworkable with the intensely individualistic Englishman of the seventeenth century. The system may have been a necessary phase of England's colonial development, but it is a striking fact that the system was always imposed upon the colonists by an external authority, and that in the councils of the Providence Company a prominent share was always taken by men like Warwick and Sir Nathaniel Rich, who were the especial upholders in the early seventeenth century of the ideas of colonisation expressed by Gilbert and Raleigh at the end of the century before.

It will be remembered that upon receiving permission from the crown to undertake reprisals against the Spaniards, a reconstruction of the company had taken place and the whole of the enterprise was placed for nine years in the hands of the adventurers subscribing for the new stock, amounting in all to about £5000. This sum was in part expended in supplying Providence with ammunition and necessaries, and the rest went to the equipment of three vessels, the *Blessing,* the *Expectation,* and the *Hopewell,* for a prolonged privateering cruise in the Indies from Providence as a base. A treaty was also entered into at Pym's suggestion with Sir Edward Conway, whereby, in return for a fifth part of all prizes taken, the company agreed to let him share in their right of reprisal with a ship he had previously been intending to send into the Indies provided with a commission from the Prince of Orange. The *Blessing* was put under the command of William Rous, who was relieved from his command of Fort Henry in Providence; John Leicester served as master of the *Blessing,* and Cornelius Billinger as master of the *Expectation.* The *Hopewell* was owned by William Woodcock, the company's husband, and was sent out on his account, one-fifth of all prizes taken being allotted to the company.

The directions given to the masters of these ships were all of a similar character, and as all subsequent regulations of the company concerning prizes were based upon them, it is worth while to consider them somewhat in detail. The *Blessing,* a vessel of about two hundred tons, was armed, in addition to what she had previously carried, with new ordnance at a cost of £182,[15] and her ship's company was increased beyond the usual complement. The master was directed to acquaint the seamen with his designs shortly after leaving the English coast and to agree with them as to their proportion of the booty. The principle of shares was to be adopted in preference to fixed wages, as making the men more ready to assault the enemy's ships and as securing the booty from embezzlement. The alternative placed before the men was the usual one, to be allowed pillage of all above deck or else one-third of the total profit obtained from the prizes. The *Blessing* was ordered to sail to Providence via Tortuga Salada,[16] where a supply of salt was to be obtained, the services of the passengers she was taking out being used in the lading. At Providence two shallops were to be obtained and these were to be manned with twenty men apiece, one to assist the *Blessing* and the other the *Expectation*. No enterprises of difficulty were to be undertaken by Rous, but after consultation with Leicester and Billinger, the will of the majority was to prevail. If a prize of poor value were taken, it was to be manned with a prize crew and sent to Providence, where her goods were to be kept safe; a prize of good value was to be brought to England, but all prisoners were to be disposed of in such a way as to avoid discovery of the ship's designs; captured negroes were to be conveyed to Providence and there disposed of, save those who could dive for pearls, who were to be retained as the company's property. The *Blessing* was permitted to consort with any English or Dutch ship,

15 Two minions, £25, 4 demi-culverins, £139-2s., 2 drakes, £18.

16 The island of Tortuga Salada, or Salt Tortuga, noted for its salt pans, must be distinguished from the Tortuga off Hispaniola. It lies not far from Punta Araya and Margarita off the coast of Venezuela.

ton for ton and man for man; if any good Spanish pilots were taken, well acquainted with the Bay of Nicaragua, the Bay of Honduras, or any part of the coast of Terra Firma, use might be made of them, but if any came to Providence, care was to be taken that their liberty did not discover the weakness of the island.

While they were employed in the first instance for prizes, trade was not to be entirely lost sight of by Rous and his fellows; strict enquiry was to be made wherever they went, where indigo, cochineal, sarsaparilla, ginger, rice, or any other commodities of value might be obtained. If gardens were found near the coast, they were to be searched for commodities fit to grow in Providence. When a suitable length of time had been spent in the Indies, the vessels were to steer for home via Bermuda, whither they were to carry any freight the governor and council of Providence thought suitable. They were to leave it in Bermuda in charge of the servants of Warwick, Saye, N. Rich, or Pym, who would dispose of it to ships trading to New England. If no suitable freight could be sent from Providence to England and the vessels were not filled with prize booty, they were to lade with wood at Tortuga or with salt at Hispaniola, and this they were to bring to Europe. In case the island of Providence was found to have been captured, enquiry was to be made at Henrietta Island, at the Moskito Cays, and on the Main to find whether any of the inhabitants had escaped. If there were no chance of resettling Providence, the passengers and the remaining colonists were to be transported to the settlement on Cape Gracias á Dios and this was henceforward to be made the headquarters of the ships; but if the enemy after its capture had wholly relinquished Providence it was to be reoccupied.

In the course of our pages very little, it will have been

noticed, has been said concerning the island of Henrietta or San Andreas, although this was included in the original patent of the Providence Company as suitable for the company's activities. As a matter of fact, although the idea had been broached two or three times, no attempt had been made at any permanent settlement of the island. San Andreas is a long low island, largely of a sandy nature, and its harbour, lying on the west side, is very unsafe and exposed to the prevailing winds. The island did not lend itself to fortification and the company, therefore, did not choose to waste upon it the labours and expense that could be more profitably expended on Providence. San Andreas, however, abounded in fine timber and became the scene of a quite respectable ship-building industry, and many shallops were built there under the direction of some Dutch shipwrights. The island was also the base for a great deal of the surreptitious preying on the smaller Spanish vessels that had to be carefully concealed from the governor and council of Providence during the early years of the colony's existence. We gather some light upon the proceedings of those who sheltered in the island from an extract or two from an extant letter of one Roger Floud to Sir Nathaniel Rich:[17] "Honored Sir—My last was by the *Elizabeth* which set sail home the 24th of March with a purpose to leave Mr. Key with Capt. Cammock, whose pinnace came here the 7th of April and without any stay went to Henrietta to saw boards for a shallop, where by an unknown accident she was burned and the people brought here by a ship of Flushing hired by Governor Hilton to bring Mr. Williams with carriages and wheels and other munitions. . . . If Mr. Williams can meet with a frigate and take it, the Dutch

[17] Manch. Pap., no. 420, Roger Floud to Sir N. Rich, Providence, 16 May, 1634.

captain will bestow the vessel on them. . . . I offered the Governor,[18] if he would let me go with 5 or 6 men to carry Capt. Cammock the news [at the Cape] I would take my shallop and bear the men safe, which was regarded as a task of desperateness. The Dutch captain and pilot, being of my acquaintance, made offer to me and others to sell his ship; if we would go with 20 men, he would serve us a twelve-month for one-third of what we should take, which offer was refused as prejudicial to the peace, yet [if] Captain Cammock's men is suffered to go and take, although but a fisherman, the breach is no less than in a plate ship.''

The Spanish fleet that attacked Providence in 1635 had previously reconnoitred Henrietta and found there only a few escaped servants, who on their approach fled to the dense woods covering the island. After burning the few huts and sheds that were made use of by the boat builders, the enemy departed to the attack upon their main objective. After the Spanish repulse, boat-building was carried on in Henrietta as before and some pinnaces of fair size were launched, among them the two that were to act as tenders to the *Blessing* and *Expectation.* Salt-making for curing the flesh of the turtle found on the shores of the island was also carried on. In March, 1636, William Woodcock, the company's husband, proposed to the company that he should send on his own account a number of men to raise commodities, especially dettee and annotto, upon Henrietta, he in return paying to the company one-fifth of the profits but bearing all expense himself. He had recently been engaging in a similar undertaking in Connecticut, where he had placed several servants to look after the flocks of sheep he had exported from England in partnership with Sir Richard

18 Gov. Bell of Providence.

Saltonstall.[19] The Massachusetts immigrants from Dorchester interfered with the peaceful occupation of his land, broke down his fences and allowed his sheep to escape, whereby both he and Saltonstall suffered considerable loss.[20] He now got ready some fifty servants under the command of one Capt. Andrew Carter and shipped them on one of his own ships, the *Hopewell*. Carter received a commission from the company as governor of the island of Henrietta and by April, 1636, everything was ready for sailing, when for some reason Woodcock resolved to defer the plantation of Henrietta for a time, and his men were ordered to Providence instead. The company wrote to the council that Woodcock had deferred his plantation upon Henrietta and consented that those who were designed to begin a plantation there should be left at Providence until a further number could be sent over. The defence of the island would thereby be strengthened, "the principal thing considerable in our designs." Woodcock's men were directed to seat themselves together on some part of the windward side of the island, that was not yet planted, and there they were to get ready provisions for their future plantation. This body of men under Carter's leadership formed an important addition to the anti-Puritan party in Providence and had a good deal to do with its ultimate loss.

The *Blessing*, the *Expectation*, and the *Hopewell* set sail from England in company in May, 1636, but soon lost

19 Mass. Hist. Soc. *Coll.*, 4th series, VI, 579, Sir Richard Saltonstall to John Winthrop, jr. See also 5th series, I, 216.

20 Lord Brooke to John Winthrop. "I am informed by Mr. Woodcock that he sent over the last year [1635] to Connecticut at least 20 servants to impale some ground, where they might improve their industry to his advantage and wherein he might feed some store of sheep." He was prevented by the Dorchester men and Lord Brooke recommends to Winthrop his demands for compensation. Mass. Hist. Soc. *Coll.*, 5th series, I, 240.

sight one of another. The *Blessing* and the *Hopewell* arrived in Providence after comparatively uneventful voyages, and William Rous having taken command of the former, she set sail on her roving commission against the Spaniards. The *Expectation's* voyage, however, was by no means so uneventful and her hundred passengers underwent terrible privations. She had not long left England when some mysterious sickness broke out on board to which Cornelius Billinger, the master, soon fell a victim. The command therefore devolved upon Giles Mersh, the mate, who, instead of landing his passengers at Providence, refused to enter the harbour and retained them on board to augment his fighting force. Two or three Spanish frigates were attacked in turn, but nothing of value was secured save a few negroes. After setting the crews of these frigates on shore near Cartagena, Mersh sailed across to the Moskito Cays and there remained for fourteen days trading for negroes with the Dutch slave-merchants in return for goods taken out of the supply he was carrying to Providence. Leaving the Moskito Cays, he again bore across to the coast of Terra Firma and there met the *Blessing,* whose captain, Rous, proposed to make a joint attack on the Spanish town of Santa Marta guided by a Spanish pilot he had captured. Though Mersh agreed to assist Rous in his enterprise, by his dilatoriness he failed to take advantage of favouring winds and the *Blessing* was left to make the attack alone. The supply of provisions on the *Expectation* had by now begun to run very short and the seamen and passengers were practically starving, though Mersh and his mate were living riotously in the cabin. The sickness again broke out on board and when, six weeks after leaving the Moskitos, the *Expectation* at last cast anchor in the harbour of Providence, more than forty of the original complement of one hundred passengers were dead and of the survivors not more than ten were whole and well.

When the *Blessing* had landed Gov. Hunt and the rest of her passengers in Providence and Capt. Rous came aboard to take command, it was to the great delight of the crew, for Rous had obtained a great name in the Indies for his profitable depredations in light pinnaces. Thomas Gage, the English Capuchin, who was sailing from Porto Bello to Cartagena late in 1636, gives us an idea of the hatred felt by the Spaniards towards the Providence colonists at this time:[21] "The greatest fear that, I perceived, possessed the Spaniard in this voyage was about the Island of Providence, called by them Sta. Catalina or St. Katherine, from whence they feared lest some English ships should come out against them with great strength. They cursed the English in it and called the Island the den of Thieves and Pirates wishing that the King of Spain would take some course with it; or else that it would prove very prejudicial to the Spaniards, lying near the mouth of the Desaguadero, and so endangering the Frigates of Granada, and standing between Portobel and Cartagena and so threatening the Galeons and their King's yearly and mighty treasure. Thus with bitter invectives against the English and the Island of Providence, we sailed on to Cartagena."

The *Blessing's* roving cruise was neither a successful nor a lengthy one, for, having, as we have seen, met the *Expectation*, and arranged to attack the town of Santa Marta in concert, the *Expectation* was becalmed and the *Blessing* entered the harbour alone. The town had been warned of the approach of the English by the Spaniards, who had been put ashore from the *Expectation* near Cartagena, and Rous met with a very warm reception. The

21 Gage, *The English American*, p. 450.

fight was too unequal to be a long one and after the English had lost several men, the rest, including Rous himself, were compelled to surrender on October 20, 1636. The prisoners were taken overland to Cartagena and there they were met on his landing by Thomas Gage. He says:[22] "I stayed in the Haven of Cartagena for the space of eight or ten days, where I met with some of my countrymen their prisoners, but especially that gallant Captain Rouse, who came unto me to complain of some affronts which had been offered unto him by the Spaniards in the ship whereby he came; which he, not being able to put up with, though a Prisoner unto them, desired to question in the field, challenging his proud contemners to meet him if they durst in any place of the Havanna (a brave temper in a dejected and imprisoned English man to challenge a Spaniard in his own country as a cock upon his own dunghill)." The temper that Rous had exhibited in Providence, he therefore carried with him into his captivity. Gage with difficulty persuaded him to abandon his attempt at satisfaction and in due course Rous was sent to Europe and arrived a prisoner at San Lucar.

He had already written from Cartagena to his kinsman Pym to secure his release, and he again wrote from San Lucar. Pym at once sent to him in Spain £20 out of his own pocket to relieve his pressing necessities, and in January, 1638, he informed the company of Rous's plight. Letters were at once obtained from the king to the English ambassador in Spain requesting Rous's immediate release and inquiring what right the Spaniards had to take our ships prize upon the coast of America.[23] But it was found impossible to do anything and on June 12, 1638, Fanshawe, the English chargé

[22] *Ibid.*, p. 452.

[23] State Papers, Foreign, Spain, Hopton to Windebank, 14 July, 1638.

d'affaires, wrote to Secretary Coke:[24] "There depends another business here concerning one, Captain Rous, who was brought likewise from the Indies to the prison of San Lucar his Lordship could procure no resolution touching him, neither can I hitherto, and it may be likely in my opinion that the issue will be as of other cases,"—that is to say that no official order would be forthcoming for the prisoner's release, but the use of bribery would be tacitly winked at and the prisoners would be permitted to make their escape from the prison of the Casa de Contratacion. The expected happened; for ten months Rous was allowed on bail in the town of San Lucar, being supported by a sum of £75 sent to him privately by Pym and by £100 borrowed from the English consul, Paul Wadworth; one of his fellow-prisoners[25] having absconded, Rous had his bail withdrawn and was cast into the common gaol of the town. In November, 1639, by dint of money provided by Pym, he managed to secure his escape along with the other surviving prisoners and at once returned to England, where he was content to settle down for a time. He was in later years elected a member of the Long Parliament, but played no very important part in its proceedings.

The story of Rous and the *Blessing* has seemed worth the telling in this detail, if only to illustrate the fact that the English sailors of Charles I's day were subject to the same vicissitudes that Hakluyt and Purchas describe for the Elizabethan sailors. There had been as yet no break of the Elizabethan tradition, the old feud was still kept up, and stories such as these going the round of English firesides made blind hatred of Papist

[24] S. P. Foreign, Spain.

[25] Edward Layfield. The ship he escaped in fell into the hands of Algerine pirates and he was again a prisoner.

Spain still the dominant motive of the ordinary Englishman in foreign politics.

The *Blessing* and her consorts had sailed from England in May, 1636, and in the same month the company was approached by Capt. Thomas Newman, with whose privateering exploits in the West Indies in the ship *Hunter* we dealt in a previous chapter. Newman proposed to the company through Treasurer Pym to undertake a voyage for reprisals in the Indies under the company's commission, either being set out by them or if he set himself out, paying them a fixed proportion of the proceeds of the voyage. Pym strongly advised that Newman should be employed and was of the opinion that it would be more profitable for the company to send him out in one of their own ships, as by this means they would secure a larger share of the booty. This was the plan accepted by the company and a fresh joint stock was started to provide the requisite capital. Nine adventurers[26] subscribed £1250 between them, and to this Newman himself added £400; a ship of three hundred tons, the *Happy Return,* was hired, together with a smaller vessel, the *Providence,* and both were well equipped with ammunition and ordnance. Some twenty servants were the only passengers sent by these vessels to Providence, as Newman desired to undertake hostilities against the enemy on his voyage out and civilian passengers would impede his activity. The vessels sailed from England in August, 1636, with the same commission and instructions that had been issued for the *Blessing;* their voyage was fairly successful until its last few weeks and we must return to some consideration of it later.

Owing to the terrible visitation of the plague that afflicted England throughout the later part of 1636, there

[26] Saye £200, Brooke £200, Rudyerd £50, N. Rich £100, Pym £200, Gurdon £50, Darley £100, Barrington £100, Woodcock £200, Waller £50.

was an entire intermission of the company's meetings from June, 1636, to January, 1637, and the small amount of business that had to be carried on was left in the hands of Secretary Jessop. In December the *James,* under the command of Capt. William Rudyerd, that had sailed to recolonise Association in June, 1636, put back into Plymouth utterly disabled. The news was carried to Pym, who was then staying with Lord Brooke at his country seat, Warwick Castle; they with Lord Saye, who was also staying at the castle, decided that the design upon Association should be abandoned, and that Rudyerd should be placed in command of a new vessel, the *Mary Hope,* and despatched to the West Indies on a prize voyage, financed by the remainder of the amount subscribed for the Association design. The instructions for his voyage were similar in form to those issued to others of the company's captains, but there was one important addition. Pym had begun to find that the company's permission to undertake reprisals against the Spaniards had a high commercial value, and that considerable sums might be made by issuing licenses or commissions to act under it for a percentage of the profits obtained. Rudyerd was therefore instructed to stay any Englishmen whom he found trading within the limits of the company's patents without their licenses. Any hostile action against Spain by other Englishmen he was to prevent in as far as he was able. Such an order was obviously futile and incapable of fulfilment, but it was a useful advertisement to the merchants, who desired to undertake privateering voyages, that the Providence Company had a valuable article to dispose of and would be pleased to do business at a reasonable rate.

CHAPTER X

THE PROVIDENCE COMPANY AND THE SHIP-MONEY CASE

In the story of the Providence Company and its activities there is, perhaps, no more striking fact to be noted than the intimate connection of its fortunes with the general history of the time. We have shown in an earlier chapter how the growing agitation against the illegal levying of ship-money had much to do with the frustration of the project of the Puritan leaders for emigration to the New World, and our investigation now leads us to consider how, in 1637, Pym and his fellows became involved in an organised conspiracy to defeat the government's plans to finance their arbitrary régime by the extension of a tax that had never received the sanction of parliament. The student of Stuart history cannot fail to notice at every turn of his enquiries, how great an influence the variations in England's foreign policy had upon the course of home politics, and here again we find the king's insoluble problem of how to secure the restoration of the Palatinate to Protestant hands playing a potent part in the affairs of the Puritan leaders.

Charles I's plans for the recovery of the hereditary possessions of his young nephew, the Elector Palatine, were marked by an irresolution and a trust in tortuous diplomatic intrigues that made his name a byword in every court in Europe. A perpetual conflict of opinion raged in his councils between those who favoured a close alliance with Spain and those who, led by the queen and her confidant, the Earl of Holland, urged an opposite course and a reliance upon French support. In December, 1636, the Earl of Arundel, who had been prominent among the pro-Spanish party, returned to England from an unsuccessful mission to the court of Vienna, so discouraged and disillusioned that he resolved to throw his influence into the opposite scale and to advise the king to an open alliance with France against Spain.[1] His assistance was particularly welcome to the Earl of Holland and the queen, and strong pressure was brought to bear on the king to force him to yield to the entreaties for overt action of his sister, the dispossessed queen of Bohemia, and her devoted adherent, Sir Thomas Roe. For months Roe had been suggesting that letters of marque for voluntary war against the king of Spain in the Indies should be granted in the name of the young Elector Palatine,[2] and in January, 1637, the foreign affairs committee of the Privy Council decided that some of the ships raised by the ship-money should be lent to the elector.[3] The greatest enthusiasm for the new plan was expressed at court and many noblemen came forward with subscriptions to aid the enterprise. While the preliminary arrangements were being made, overtures were received from Richelieu for a close treaty of alliance between England and France, and it appeared as though the king would at last be able to strike out a clear course in foreign policy, that would meet with the approval of the nation at large. On the 7th of February, all the twelve judges to whom the question of the legality of ship-money had been referred returned an answer in the affirmative and Charles was sanguine enough to sup-

1 Gardiner, VIII, 202.

2 *C. S. P. Dom.*, 1636-1637, Oct. 19. See also p. 504 and S. P. Dom., cccl, no. 77. For Roe's propositions in 1637 for the formation of an English West Indian Company, see *C. S. P. Dom.*, 6 Aug., 1637, and Col. Pap., IX, 61, 62, 63.

3 Gardiner, VIII, 204.

pose that this answer would soon put a stop to the agitation in the country about the obnoxious tax, and that he would soon be in possession of a revenue ample enough to permit him to undertake hostilities with every hope of success.

While the meetings of the Providence Company in London had been intermitted owing to the plague, some most important overtures from the West India Company of Holland had been made to the Earl of Warwick and his partners. The period of the greatest activity of the Dutch company was just opening, and active preparations were being made for the despatch of Count Joan Maurice of Nassau with ample resources to develop the Dutch empire in Brazil as supreme civil and military commander. In order to divide the Spaniards' attention a great diversion in the West Indies was contemplated and it was therefore suggested that the Providence Company should transfer their rights in the island to the West India Company of Holland, who would undertake the maintenance of the colony and would make it a base of attack upon the Panama trade. That the negotiations might be carried on, it was necessary for the Providence Company to obtain permission from the crown to part with the island, if a decent price could be obtained. The Earl of Holland was therefore requested to approach the king and to report to the company the result of his petition, but the request was made at the height of the new enthusiasm at court for anti-Spanish projects and the moment was evidently inopportune for the granting of the desired permission to part with an English possession that would form so suitable a base for offensive operations against the Spaniards.

On February 9, 1637, the Earl of Holland made his only appearance at the general court of the Providence Company to convey the decision of the king concerning the island "for the parting from which his Majesty was pleased to promise leave to the company some time since, it proving hitherto a place of charge rather than profit." "Forasmuch," said he, "as the Dutch ambassador had declared to his Lordship the Hollander's uncertainty and delays in resolution and their unwillingness to part with so great a sum as might be expected by the company, he had moved his Majesty to retain the island still in the hands of his own subjects, and the rather because of some designs in resolutions to be attempted about those parts. And to that end his Majesty would be pleased either to allow the company a convenient sum of money for recompense of their charges, or to furnish them with means to secure the place until his Majesty shall think fit to take it of them." The negotiations with the Dutch were therefore to be broken off and the company were directed to prepare propositions for carrying on the work. In accordance with this direction the general court appointed a standing committee for the launching of a new scheme, and the last reconstruction of the company was begun. The work occupied rather more than a year, and in April, 1638, a large expedition was sent to strengthen Providence, under the command of the celebrated Capt. Nathaniel Butler as military governor. The negotiations that led up to the despatch of this expedition had, of course, a great influence on the fortunes of the colony and will demand our attention from that point of view, but they are of wider interest as a part of the activity of the Puritan leaders and it is from this standpoint that we must first consider them.

When the king refused his permission for the sale of Providence and recommended a reconstruction of the company in February, 1637, his affairs had to the inexperienced eye never seemed in a more prosperous condition; when in April, 1638, the reconstruction was complete and Butler's expedition was despatched, this hollow show of prosperity had vanished before the menace of Scottish rebellion, and even the least capable student of affairs could see that a crisis was at hand, and that the struggle between crown and parliament, that had apparently closed in 1629, still remained to be fought to an issue. Through these months of preparation the doings of the Puritan leaders are wrapped in obscurity, and any indirect light that can be thrown upon them is of value where evidence is so lacking. Some such light it is possible to obtain from the Providence records, and, though its gleams are scant and fitful, yet where more definite information cannot, of necessity, be obtained, it may aid us somewhat to pierce the gloom. Nothing less was in process of formation during these months than the first organised political party of opposition to an English government, a task whose difficulty can hardly be grasped by the modern Englishman, to whom nothing is more natural than the existence of "His Majesty's Opposition," bound as closely to constitutional courses as any other party in the state. As in nature the shock of an external impulse will cause the saturated fluid to congeal round a tiny nucleus into a solid mass, so did that congeries of discordant units, the England of 1637, form itself round the nucleus of the Providence Company into the opposition of 1640, stiffened in active resistance to absolutism by the external impulse of the Scottish Wars.

The men of the next generation realized what an important part the meetings of the Providence adventurers played in the organisation of the opposition, for we may learn from the pages of Anthony à Wood that: "At Saye's house in the country at Broughton [near Banbury] the malcontents used to meet, and what embryos were conceived in the country, were shaped in Gray's Inn

Lane, near London, where the undertakers for the Isle of Providence did meet.'"[4] Hostility to the second writ of ship-money had been most noticeable in those counties where the Puritan leaders could especially exercise their territorial influence, and the State Papers for 1636-1637 bear this out in detail. Fawsley, Broughton, Hatfield Broad Oak, Great Hampden, and Harrow-on-the-Hill are names that are constantly recurring in the sheriffs' complaints of their inability to collect their quotas,[5] and the conviction is borne in upon us that a concerted plan of resistance to the impost had been agreed upon. Saye, as the Puritan leader who had been most often engaged in similar contests with the government, determined, if possible, to test the legality of the hated tax in the courts of law, and chose one of his Lincolnshire estates as the case for conflict. Some of his goods had been distrained upon for payment of his portion of the ship-money and Saye in consequence sued the constable for illegal distraint;[6] in reply the constable pleaded the king's writ and to this Saye demurred as an insufficient authority. The government declined to take up the battle on such grounds and Saye was proceeded against in the Star Chamber for depopulation of his estates, an entire shirking of the issue. Nor could Warwick, even though he openly protested to the king, secure that his case should be brought before the courts, while he found it difficult to secure the signatures of any but his own

[4] Wood, *Athenæ Oxonienses*, ed. Bliss, III, 547.

[5] A few instances only will suffice: *C. S. P. Dom.*, 1636-1637, 20 March, 28 March, 10 October, difficulty of collection from Knightley's tenants at Fawsley; 12 Sept., distress to be levied on Saye's Gloucestershire tenants; many other entries re Saye; 4 Oct., Sir Gilbert Gerrard refuses to pay ship-money at Harrow; p. 214, very refractory in payment among Barrington's tenants at Hatfield Broad Oak; 17 Nov., 17 Dec., the Earl of Warwick refuses to pay.

[6] *C. S. P. Dom.*, 1636-1637, pp. 155, 252.

immediate party to the public protest against the ship-money with which he meant to approach the king. Charles's presentation of the question of legality to the judges was intended to put an end to all hopes of a direct trial of the issue, and the public reading of the judges' answer on February 14, 1637, finally clinched the matter as far as the majority of people were concerned.[7] But although Lord Keeper Coventry had hinted his belief that any lawyer would be very foolish to take up so desperate a case as the contest of the legality of ship-money in face of the unanimous decision of the judges, the Puritan leaders were not of the same mind.

On the 24th, 26th, and 27th of February, 1637, we find from our records that meetings of the Providence Company were held at Preston Capes in Northamptonshire, only half a mile away from Knightley's seat at Fawsley and where he may have possessed a second residence. The adventurers attending these meetings were Saye, Brooke, Mandeville,[8] Knightley, and Pym, together with the company's husband, Woodcock, whom we may neglect. The presence of John Hampden at Preston may also be confidently assumed, for his seat at Great Hampden in Buckinghamshire was only a few hours' ride away. Among Knightley's guests there is no doubt that the Providence Company's affairs would demand very little share of the conversation, but the one absorbing topic would be the recent answer of the judges and

[7] Gardiner, VIII, 209.

[8] Edward Montagu, Viscount Mandeville, had begun to take a prominent part in the company's work after the death of Sir Nathaniel Rich on 29 May, 1636. From a letter of Matthew Cradock to John Winthrop, 15 March, 1637, we learn that Sir Nathaniel's life was shortened by the immoderate use of a new quack medicine, the "Antimoniall Cuppe" (Mass. Hist. Soc. *Coll.*, 4th series, VI, 125). Mandeville was Rich's executor and succeeded to the whole of his holding in the company, and to his papers. This accounts for the presence of Rich's papers in the Manchester collection. Rich's will is extant at Somerset House.

the best means of compelling the government to take up a definite challenge in the law courts. Pym could speak for the wealthiest and most respected Puritan in England, the Earl of Bedford, as entirely sympathetic to the object in view, and the services of the two lawyers, Holborne and St. John, to whom the management of the whole of the vast Russell law business was entrusted, might be depended upon for the proper presentation of the case. On the 9th of March,[9] the plans of the conspirators were put into action, a writ of *certiorari* was directed from the Chancery in respect of Hampden's refusal to pay the twenty shillings of ship-money assessed on his lands in the parish of Stoke Mandeville, and before the year 1637 was out the names of John Hampden and Oliver St. John were the most famous in England.

Throughout the early summer of 1637 the business of the Providence Company was transacted at Brooke House in Holborn by a committee consisting of Saye and Pym, with Brooke, Warwick, Rudyerd, and Darley as occasional attendants. On July 24, however, we again find Saye, Brooke, Pym, and Mandeville meeting at Fawsley. Between July and November no meetings were held owing to the immersion of Pym in the preparations for the coming case. Pym and St. John were Hampden's close counsellors in the interval before the public trial, and six months[10] were passed in preparation on both sides. While the public arguments on the case were proceeding in the Exchequer Chamber,[11] there was a full assembling of the Puritan leaders in London. On November 27, Saye, Brooke, Pym, Waller, Barrington (now a very rare attendant), Darley, and Woodcock met

[9] Nugent's *Mems. of Hampden* (5th ed., pub. Bell), p. 108.

[10] Forster's *Life of Pym*, p. 76.

[11] 6 November to 18 December, 1637.

at Brooke House; on December 9, Saye, Brooke, Pym, Warwick, Mandeville, Darley, and Woodcock and two days later Saye, Brooke, Pym, Darley, Waller, Barrington, and Woodcock met at Brooke House. The regulations enforcing upon country gentlemen residence upon their estates were particularly strictly enforced at Christmas, 1637, and orders were issued that all must leave London before December 12. It is now for the first time that we find Pym taking charge of the business of the Puritan party during the absence of its members from London and a special petition was addressed from the Providence Company to the king asking permission for him to remain along with Darley to look after the business, and in the return of the Middlesex justices[12] to the government, we find his name recorded as residing during the early part of January in St. Andrew's parish, Holborn. Against some of the names given, mention is made that permission to stay had been accorded, but there is no record of the sort against Pym's name and it is possible, therefore, that he stayed without any proper warrant and in despite of the royal order.

From the end of January, 1638, onwards, full meetings of the company were resumed at Brooke House, and Saye, Brooke, Warwick, Pym, and Mandeville were regular attendants. At this period the outlook of affairs was so black for the Puritan party, and there seemed so little chance of making headway against the tide of absolutism and Arminian innovation, that once more the idea of emigration presented itself to the leaders and preparations began to be made for them to proceed to Providence and the Main. On January 31, 1638, Lord Saye announced to the company his intention of emi-

[12] S. P. Dom., Car. I, ccclxxviii, No. 94, 16 Jan., 1638. Return by John Heme and Geo. Long, justices of the peace for Middlesex, of such persons of honour as have continued in London since 12 December last.

grating to the island as soon as he could clear up his affairs in England, and on February 15 the Earl of Warwick, Lord Brooke, and Henry Darley signified that they had the same intention, thus reviving the idea that they had been compelled by governmental pressure to abandon in 1633, when their intended goal was New England. The feelings of profound discouragement that filled the hearts of the Puritan leaders were even deeper in 1638 than in 1635, and Gardiner has described for us[13] how these feelings had spread even to those least in sympathy with Calvinism, and has shown how the gentle Milton of "L'Allegro" was waked "to the scornful indignation of the time that sounds forth with so stern a note from among the graceful lamentations of Lycidas." Almost as striking a note is heard in a brief letter that John Pym addressed to his old friend, John Wandesford, then consul of the English Levant Company at Aleppo. This letter has found its way into the State Papers, and this fact may indicate that the government, even in 1638, were beginning to suspect Pym of being the business man of the Puritan party and were intercepting some of his correspondence in the hope of finding evidence of treasonable communications with the malcontent Scots. The letter, though brief, is of interest as being one of the very few personal communications from Pym that have come down to us. He says: "I have passed through much variety of occasions since I last writ to you, and they furnish me matter of excuse of several kinds, which will not yield any the least charge or touch of disrespect or forgetfulness to be laid upon me. Now, being again to go into the country, where I have been for the most part of those two years last past, and it being a time which threatens great change and trouble, I have thought good now to salute you with this

[13] Gardiner, VIII, 244 sqq.

short letter and to assure you that you have always had a place in my thoughts and affections of much estimation and respect, and that I think myself indebted to you for many kindnesses and expressions of love, which I cannot deserve. How God will dispose of me I know not! If the public peace continue, I hope to write again in Michaelmas Term; if distemper and confusion do overwhelm us, in whatever condition I am, I shall live in a resolution, both by my prayers and endeavours, always to express myself your very assured friend and servant Jo: Pym.''[14]

In March, 1638, the adventurers were determined to depart and a formal petition was presented to the king through the Earl of Holland, praying for permission for the principal members of the Providence Company to leave England for Providence in order to settle there the affairs of the island. In the distractions of the conflict in Scotland that was rapidly moving towards war, the West Indian designs of 1637 had been entirely forgotten and it was hardly likely that the government would consent to lose sight of notorious malcontents, such as Saye and Brooke, who were suspected with very good reason of being in intimate relations with the Scottish rebels.[15] A single entry in the Providence records under date February 20, 1638, tends to confirm this. Lord Brooke desired the company to acquaint Lord Forbes ''that they had thought of his brother as a gentleman well qualified for the government of Providence,'' and Lord Forbes was to invite his brother to accept a proposition of the company. Nothing came of the plan, but the entry is of interest to us when we remember that Lord Forbes was one of the most celebrated Scottish soldiers of the time, was deep in the

[14] *C. S. P. Dom.*, 20 July, 1638, John Pym to John Wandesford.
[15] Gardiner, VIII, 335.

counsels of the Scots leaders and a year later was one of those who, out of his military experience in Germany, recommended Alexander Leslie for the command of the Covenanting forces. No answer was returned by the king to Saye's petition and the only trace of it that has remained outside our records is, as we showed in a previous chapter, the tradition preserved by Bate and Dugdale that the Puritan leaders were contemplating emigration to America in 1638.

CHAPTER XI

FINAL RECONSTRUCTION OF THE COMPANY

We have now to retrace our steps a little and take up again the thread of our story where we dropped it with the king's suggestion for a reconstruction of the Providence Company in February, 1637. The standing committee appointed to draft a scheme laboured diligently under the presidency of Pym, and by June their plans were ready and were submitted to the company at large and to many outside members of the Puritan party, who were thought likely to join. As their scheme is recorded in the company's minutes, it bears a striking resemblance to a modern company prospectus and it is worth while to examine it for a moment. For the good of the kingdom it is fitting that the design of Providence should be pursued because of: "1. The strength and opportunity of that island to become the foundation of very great enterprise by annoying the Spaniard and intercepting his treasure, whereby he hath troubled and endangered most of the States of Christendom and doth foment the wars against the professors of the reformed religion. 2. The facility of transporting colonies from thence to the Main Continent being, as [the company] hath [been] informed by divers that have viewed it, as rich and fertile as any other part of the Indies, where there do already grow commodities of very good use, which may by the industry of many hands be brought home in great quantities; and the soil capable of the richest drugs and merchandize, which come from America." The king has promised the company freedom from all customs both for outlading and inlading for twenty-one years, freedom from the new impositions on ordnance and ammunition, to be accountable to no admiralty but their own, and to be free from all the proclamations set forth against going into America.

The committee therefore propose that a stock of £100,000 shall be raised by instalments of £20,000 a year for five years. One thousand pounds shall be a whole share with four votes and £250 to have one vote; no man shall be obliged to pay in to the first supply before twenty whole shares have been subscribed, nor into the final supply till fifty whole shares. Three principal members of the company shall go out to govern the colony as[1] soon as the company is provided to set them forth, but until then a soldier and a gentleman shall be set forth as governor with one hundred well-armed fighting men and supplies to prepare the way. Further light is thrown on the designs of the company by an extant letter from Sir Edmond Moundeford to Sir Simonds D'Ewes, the antiquary, inviting him to subscribe to the new stock:[2]

Sir

I have received your command to inform you concerning the Isle of Providence. Lately we finding our strength too weak longer to support so great a burden, the Company were resolved to sell it to the States of Holland, they then offering us for it £70,000; we, by the Earl of Holland, our Governor, petitioned his Ma^{ty} for leave to sell; our answer was very gracious that he hoped it might be useful to him in his present designs, therefore would not as yet have it sold, but desired we would go on with the work and we should have such helps from him as in compass of reason should be desired, which accordingly were

1 This provision is of interest as showing that even thus early it was recognized that Massachusetts had succeeded better than other colonies because it was governed by members of the company on the spot.

2 Brit. Mus., Harl. MSS., 287, fo. 265.

upon our petition granted with promise of further addition of his favour. I shall relate some of those things we obtained as my memory will help.

(Here Moundeford recites most of the privileges above enumerated and adds): Freedom from the proclamations set forth against going into the American plantations. So that we may send or carry whom we will, without disturbance or further trouble. . . . It was resolved before I came out of town that three of our company should go in person . . . and five hundred men to be sent with them. Some of the Lords and others of great quality are resolved to go.

It is thought a great part of the stream will be carried from the late intended course and fall upon this plantation instead of New England, we having there many good people and very considerable teachers. The place is highly commended for health and plenty. I will not now trouble you further; so soon as I hear from London I will send to you, being desirous to see you added to the honourable Company, of whom, you know, many will be glad of your society, and so shall I who crave to have my service presented to your noble lady

and to be ever your affectionate friend

To his much honoured and ally
friend and kinsman Ed. Moundeford
Sir Simonds D'Ewes, Knight, these at his Stowhall, Suff[k].

The idea expressed in the last paragraph of this letter, of diverting the stream of Puritan emigration from New England, marks how far the Puritan parties in England and America had become estranged one from another in seven years, and the company's efforts to carry it out will demand our full consideration in a subsequent chapter. Owing to the troubles in which England became immersed in the latter part of 1637, no new adventurers could be persuaded to take up shares in the new stock, and finally £6000 had to be subscribed by Warwick, Saye, Brooke, Mandeville, and Pym in order to keep the enterprise running.[3] It was impossible to secure from the king any ratification of the privileges he had promised, as he had rapidly lost all interest in the western design and had begun once more to desire a rapprochement with Spain.

The new expedition, however, was got ready by April, 1638, and placed under the command of an old protégé of the Earl of Warwick, Capt. Nathaniel Butler, whose name was particularly well known in the Western Hemisphere.[4] Butler, who came of a good Bedfordshire family, had led a very adventurous life and had probably had his first American experience in one of the early Guiana voyages. In 1619 he was appointed by the Earl of Warwick's influence to the governorship of Bermuda, which he held till 1622. His governorship was marked by the difficulties concerning the ship *Treasurer*, that we have dealt with in an earlier chapter, and by some very questionable proceedings concerning a Spanish wreck. The Spanish government took up the matter so vigorously that Butler had to be superseded, and he proceeded to Virginia in the autumn of 1622. There he led an expedition against the up-river Indians and, returning to England, published in April, 1623, the

3 Warwick, Saye, Mandeville, Pym, £1000 each, Brooke £2000 in two instalments.

4 For an outline of Butler's life, see Brown, *Genesis*, II, 836. He makes the usual confusion between Sta. Catalina and the Bahamas and says that Butler ''was probably the person who was committed to Newgate for dispersing treasonable and scandalous books in June, 1649.'' This guess is demonstrably wrong; the prisoner was the well-known Nathaniel *Butter*, the publisher of so many of the tracts in the Thomason Collection, who often got into trouble with the authorities for his publications. Butler was the author of a work upon seamanship, which was fairly well known in the seventeenth century. The original draft of the work is in the British Museum (Sloane MSS., 758). The work must have been written in part while Butler was governor of Providence, for many pages of the MSS. are filled with notes concerning the island's affairs and the volume also contains a very full diary of events in Providence.

venomous attack upon the administration of the colony called *The Unmasking of Virginia.* After the dissolution of the Virginia Company he was placed upon the council for the government of the colony, but did not serve for long. In the Cadiz expedition of 1625 he commanded the hired merchant vessel, the *Jonathan,* of two hundred and fifty tons[5] and he served also in the expedition to Isle de Rhé. In 1637 he was appointed to the command of H. M. frigate *Nicodemus,* and must have relinquished this command to take up the governorship of Providence. To the colonists the company recommended Butler as "a man of very good parts and experience, being an ancient soldier at sea and land and heretofore employed in good places of trust and command, and a man of very good esteem here, the defence of the island requiring at this time a man of ability in regard of the danger from the Spaniards."

Gov. Hunt had been sent out to supersede Capt. Philip Bell in 1636, as having had some acquaintance with the military art, but his governorship had been noticeable only for a bitter recrudescence of the quarrels that Bell had vainly attempted to assuage. The first governor had always endeavoured to hold an even balance between the Puritan zealots who, under the leadership of Rishworth and Rous, sided with Sherrard, the minister, and the party who desired a relaxation of the rigid Puritan regulations that had been imposed by the company. The zealots desired to confine the attention of the colonists to planting and wished to expel from the island everyone who did not satisfy the exacting demands of the minister for orthodoxy, even though the defence of the island were thereby weakened; their opponents under the guidance of Daniel Elfrith and Andrew Carter cared

[5] S. P. Dom., Car. I, VII, 47. See also Nicholas's lists, cclxx, 65, cclxxxiv, 84.

nothing for religious matters and very little for planting, but they wished to rob the Spaniard with as much ease and security as possible, and to have a ready market for their booty with the Dutch and French ships that came to the island. Gov. Hunt, as a rigid Puritan, boldly sided with the zealots, and as soon as he had recovered from an illness that attacked him on his arrival in Providence, lent his aid to an attack on Bell for acts done as governor. As we have seen, Bell had to suffer many annoyances, but he soon left for England, and the zealots then turned their attack upon Elfrith. Even under Bell's governorship a petition had been presented by certain members of the council for his dismissal from all his offices and for his punishment "as a carnal and ungodly man"; the zealots were, however, in a minority and the governor refused to receive the petition. The change of governors gave the Puritans a majority, and within a few weeks Elfrith was deprived of his offices of councillor and admiral amid the rejoicings of Sherrard and his adherents, though they must have been very much damped when they received a letter from the company denouncing the whole of their proceedings and stigmatising them as "a mere nullity."

The other Christian virtues seem to have found little place in the hearts of the zealots beside their fervour for orthodoxy, for the company were compelled to point out to them that when Gov. Bell helped starving newcomers out of the company's stores in defiance of the wish of Rishworth's party in the council, he was only exercising the virtue of Christian charity and was to be commended rather than blamed. In other colonies the ministers were supported by the voluntary offerings of the planters, but in Providence the company was expected to bear the whole charge; nor were the planters forward in contributing to the upkeep of the church, for the company heard with regret that more trouble was lavished upon private dwellings than upon God's House; they therefore exhorted the planters to repair the church and keep it in a decent manner, this "being commended to Christians by the practice of the very Pagans themselves." The absence of many of the most unruly spirits from the island on the privateering voyages that were undertaken from 1636 onwards, left the Puritan party in the ascendant throughout the whole of Hunt's governorship, but the arrival of Capt. Butler as governor, the capture of Rous in the *Blessing,* and the return of Samuel Rishworth to England, weighed down the balance on the other side, and it may be well here for us somewhat to anticipate events and complete the story of the colony's religious troubles. Our information concerning the end of the long conflict is derived not only from the colony's records, but also from the narrative communicated by one of the ministers of the island, Nicholas Leverton, to Dr. Edward Calamy and reproduced by him in his *Nonconformist's Memorial.*[6]

Nicholas Leverton, B. A., of Exeter College, Oxford, was born at St. Wall, Cornwall, about 1600. After leaving Oxford, he kept a little school at Padstow, "but being ordained he went to Barbadoes, and there met with good acceptance. Though he had yet little seriousness, he soon grew weary of the profligate morals of the people and went as chaplain to a ship's crew who designed to begin a plantation upon Tobago.[7] By this means he met with a variety of remarkable providences, which God blessed to awaken him to a serious sense of religion."

[6] Calamy, *Nonconformist's Memorial,* I, 371.

[7] Tobago had been colonised by a party of Zeelanders from Walcheren under the auspices of Jan de Moor, burgomaster of Flushing. This colony was destroyed with great cruelty by Spaniards and Caribs from Trinidad in 1637 and Leverton's visit to Tobago was soon after this. See Edmundson, *Eng. Hist. Rev.,* XVI, 643.

The attempt at the colonisation of Tobago ended in complete failure, more than half of the company of between thirty and forty men being killed by the Caribs. The survivors managed to recover their boat with difficulty and put out to sea. "Not being able to return to Barbadoes or any of our English plantations on that side, because of contrary winds, they resolved to make to the Isle of Providence, which was five hundred leagues off near the line. Notwithstanding many fears and difficulties they had a prosperous voyage and a welcome reception from their countrymen there.

"Most of the inhabitants were such as had left their native country upon a dissatisfaction with the English hierarchy and settled there as others did in New England. They had but one minister among them, viz., Mr. Sherwood,[8] who was also dissatisfied with conformity. Yet some of the inhabitants were for the English ceremonies and upon Mr. Leverton's arrival would have had him minister to them in their own way." It is evident that the laxer party in the island were here endeavouring to set up a rival minister to Sherrard in order to cloak their proceedings under guise of attachment to Arminian doctrines. "Hitherto [Mr. Leverton] had never considered the controversy, but his impressions of religion were such as the general custom of his country and education had made. But now, being made very serious by the remarkable providences he had met with and finding Mr. S. a pious person, he was disposed to hear his reasons for Nonconformity, which induced him heartily to fall in with him in the same way." Gov. Butler reached Providence in October, 1638, and at once took sides against the extremists of the Puritan party and the ministers, and wrote home to the company to their detriment. The company were not prepared to

8 That is, Sherrard.

listen to these stories and exhorted Butler to give Sherrard and his particular congregation every liberty and favour. "God makes no difference," they told him by the hand of Pym, "between them that do faithfully and heartily seek him, though there be in the appearance of men some difference between them in opinion and practice concerning outward things." He was exhorted to take away all occasion of faction among the colonists and of any breach with the churches of New England, who, on their side, they hoped would carry themselves modestly and be content with their own freedom, leaving others to theirs. The communication between Providence and New England had been constant ever since 1637 and the Puritan party were now applying for active help from the churches in Massachusetts. Of their intention to support him against his enemies, the company assured Hunt, the leader of the Puritans, by the same ship: "Our main desire," they wrote, "is that Godliness may be furthered and vice beaten down, and though all honest men shall not agree in their opinions and practice concerning outward things, yet we hope they will agree with those which are apparent for God's glory and the furtherance of the public good, which is a disposition which, we hope, is in yourself." To the governor and council in their public letter they wrote: "We heartily pray God to bless and direct you in your plans that you may be Instruments of His glory, and for the furtherance of that great work of subverting the Spanish Tyranny in those parts and planting the Gospel, which is the main thing that drew us to bestow our care and money upon this Design."

Butler's ideas for the subversion of the Spanish tyranny did not involve attention to the duties of his governorship, but ran rather in the direction of piratical attacks upon Spanish ports. Within six months after reaching Providence he got together a mixed fleet of Dutch and English ships and set forth on a regular piratical cruise against the Spanish coasts. Butler supplies us in his diary with full details concerning the expedition, but these need not detain us. It wound up with the surprise of Truxillo, the chief port of the province of Honduras, which had successfully repelled the attack of Sir Antony Sherley and Capt. Parker in 1597.[9] The town was much decayed and was unable to offer resistance to the corsairs' attack. The citizens compounded for the town's freedom from sack for a ransom of 16,000 pieces of eight, paid partly in bullion and partly in indigo, the chief product of the province. After so satisfactory an adventure, Butler felt no inclination to carry out his bargain with the Providence Company, but determined to leave for England without delay. Returning to Providence in September, 1639, he, without consulting the rest of the council, appointed Capt. Andrew Carter, the leader of the anti-Puritans, to act as deputy-governor, and took his departure for England in great haste in February, 1640. Carter lost no time in taking his revenge upon the Puritans for their proscription of Elfrith and other of his friends, and Leverton's story goes on to tell us that "at length the governor leaving the island, a difference arose in the colony. He named his successor, but the people pleaded a right by charter to choose their governor and fixed upon a person of their own nomination, one Captain Lane.[10] But the other [i.e. Carter] privately arming some of the under sort, seized Lane and both the ministers and sent them prisoners[11] to England, with

9 Hakluyt, VII, 220.

10 This was the Richard Lane, a protégé of Lord Brooke, who had been employed in the company's trade at Darien.

11 Lane, Leverton, Sherrard, and Henry Halhead, were sent prisoners in the *Hopewell* and arrived in England in January, 1641.

an information against them to Archbishop Laud, that they were disaffected to the liturgy and ceremonies of England. When they arrived here, the state of things was changed and Laud was in custody of the Black Rod.[12] They were kindly received by the Lords Patentees or proprietors of the island and encouraged to return." Before they did so, however, much had taken place and none of them saw Providence again.

From the economic point of view the period of the colony's life that succeeded the supersession of Gov. Bell, in 1636, is marked by the great rapidity with which Providence approximated to the ordinary type of a West Indian colony that subsisted with very little change down to the end of the eighteenth century. Barbadoes and St. Christopher long had a large majority of whites over negroes and carried on the production of tobacco and cotton by the labours of indentured white servants, as did the English planters of Jamaica for some years after its capture, but Providence, owing to the privateering carried on from thence, was always able to obtain unlimited supplies of negroes at very cheap rates, and by the end of 1637 there were almost as many negroes as white men in the island. The company strongly objected to the constant increase in the number of negroes as endangering the safety of the island, but owing to their difficulties in England, they were unable to supply white servants to the planters in anything like sufficient numbers, and had great difficulty in getting the planters to accept even those they did send. The servants were contracted with for three or four years' labour in return for food, lodging, and clothing, and at the end of their time they were to receive £10 each from their masters and a parcel of land from the company. These terms the

12 Laud had been committed to custody by the Lords on December 18, 1640.

planters became more and more disinclined to assent to as time went on, and the company complained that the increased employment of negroes "brought down the bodies and labours of men to such cheapness that we shall not be able to supply servants as we have done formerly." Those servants who could not be disposed of to the planters were combined into families of twenty or less and set to work on tobacco and cotton raising for the company's profit. A store was accumulated from these profits to pay the £10 due to each on the expiry of their indentures, and inspectors were appointed by the council to view the plantations every three months and see that the arrangements were working satisfactorily.

None of the company's efforts to stop the influx of negroes met with any measure of success. It was ordained that every planter keeping a negro should maintain a servant one day in every week upon the public works. Those having no negroes were to be excused labour upon the public works, their places being filled by the negroes belonging to the company. When this arrangement was found of no avail, it was directed that to every two Englishmen upon a plantation, one negro might be received, but no more, and for each of these negroes forty pounds of tobacco was to be paid per annum to the company's store. In addition to this each negro was bound to labour sixteen days in the year on the public works, "since they are cheaper and are perpetual servants, and the rather that the desire of English bodies may be kept, we depending on them for the defence of the island." Negroes were only to be bought from the Dutch on the company's account for disposal in Virginia and the Somers Islands, "we well knowing that if men be left at liberty to buy as they please, no man will take off English servants. And therefore we think fit that whosoever buys a Negro, shall be bound to take off two English servants at the common charge of transportation and otherwise."

The sale of negroes to other plantations was becoming a very important part of the colony's activities, and both Capt. Newman in the *Happy Return* and Capt. Rudyerd in the *Mary Hope* were constantly landing captured negroes in the island and there disposing of them to ship-masters from Virginia and New England. From 1637 onwards the traffic between Providence and the northern colonies became a regular one and from Winthrop's journal, as well as from the Providence records, we can learn that William Peirce,[13] the well-known New England ship-master, was a frequent visitor to the island. After the victory of the Massachusetts colonists over the Pequot Indians in July, 1637, Winthrop says:[14] "We had now slain and taken in all about seven hundred. We sent fifteen of the boys and two women to Bermuda by Mr. Peirce, but he, missing it, carried them to Providence Isle."[15] Peirce returned to New England in February, 1638, and Winthrop in his journal for that month gives us a fuller account of the island.[16] February 26, 1638, "Mr. Peirce in the Salem ship *Desire* returned from the West Indies after seven months and brought some cotton and tobacco and negroes from thence and salt from Tertugos.[17] Dry fish and strong liquors are the only commodities for those parts. He met there two men-of-war set forth by the Lords of

[13] William Peirce was in command of the *Lion* in Winthrop's voyage of 1629 and was by far the best-known master in the New England trade, in which he had been engaged at any rate from 1623. Bradford's *Hist. of Plym. Plant.* (ed. 1912), I, 309 and note 2.

[14] *Journal*, I, 228 (1905 ed.).

[15] Mass. Hist. Soc. *Coll.*, 5th series, I, 277.

[16] *Journal*, I, 260.

[17] This may be either Tortuga Salada or Association. Salt was being made at both places in 1637.

Providence with letters of mart, who had taken divers prizes from the Spaniard and many negroes.'' Some of the negroes sent from Providence to New England were very savage and had to be at once returned, for soon after one of Peirce's voyages we find the company giving special caution to Gov. Butler to take great care of ''the cannibal negroes brought from New England.''

The company's fears of trouble arising from the large number of negroes in the island were only too well founded. Large numbers of them escaped to the woods covering the highest parts of the island, and great difficulties were experienced in bringing about their submission, though those who surrendered voluntarily were well treated, while those who resisted were barbarously put to death. Matters came to a head at the end of 1638, when the escaped slaves in concert with those negroes still in servitude rose in rebellion against their masters. It was only with the greatest difficulty that the revolt was suppressed and the island was gravely weakened by it, for it emboldened the Spaniards from Cartagena once more to renew their efforts to clear out their English foes.

As has been shown in earlier chapters, the company had entirely abandoned the sending of magazines to the island, for those sent had proved very unprofitable. During the later years of the colony's existence entire freedom of trade was permitted subject to the payment of customs dues to the company. These were fixed at a higher rate for Dutch ships than for English in order to comply with the royal commands restricting intercourse with the Hollanders, and for reasons which the company expressed thus: ''For every pound of tobacco the Dutch shall receive out of the island in exchange for any goods you require of them, vi[d] is to be paid there, and so for every pound of cotton, which are about the usual rates of custom paid here, and so for other commodities. The customs on tobacco in England are very high, whereas in Holland it is low and so the Dutch can sell their tobacco and other commodities at a cheaper rate than can be obtained from commodities received through London, whither [the Company's] ships are bound to return." In order further to mark their hostility to foreign interlopers, the company ordered that any fort or bay having a Dutch name was to be renamed in English, and the Dutchmen in the island were to be treated very coldly. So difficult and precarious were trade conditions in England in 1639, that the company resolved to attempt to make the cloth they required for clothing the colonists from the cotton in the island itself; weavers and spinners were hired and sent out in the *Mary* in June, 1639, with engines "to weave the cotton into fustians and dimities;" and it was resolved also to trade as much as possible with New England for the commodities the island required. Orders were given that any hides, tallow, or sarsaparilla captured by the company's ships were to be disposed of in New England, whence they might be despatched through the Straits of Gibraltar to Mediterranean ports or to France, so as to save the customs and impositions in England. That this course was in fact adopted, we may learn from many entries by Massachusetts writers.

In September, 1638, Capt. Newman sent to Massachusetts a captured Spanish frigate with hides and tallow,[18] and in November he arrived there himself in his pinnace, the *Providence*.[19] "One Captain Newman, being set forth with commission from the Earl of Holland, Governor of the Westminster Company, and the Earl of Warwick and others of the same company, to spoil the Spaniard within the limits of their grant in

[18] Winthrop's *Journal*, I, 278.

[19] *Ibid.*, I, 283.

the West Indies, after he had taken many of their small vessels, etc., returned home by the Massachusetts in a small pinnace, with which he had taken all his prizes (for his great ship was of no use for that purpose). He brought many hides and much tallow. The hides he sold here for £17-10s. the score; the tallow at 29s the hundred; and set sail for England on the 1st of December." Newman's adventures after leaving Massachusetts are of interest to us as involving the Providence Company in a lawsuit that was undecided for many years and was still debated long after the colony had been destroyed.

The *Happy Return,* Newman's larger vessel, had reached England safely in April, 1638, and had landed a cargo of tobacco, tallow, and hides to the value of about £4000. Sarsaparilla to the value of about £900 had been disposed of in New England, so that the company for their share got about £3000 out of the cargo. Newman in the pinnace *Providence* was sailing up the Channel on Christmas Day, 1638,[20] after a favourable passage from New England, when less than two leagues off Dungeness the vessel was attacked by a Dunkirk ship, belonging to one of the principal officers of the town. Five sailors were wounded and three killed in the fight and the *Providence* was finally overwhelmed by force of numbers and compelled to surrender. The officers and sailors were stripped to their shirts, carried to Dunkirk and there tied two by two and thrust into a dungeon below the town ditch. The cargo of the *Providence,* when discharged, was found to comprise valuables of all

[20] Many depositions about the case exist among State Papers, Domestic, State Papers, Foreign (Flanders), and the Admiralty Court records. Some of these have been calendared under a misapprehension as having to do with the great fishing company of the Earl of Pembroke that was also having trouble with Dunkirkers about this time.

sorts,[21]—twenty-five packages of indigo, divers packages of sarsaparilla, a gold chain three ells long, a sack of ambergris, four diamonds, a large quantity of pearls, several bags of gold and silver, some silver plate, two large and heavy lumps of gold as heavy as a man could lift, the whole being of the value of about £30,000. No sooner had the company heard of Newman's capture than they began through the Earl of Holland to move the king to secure his immediate release. Sir Balthasar Gerbier was directed to make the most strenuous representations to the Cardinal Infante, the ruler of the Spanish Netherlands; Sir Arthur Hopton was ordered to do the same to the Spanish court, but not the least progress could be made, for Newman was held at Dunkirk to be "the greatest English pirate unhanged." Gerbier's representations to the Cardinal Infante himself were received with studied rudeness, and his letters home pointed out that his pleadings for a notorious pirate damaged badly the more important negotiations he was constantly being charged to deal with. The only boon secured after nearly two years' negotiation was the release of the prisoners on the payment of their very heavy charges. Newman at once returned to his piratical exploits and from Winthrop[22] we learn that "he was afterwards cast away at Christopher's with a very rich prize in the great hyrracano, 1642." The matter of the captured cargo was brought before parliament in 1641,[23] but stood still during the troubles, until in 1649 we find the surviving members of the Providence Company claiming a share of the value of the celebrated Spanish vessel, the *Santa*

[21] These details are derived from Sir Balthasar Gerbier's representation to the Cardinal Infante. S. P. For. Flanders, 4 Jan., 1640.

[22] *Journal*, I, 283.

[23] "House of Lords, MSS.," Hist. MSS. Com., *Fourth Report*, 20 April, 28 June, 6 July, 1641, 12 Oct., 1643.

Clara, that had been seized in Portsmouth harbour. No conclusion could be arrived at and on January 25, 1650, the matter was left in the hands of the Rump Parliament to be dealt with, but apparently without result. The last mention of the affair is found in a petition to the Restoration House of Lords in the session of 1660.

Attempts might be made by the company to secure redress from the Dunkirkers, though the attempts might be vain, but no redress could be sought from the Algerine pirates, who swarmed in the Bay of Biscay and the entrance to the English Channel. The reinforcements for Providence for the year 1639 were sent out by the *Mary,* a ship belonging to the well-known merchant, Maurice Thompson, which was bound for Barbadoes and was chartered by the company for their service after leaving there. She carried a few servants for Providence and one or two Puritan families under the lead of John Symonds, a client of Lord Mandeville, who was returning to his wife in Providence. Hardly had the *Mary* left the Channel (July, 1639), when she was captured by an Algerine corsair and her passengers and crew carried into captivity. The first news from them arrived in a letter written by Symonds from Algiers in November, 1639, and still extant among the Manchester Papers.[24] Symonds writes to Lord Mandeville to beg the company to ransom the poor captives from their slavery. "When I considered," he says, "that the soul into which God hath distilled most grace, and [which] hath tasted the joys of God's spirit is ever compassionate, having a fellow feeling of the miseries of others,

[24] Manch. Pap., 423, 20 Nov., 1639. The letter is very badly written and has been calendared (Hist. MSS. Com., *Eighth Report,* App. 2) as coming from "Aryter most probably Henrietta"(!), a misreading of *Argier,* the seventeenth century form of the name Algiers. The précis of the letter is badly done.

that consoled me to trouble your Lordship humbly beseeching that you would commiserate the miserable condition of a company of poor people. We expect not that the honourable Company should disburse money for our redemption, for the sum will be great, we being about 30 that were shipped for the island. Right Honourable, if it may be done with conveniency [we pray you] to move our gracious King in our behalf; there are 2000 English Christians besides Renegadoes. . . . There are some forced to filthiness, some to despair, and so to turn their back upon Christ. Myself have been much solicited, but God hath established my heart. . . . I have been a suitor through Mr. Carter to their honours Lord Saye and Lord Brooke, and the same suit I present to your honour. There is a gracious woman weeping, as I humbly beseech your Lordship to think, upon your poor island.'' Symonds's pathetic plaint did not fall on deaf ears, for by February, 1640, the company had arranged to ransom at any rate some of the captives.

The possession by the Providence Company of permission from the crown to undertake reprisals against the Spaniards was a very valuable asset to them, and they were constantly being approached by speculators during the later years of their existence as a company for the issue of commissions for ships to undertake privateering voyages in the West Indies in return for a share of the proceeds. The company always refused to invest money in fitting out these privateer ships, but granted the desired commissions to the adventurers in return for a fixed payment of one-fifth part of all booty taken. The last ships fitted out by the company themselves were two pinnaces, the *Swallow* and the *Spy*, despatched in July, 1638, under the command of Capt. Samuel Axe, his son Andrew Axe, Capt. Nicholas

Parker,[25] and Matthew Harbottle. In October, 1638, the Earl of Warwick, who had bought out the rights of Philip, Earl of Pembroke, over the islands of Trinidad, Tobago, St. Bernard [Fonseca], and Barbadoes,[26] despatched two pinnaces to commence a plantation upon Trinidad, and these received from the Providence Company commissions for reprisals against the Spaniards. In June of the same year a grant of incorporation was issued by the company to William Claiborne, the Virginia and Maryland planter, for the settlement "of an island by him and his associates discovered within the Company's Patent to be called Rich Island in honour of the Earl of Holland." This was the island of Ruatan (Rattan), the principal of the Bay Islands, off the coast of Honduras; the first settlement of the island by Englishmen did not last long, for they were expelled by the Spaniards in 1642,[27] but the connection of England with the Bay Islands subsisted through the eighteenth century and the claims to their possession were only abandoned some fifty years ago.

In July, 1639, Capt. John Dell was provided with a commission for his ship, the *Advantage,* financed by Abraham de Leau, a prominent Huguenot merchant in the City of London, and some of his partners, and in January, 1641, there returned to England Capt. William Jackson with a prize richly laden with indigo, which had been captured under the company's commission and brought into their coffers over £3000. In the turmoil of the time Capt. Jackson's name has been entirely forgotten by succeeding generations, but by the English-

[25] Capt. Parker filled an important part in later West Indian history and became a trusted employé of the Commonwealth. In 1660 he was consul at Algiers.

[26] Brit. Mus., Sloane MSS., 3662, fo. 45, Scott's account.

[27] Brit. Mus., Sloane MSS., 793 or 894. Alcedo y Herrera, *Piraterias y agressiones en la America Española,* Madrid, 1883, p. 123.

man of 1642 his exploits were as proudly thought of as those of Drake and Hawkins. No account of his doings appears to have been printed, but among the Sloane MSS. in the British Museum there is a little manuscript volume entitled "Mercurius Americanus,"[28] giving a full account of the last expedition in the Elizabethan manner against the Spanish Indies, carried out under Jackson's command in 1642-1643. The account is written by an eyewitness of the exploits and is quite after the Hakluyt fashion. At some future time it may be possible to rescue Jackson's story from its undeserved oblivion. Both his voyage of 1639-1641 and the later and greater expedition were carried out under the Providence Company's commission for reprisals. The first voyage was financed by the well-known merchant, Maurice Thompson of London, and some Cornish merchants interested along with the Killegrews in the privateering trade.[29] Jackson left England some time in 1638 and obtained little success on his outward voyage; he put in to Providence to revictual in April, 1639, while Gov. Butler was absent from the island and the government was vested for the time being in the hands of Capt. Andrew Carter. We showed in the previous chapter to what lengths of injustice Carter proceeded when the government was definitely vested in him, but even thus early he displayed the same spirit.

One Robert Robins, a native of Penrhyn in Cornwall, had long been a planter in Providence and a prominent supporter of the Puritan party. Having in some way offended the governor, he was arrested, clapped into

28 Brit. Mus., Sloane MSS., 793 or 894.

29 "House of Lords MSS.," Hist. MSS. Com., *Fourth Report*, App., p. 63. *Lords' Journals*, IV, 248. The majority of the details given in the text are derived from the original petition of Robert Robins to the House of Lords, 22 April, 1642, calendared very briefly, *Fifth Report*, App., p. 18.

irons, and refused communication with his wife, servants, or family; the following day, being brought before Carter, an order of banishment was pronounced against him without any trial and he was forcibly conveyed aboard Jackson's ship, then lying in the harbour. The Puritan party of the council, hearing of Robins's plight, approached Carter under the leadership of Sherrard and Halhead and offered to stand bail for his appearance at a public trial either before the council or in England before the company. Carter entirely refused to listen to them and maintained that what he had done was within his prerogative as governor. Jackson was then bound on a daring raid up the Nicaragua River or El Desaguadero, and Robins in his own words was "in fearful storms of thunder and foul weather forced to work, stand sentry, watch and fight, he being a prisoner. The pillage that he got was taken from him, also he suffered miserable afflictions for want of clothes by mosquitoes and other venomous vermin and flies, daily in danger of his life." Jackson's raid was very profitable, but Robins for all his sufferings was only granted a single share. "When the goods were being shared, one of the company, pitying his cause, promised him a single share, being half so much as the boys have, yet they had made him cook for the whole company and divers others, strangers and negroes, and four shares belonged to the cook by order of the Trinity House." Robins was sent ashore in Providence and told to shift for himself, while Jackson sailed to New England to dispose of the booty.

On August 27, 1639, Winthrop writes in his journal:[30] "Here came a small bark from the West Indies, one Captain Jackson in her, with commission from the Westminster Company to take prize, etc., from the Spaniard.

[30] *Journal*, I, 309.

He brought much wealth in money, plate, indico and sugar. He sold his indico and sugar here for £1400, wherewith he furnished himself with commodies and again departed for the West Indies." For another year Jackson continued his roving cruise in the Indies and met with very fair success, but about the end of 1640 he set sail for England with the large indigo-laden prize we have before mentioned. Robins had succeeded in collecting some of the debts owing to him in Providence, and having with great difficulty secured from Carter permission to leave the island, he paid for his passage to England on one of Thompson's ships. But his troubles were not yet over. "The petitioner shipped himself a passenger for England with one Thompson and delivered him his ticket[31] for his free departure out of the island, yet within three weeks of their being at sea, in the Gulf of Florida, Jackson and Thompson combined together and violently took and carried the petitioner aboard Jackson's man-of-war, kept all his goods and much of his clothes, gave special directions to the master of the ship to keep him in irons and convey him to New England to be hanged and his goods to be spent upon the seamen. Then the petitioner demanded his ticket, being his relief from imprisonment, and a bill of lading for his goods, but Jackson and Thompson said he was a prisoner and should have none of them nor any bill of lading for them." Robins suffered a great deal of misery and "was forced to eat tallow for the most part of his meat for a long time, which caused a dangerous sickness when he came ashore, being almost starved and naked." The vessel in which he was a prisoner did not sail direct to England, but put into some

[31] The "ticket" was a paper signed by the governor and certifying that the person named in it had full permission to sail for England.

Irish port and there disposed of a large part of her booty.

There is no room to doubt that the Providence Company were not being honestly dealt with by those who plundered the Spaniards under their commission, and it is certain that Jackson paid over to the company much less than the fifth due to them under their agreement. He also endeavoured to cheat some of his partners and the journals of the Long Parliament contain many references to the disputes that resulted in consequence of his sharp practice. Robins found it impossible to get redress for his wrongs either from Jackson or from "the honourable Company of Adventurers into Providence in respect of State affairs, all of them being members of Parliament . . . and now," wrote he in 1642, "all his witnesses are bound to sea, and also Captain Jackson is bound to the West Indies on the first of April next [1642], so that the petitioner is likely to lose all his goods, suffer all their wrongs and return to his friends begging, in respect he can get relief in no Court in England, but in this hon^ble^ House, and except your Lo^ps^ hear his case." It is to be feared that Robins got very little satisfaction even from the House of Lords, for though Lords Brooke and Robartes were appointed as a committee to examine the matter, no conclusion was arrived at before England was plunged into the throes of the Civil War, and all good government was at a standstill.

CHAPTER XII

TRADE WITH THE MAIN; FRENCH CAPTURE OF TORTUGA

While the course of events in Providence and Association was proving fatal to all the company's hopes of profit and success, their scheme for founding a prosperous colony and trading post upon the mainland coast was flourishing no better. In 1634 a large vessel, the *Robert,* had carried out a valuable cargo of trade stuff to Capt. Sussex Camock, the company's agent at Cape Gracias á Dios, but the voyage was an entire failure, and when the *Robert* returned to England in June, 1635, the company were disgusted to find that Camock had wearied of the work he had contracted to do, and had returned home in defiance of all engagements.[1] Camock had left in charge of the colony Capt. Samuel Axe, who had done much for the company's interests while in charge of the depot at the Moskito Cays. Axe was well seconded in his efforts to carry on a successful Indian trade by a Dutch sailor, who had long served as mate in the company's ships. This Abraham Blauvelt, or Blewfield (Bluefield)[2] as the English called him, was a daring and resourceful sailor who was constantly undertaking voyages of exploration and trade up the rivers

[1] Camock left the company's service on his return to England. In 1636 the State Papers show us (3 June, 1636) that he became captain of Landguard Fort at Harwich and there he was still serving during the early years of the Civil War.

[2] The name is frequently spelled Bluefield or Bluefields.

of the coast, and who has left his name permanently in at least two places on the map of the West Indies. We first hear of him as doing shipwright's work in the repair ships at Providence, and later building shallops for the company from the cedar-wood that grew in profusion in Henrietta Island. In a pinnace that he himself had built, he began his exploration of the rivers of the Main, and with her he maintained communication between the island of Providence and the men engaged in preparing silk-grass at the Cape. In 1637 he returned to England as mate of the *Expectation* in order to give an account to the company of his explorations of the mainland coast. He told them that at Monkey Bay he had discovered a good harbour a mile and a half broad at the mouth and capable of strong fortification by means of some islands lying in its entrance. This harbour provided an excellent anchorage for ships, and was surrounded by fertile country overgrown with silk-grass and containing many other excellent commodities. Into the harbour flows an important river now called, after its discoverer, the Blewfields River and by the Spaniards the Escondido; this river Blewfield explored for a considerable distance into the Main. He recommended the harbour to the company as a suitable place for the establishment of a trading station and settlement, but their preoccupations rendered it impossible for them to act upon his suggestion. At a later period, however, the buccaneers made the harbour one of their principal rendezvous, and the town there established is still called after the name of the discoverer of the harbour, Blewfields. After the capture of Providence by the Spaniards, Blewfield entered for a time the service of the Swedish West India Company, but he found privateering a more profitable occupation than trade, and in 1644 we find him commanding a ship of his own and sailing from

New Amsterdam[3] to prey upon the Spaniards. At this time, or perhaps later, he occasionally made his headquarters at a harbour in the southwest of Jamaica and this is still called Blewfields Bay. The publication of the treaty of Munster in 1648, by which the long war between Holland and Spain was closed, prevented him from bringing his prizes safely into New Amsterdam, and he began to dispose of them instead at Newport in Rhode Island. There he got into trouble with his crew of many nationalities and we hear of him in a letter from Roger Williams, who was much put about at the ill-name his unlawful proceedings would bring upon the Rhode Island colony.[4] We last hear of him in a list of buccaneers in 1663 as "Captain Blewfield, belonging to Cape Gratia de Dios, living among the Indians." His ship was a barque with fifty men and three guns.[5]

The trade at the Cape, although it never attained to any considerable proportions, was maintained by the Providence Company throughout its existence, and in the later years, when they realised that Providence might at any time be overwhelmed by the Spaniards, the masters of their ships were instructed to carry their passengers to the Cape, if Providence were found to have been captured. In 1638 Capt. Axe described the land surrounding the settlement in these terms: "At the Cape [Gracias á Dios] there is good store of victuals, a good country for corn, the grass not troublesome as in the Island, store of honey, yet not to make a commodity. Reasonable store of flax, greater store at

[3] O'Callaghan, *Hist. of New Netherland*, I, 296; *New York Documents*, I, 397-399. In 1650 he owned and commanded the French ship *La Garse.*

[4] Mass. Hist. Soc. *Coll.*, 4th series, VI, 272. Roger Williams to John Winthrop, jr., Narragansett, 25 Oct., 1649, and 9 Nov., 1649, "Here hath been great bickerings about Blewfield's ship at Newport."

[5] Rawlinson MSS., quoted by C. H. Haring, *Buccaneers of West Indies*, Lond., 1910, p. 273.

Monkey Bay, but then they that gather it must go strong in regard of the Spanish neighbourhood.[6] The flax after cutting will grow again in 6 or 7 months. As fair sugar canes as any in the world. The air is temperate; it agrees with English bodies and is very healthful; the soil some miles from the coast is very firm. The Cape River is navigable with small vessels, but the entrance is unhealthful in regard to the drowned grounds thereabout, which may be avoided by going up the river at Many Bay for about 10 miles, which will bring one into the Cape River above the 'moorish"[7] grounds. Some quantity of deer, good materials for brick, good trees for building. The only clothes requisite are linen, shoes and hats. Annotto thrives well and in great abundance, and there is plenty of cotton. The tobacco is like to exceed that of the island in goodness."

Axe had been less successful than other employés of the company in dealing with the Indians and the only occasion on which we hear of any Indian fighting in the colony's history is soon after his taking over from Camock the command of the enterprise on the Main. The affair appears to have occurred during one of his exploring voyages up the Cape River and he came in for a very severe reproof for undertaking any hostility whatever against the natives. "We desire to receive explanations," wrote the company, "concerning the slaughter of the Indians by the English under your command upon the Main. We know that the law will not take notice of it, yet the Lord is the avenger of blood and His justice will certainly requite it. Besides we are yet ignorant

[6] The Spanish friars had made many attempts to convert the Moskito Indians and many had suffered martyrdom, e.g., Fray Martinez in 1624. Axe's allusion may point to some fresh Spanish missions on the Ascondido, v. Juarros, *Hist. of Guatemala*, p. 361.

[7] For "mere-ish." Covered with shallow sheets of water filled with reeds.

how the guilt of your crime may redound to the blasting of our own designs. We expect your defence by the next ship, but as the matter now stands, we cannot clear you from a crime of very high nature, though we do not hold you guilty till we hear your defence. Remember that the eye of God is upon you and cannot be deceived. If you are not able to take off the guilt of blood from your conscience, we advise you to humble yourself before the Lord by unfeigned repentance and to give public testimonies of the truth of your humiliation."

The chief difficulty the company had to labour against in carrying on both their trade at the Main and the plantation in Providence itself was the great disinclination of the colonists for steady and laborious work and their preference for the free and easy life of the rover, who though one day he might be starving on a meagre allowance of raw turtle, might the next be master of a rich prize of sarsaparilla or indigo that he could dispose of to the merchants in New England for what was a fabulous sum to a poor sailor. The fascination of this roving seems to have been almost irresistible and most stringent penalties had to be enacted by the company in order to prevent their servants from stealing away in shallops or canoes to seek for wealth at the Spaniards' expense. "If any man shall offer to run away from the island in boats or otherwise, upon discovery of his purpose," wrote the company to the council, "you are to sentence him to be whipped and then to be laid in irons and afterwards to be condemned to perpetual service on the public works till we give other order, having such reasonable food allowed him as may keep him in strength only. If frequent attempts are made, some of those so attempting are to be sentenced to death in order to make an example." But these harsh penalties proved ineffectual and the perpetual leakage went on, even though men learned of the hard fate of some of those who had escaped. On February 15, 1639, an alarm was given from the lookout stationed upon Fair Way Hill that a large ship was making for the harbour without showing the private signal; her navigators were evidently strangers to Providence, for she fell among the narrow channels to the northwest of the island and was deserted by her crew. Nor were they in their shallops able to find their way into the harbour until Gov. Butler, going out in his barge to reconnoitre, found the vessel to be a Dutch privateer with a commission from the Prince of Orange, and guided them into the harbour, where they were hospitably entertained. Among those on board the Dutch vessel was an Englishman, who with four companions had escaped from Providence long before in a shallop they had stolen by night in the hope of intercepting one of the small Guatemala frigates that crept along close in to the shores of the Main. But a gale springing up, they had been driven far from their intended course to the northward and their boat had been dashed to pieces on the tiny sandy islet of Roncador or "The Snorer," some ninety miles to the east of Providence. The islet had received its name from the continual noise made by the breakers upon the sunken rocks surrounding it and was avoided by every mariner. It is quite barren and without fresh water, but in the breeding season is the haunt of sea-birds. There for two and a half years the Englishman had lived a miserable existence upon the fish and sea-fowl he caught, and the rain that gathered in the hollows of the rocks. One by one his companions had perished, and for the last ten months he was quite alone, till the crew of the Dutch vessel espied and rescued him. So striking was his deliverance thought to be after so many vicissitudes that Minister Sherrard could not resist the opportunity of pointing a moral, and the following Sunday at the evening service in the presence of the governor and council, the rescued man was introduced after the sermon to offer up public thanksgiving for his deliverance, to make confession of his vicious life, and to register a vow of future atonement.

The passion for wandering from island to island in search of an easy road to wealth is a most noticeable trait of the early colonists in the West Indies, and it was many years before the English colonies settled down into well-organised and stable communities. The average man who had once abandoned the ordinary equable course of his life in England in order to emigrate either to New England or the Caribbean must have had in him some latent love of adventure for its own sake, and the zest for novelty once having been roused was hard to quell, and it was difficult for him to settle down again to a life of monotonous toil. This restlessness is noticeable as it affected many among the New England colonists, but there the conditions of the community soon became practically stable and the social system was after all not very different from what the colonists had left behind in the old country. The general trend of affairs in New England, therefore, was towards stability and so remained well on into the eighteenth century; in St. Christopher, Providence, and Barbadoes everything tended in the opposite direction. The climate and the surroundings of the settlers were entirely different from those they had left in England, different methods of cultivation must be adopted, and to secure good profits from the soil constant effort was necessary. Unremitting effort is always difficult for a white man beneath a tropical sun, but it was especially hard for a new-landed emigrant when he had before his eyes the spectacle to be seen daily in the houses round his harbour, where the rovers would congregate after their voyages to squander their gains in revelry and to boast of the wealth to be won at the Spaniards' expense. One of the greatest masters of English fiction has imparted to the pages of his *Treasure Island* the glamour of this spirit of adventure in a way that a prosaic summing up of details and statistics would entirely fail to do; but even the most cursory reading in the records of the early seventeenth century must convince us that the spirit of adventure was as real a factor in the history of the Caribbean as it has been in the history of the western frontier of America.

Just as Providence lost settlers to other colonies, so did it receive them; we have already mentioned the arrival of the minister Leverton and his followers from Barbadoes and Tobago, and many others migrated from Barbadoes to Providence at a later date. In the space of four months in the early part of 1639, forty-nine persons arrived from Barbadoes and twenty-seven from St. Christopher, besides stragglers from Virginia and Bermuda on their way to Claiborne's projected settlement in the Bay Islands. Tortuga had been deserted by the majority of its English colonists in 1637, but it did not remain uninhabited for long, for many of the old planters who had abandoned it in favour of a settlement upon the main island of Hispaniola soon returned and were joined by several Englishmen from St. Christopher. One William Summers[8] with several companions attempted in 1638 to found a settlement at the Great Salt Pan in St. Christopher on territory which had up to then been occupied neither by English nor French.

[8] Brit. Mus., Eg., 2395, fo. 508. An account of the early history of St. Christopher by fourteen of the oldest planters, given to Gov. Stapleton in 1675 and forwarded by him along with John Hilton's account. The covering letter is to be found in Col. Pap., xxxiv, No. 85. For migration of French stragglers to Tortuga, see Charlevoix, III, 7.

Finding, however, that no water was to be had there without much labour and toil, Summers and his settlers determined to leave St. Christopher and to settle in the abandoned colony of Tortuga. By the end of 1639, therefore, Tortuga no longer lay deserted but was occupied by some three hundred inhabitants, mainly English, but with a large admixture of Frenchmen. They had gathered there from all parts of the West Indies and appointed as their governor Capt. Roger Floud, who had at one time been sheriff of Providence Island. Floud failed to give satisfaction to the colonists and they elected in his stead one James, who chose to call himself "president" as a more fitting title than governor for the head of a self-governing community. Remembering the assistance the Providence Company had given to their old Association colonists in Tortuga, James wrote to them in 1640 to beg for a supply of arms and ammunition, in return for which he promised that the colonists would pay to the company a poll-tax of so much per head. The active members of the company were disposed to furnish aid upon these terms and in June, 1640, John Pym was given a free hand to carry out all the necessary arrangements. This, however, he was unable to do before news arrived that Tortuga had fallen into the hands of the French[9] and that the English had been expelled.

9 Our authority concerning the French capture of Tortuga in 1640 is derived from three sources, all French. J. B. Du Tertre, *Histoire des Antilles Françoises,* Paris, 1667, gives original information derived from Hothman, the governor of Tortuga in 1650. J. B. Labat, *Nouveaux Voyages aux Isles de l'Amérique,* Paris, 1722, copies Du Tertre. P. F. X. Charlevoix, *Histoire de l'Isle de St. Domingue,* Paris, 1730, bases his work on original sources of information in the French colonial records, see Vol. II, p. 7, etc. Esquemeling's celebrated *History of the Buccaneers,* where tested for this period, has proved worthless. He calls Le Vasseur "Le Passeur," and dates the capture of the island by the Spaniards in 1635, in one place in 1630, and in another in 1664 under D'Ogeron. The compilation had a tremendous

According to Charlevoix, the historian of St. Domingo, there were four sorts of inhabitants in Tortuga in 1640, *Buccaneers* engaged in the chase, *Filibusters* who roved the sea, *Habitans* or planters who cultivated the soil, and *Engagés* or servants, who were supplied by merchants of Dieppe to the planters on three-year terms. A democratic government had been established and an Englishman of resolution had been chosen by both English and French as captain;[10] but he seized the entire power for the English and treated the French settlers with considerable injustice. One of them embarking secretly for St. Christopher there informed De Poincy, gouverneur géneral des Isles du Vent, that the English were now masters of Tortuga to the oppression of the French. He begged assistance to seize the island for France, which might be done without much difficulty. De Poincy had been getting into considerable trouble in France for nurturing Huguenots in St. Christopher and saw here an opportunity of getting rid of many of them by sending them to the assistance of their countrymen in Tortuga, many of whom were Huguenots. He therefore offered

vogue in Western Europe and seems to have been got up to sell by its sensationalism. Early buccaneering, at any rate, was a good deal more prosaic than Esquemeling makes out. Two works have recently appeared which deal critically with the history of Tortuga, C. H. Haring, *The Buccaneers of the West Indies in the Seventeenth Century,* London, 1910, a work largely based on Esquemeling, and P. de Vaissière, *Saint Domingue,* Paris, 1909, an excellent historical work dealing with the social life of the French colony in the eighteenth century but incidentally touching upon the early history of Tortuga and giving in full some original letters from De Poincy from the French archives.

10 Charlevoix calls this man Willis and all subsequent writers have copied this from him. Du Tertre says simply: ''Quelques Anglais s'y etant remis y ayant attiré, quelques Français, boucaniers, ils se trouverent jusqu'au nombre de 300, desquels *un Anglais* s'etait fait le chef.'' The Providence records repeatedly give the leader's name as President James. His real name may have been *William* James for Charlevoix's spelling of English names is very erratic, e.g. Waemaerd for Warner.

one Le Vasseur, a companion of D'Esnambuc in the first settlement of St. Christopher, liberty of conscience to himself and any Huguenots who would accompany him if he would lead the expedition. Le Vasseur, knowing Tortuga and its advantages, accepted the governor's offer and, gathering together a small force, set sail. For three months he remained sheltered in a small harbour on the Hispaniola coast some twenty miles from Tortuga and there he drilled his small force into something like discipline. On the last day of August, 1640, hearing that many of the English rovers were absent, he suddenly entered the harbour of Tortuga and landed without opposition. He at once summoned the English to surrender and leave the island within twenty-four hours or no quarter would be given; they, staggered at the sudden onslaught and at the defection of the French colonists who at once joined Le Vasseur, gave way without striking a blow. The flag of the French king was hoisted over the primitive fort and thenceforward Tortuga remained in French hands.[11] The conquest was more important in reality than it appeared, for from this modest beginning sprang the greatest French colony of the eighteenth century, the "Saint Domingue" that was the richest and best cultivated of the West Indian islands.

[11] The Spaniards again attacked Tortuga in 1643 and 1654 but were both times repulsed.

CHAPTER XIII

THE COMPANY AND NEW ENGLAND

The intimate accord that had subsisted throughout the early years of Massachusetts' history between the colonists and the English Puritan leaders, was first disturbed by the reply of the colony's leaders to Saye's propositions for government in 1636. A slight, but gradually widening, estrangement began to divide the two branches of Puritans, and aided by many causes this estrangement had by the end of 1638 rendered the Puritan leaders in England almost as hostile to the ruling oligarchy in Massachusetts as were King Charles and Archbishop Laud. The constitutional development of the colony had been all in the direction of an intolerant theocracy and this growth in the power and influence of divines like Peters and Cotton, was profoundly distasteful to the thorough Erastian English spirit of Saye, of Brooke, and of Pym. Convinced Puritans as they were, they were not Separatists in the least, for though they hated Laud bitterly for his narrow ecclesiasticism, they hated him far more for his innovations in the semi-Calvinism of that Elizabethan Church of England in which they had been brought up and to which they were deeply attached. The rule of ecclesiastics has never been palatable to Englishmen, and the harsh dogmatic government of the archbishop was not only in itself a mediæval anachronism in the seventeenth century, but was also profoundly foreign in temper to the compromise-loving English country gentlemen, who, whether Puritan or Arminian, liked a parson well enough only as long as he knew his place and did not dictate to his betters. In Massachusetts matters were entirely different; almost all those passing to the colony in its earlier years were moved by religious fervour and looked up to their ministers as messengers of Heaven; the rulers of the colony were profoundly religious men in whom, with the exception of Winthrop, the religious spirit was deeply tinged with fanaticism. Everything, therefore, tended to exalt the ministers' power in the community and, as always, clerical rule was wielded with a ruthless dogmatism and a hard logic that were fatal to compromise or tolerance. The attack on Gov. Winthrop's administration[1] in 1636 for its lenity and remissness was submitted for adjudication to the three principal ministers of the colony, who practically forced him to admit his error and administered to him a severe admonition to observe greater strictness of discipline in the future. Young Henry Vane, who succeeded to the governorship in 1636, found his position untenable owing to the bitterness and intolerance of the theological disputes of the ministers with the Antinomians. So out of tune with the ruling oligarchy did he find himself that at the election of 1637 he was excluded from the government and left Massachusetts for England in August of the same year.

Vane's report to his friends in England of his American experiences must have done much to add to the estrangement already existing and have aided in convincing the leaders that it would be well to divert future emigrants towards Providence, if possible, rather than to allow them to strengthen further the aggressive community in New England that had already diverged so far from the good old type of English society. It was this aim of diversion that actuated Pym and his fellows

[1] Doyle, *Puritan Colonies,* I, 128; Osgood, *The American Colonies in the Seventeenth Century,* I, 238-246.

in the final reconstruction of the Providence Company, as is shown in Moundeford's letter to D'Ewes,[2] and many persuasions were brought to bear on ministers and emigrants proceeding to New England to urge them to change their direction and sail to the Caribbean. The success obtained in procuring emigrants for Providence was very small, but the tide of emigration to New England began in 1637 to slacken, and we may justly attribute some part of this slackening to the efforts of the Puritan leaders and their friends. These efforts of course became immediately known to the rulers of Massachusetts and naturally embittered their feelings against their old allies. They consequently resolved as a set-off to accede to the prayers of the extreme Puritan party in Providence for assistance against their governor and the demands of the company. That communications between the colonies were frequent from 1638 onwards, we have already seen, and that assistance against their enemies was sought by the Providence Puritans we can learn both from the records and from Winthrop's journal. In June, 1639, the company wrote to Gov. Butler urging him to take away all occasion for breach with the New England churches and expressing the hope that "they likewise of New England will carry themselves moderately, be content with their own freedom and leave others to theirs."

The bitterness of the Massachusetts rulers against those who disparaged the colony, was the greater in these years, 1639-1640, because many causes in the colony itself were tending to discourage the settlers and persuade them to abandon the enterprise. The falling off of emigration, the long conflict over the Antinomian heresy, ending in the expulsion among scenes of hardship of Mrs. Hutchinson and her followers, the disputes over

[2] See p. 249.

boundaries in which Massachusetts became involved because of her claims under her charter, the constant dangers to be apprehended from the Indian tribes, Pequots, Narragansetts, and Mohegans, the incessant strain of labour against the hard New England winters, the exhaustion of the supplies that had been brought from England, and the almost utter absence of money to procure more,—all these causes had produced in the minds of many of the Massachusetts colonists feelings of the deepest depression and a conviction that after all they had been deluded in fancying that God had directed them to New England as the "promised land."[3] Those who gave way to these counsels of despair found a rallying point in the person of one of the earliest leaders of the Massachusetts enterprise, John Humphry. We have already said something of Humphry's earlier career; in the colony he had always stood to a certain extent aloof from the rest of the ruling group, and Cotton in his reply to Lord Saye's proposals of 1636 tells us[4] that Humphry was the only freeman of the colony who was not a member of a church. This lack of church membership, Cotton puts down to the unsettledness of the place where Humphry lived at Saugus, but the excuse seems very weak when we realize that Saugus lies only a very few miles from either Boston or Salem. Humphry had reached Massachusetts with higher hopes and far more resources than most of his fellows, but he had failed in his struggle with the conditions of New England, and had sunk lower and lower in estate until he was compelled in 1638 to beg from the Court of Assistants pecuniary help to tide him over his difficulties. His first application was favourably received, but on a second

[3] Cf. Strong, "A Forgotten Danger to the New England Colonies," *Report*, American Historical Association, 1898, 79-81.

[4] Hutchinson, *Hist. of Mass. Bay,* I, 498.

appeal the court refused to do anything, probably at the motion of Endecott. There was some ill will between the two men, for later we find Humphry bringing certain charges against Endecott at Salem and being compelled to withdraw them.[5]

It had been suggested in the colony that in view of the slackening of emigration it would be well to employ an agent in England to secure men or money, or both, and for this service the employment of Humphry had been suggested, but against the whole plan Endecott protested most strongly to Gov. Winthrop. He wrote late in 1639:[6] "For the project for an agent or agents to be employed by the country or council to procure men or money or both for us from England, we (submitting to better judgments) think it may prove more hurtful than helpful to us in divers ways. For first it will confirm my Lord Say and others of his judgment that *New* England can no longer subsist without the help of *Old* England, especially they being already informed of the forwardness of divers amongst us to remove to the West Indies because they cannot here maintain their families. . . . Touching the persons, some of them, who are thought to be most fit to be employed in this design, I do think [them] most unfit. In general take notice that they are men well affected to the West Indies."

The idea of migration to the Caribbean was making so great a headway among the Massachusetts colonists at this time as to cause the greatest uneasiness among their leaders, who put down the whole cause of the unrest to Lord Saye and the rest of the Providence Company.[7] So strong were the expressions of feeling

[5] Mass. Hist. Soc. *Coll.*, 4th series, VII, 145; see also, VII, 96.

[6] Mass. Hist. Soc. *Coll.*, 4th series, VI, 138.

[7] This projected migration has been dealt with by Strong in the article already noted.

among the members of the Court of Assistants on the subject of these disparagements that in March, 1640, Gov. Winthrop wrote personally to Lord Saye a strong letter of protest.[8] The letter itself is not extant, but it drew forth a lengthy reply from Saye, which has been preserved for us among the Winthrop Papers.[9] Saye begins his letter by reproving Winthrop for taking God's name in vain. He says: "I received a letter from you dated the 20th of March wherein upon hearsay you fall into a reproof of me backed with intimations that I may expect and fear judgments, as the ten princes of Israel found, for bringing up an ill-report upon your land and diverting men's intentions from coming to you, as they did the Israelites from going into the land of Canaan. . . . For the matter itself, the substance of what you charge me with, is that my authority (which you advance as very effectual) hath diverted many from coming to you and cast their affections another way. . . . Why should you or any other man be grieved that men follow their own judgments in transporting themselves when it is free for them so to do, . . . why am I so sharply dealt withal for speaking that which is a truth in my judgment to any that shall advise with me? But you will say I disparage that plantation to advance another: it is meet for him that will judge, to hear both sides first and to be sure of his grounds: if you knew how falsely and basely that other plantation of Providence hath been disparaged by those affected to yours for the end for

[8] Winthrop's *Journal,* I, 335.

[9] Lord Saye and Sele to John Winthrop, 9 July, 1640. Mass. Hist. Soc. *Coll.,* 5th series, I, 297, and *Life of Winthrop,* II, 248, and App. VIII, p. 422. Saye wrote his letter among the most pressing distractions, for he and the other Puritan leaders were at the time deep in secret negotiations with the Scots, carried on through Henry Darley. The celebrated letter from the associated peers to the Convenanters is dated July 8, see Gardiner's *Fall of Monarchy,* I, 402.

which you suspect I had done the like to you, then you would better know where to place and apply your reproof. For my part, my prayers have been and shall be for the good and advancement of those faithful people and pure churches I know to be there; and to that very end have I, according to my judgment, persuaded men to think of a more southerly part of that continent where they might find a commodious place for such a body as they already are, and are likely to grow into quickly by accession of those who would there come unto them, or they would be able to bring unto them if poor, by the ability that such places would afford them.'' Saye evidently here alludes to Pym's project for the great mainland colony at Cape Gracias á Dios that had so gripped the imaginations of all the Providence leaders. That his aims were not centred on Providence alone, we can see from his following sentence which, approximating closely to the unpalatable truth, greatly roused Winthrop's ire. ''Now [the Massachusetts colonists] are so placed that rich men grow poor, and poor men, if they come over, are a burden, the rich only maintaining the market for a time until that be spent which they bring out of England, which land flood will have an end. . . . In a place where staple commodities already are, and the soil and climate known to be fit to produce the richest and thereby to carry on so great a work as the framing of a commonwealth and the settling thereof for posterity, there will be no place for this [impoverishment] and by this, I hope also, I shall not be thought to have a little island and the advancement thereof only in my contemplation in all this proposition.''

Saye went on to suggest that God had appointed Massachusetts only for a *temporary* abiding place and did not mean His people to settle there forever, but into these arguments and his reiteration of the objections to the system of government of the colony as set forth by Cotton, we need not follow him, for in his prediction of a prosperous future for the colony on the Main, he had laid himself open defenceless to Winthrop's retort. The full text of this does not appear to have been preserved, but upon the back of Saye's letter Winthrop jotted down a few heads for his answer and its general purport may be conjectured with fair probability.[10] He would protest against the lords taking Humphry and other broken men as reliable guides as to the condition of affairs in Massachusetts, for they had already run through their estates by bad management and had everything to hope for from a new start. Gurdon and Darley could bear witness to Humphry's poor financial position. It was notorious that the Providence planters were terribly discontented with their position and prospects, not only from a material point of view, but also from that of religion; Gov. Butler was quite alien in sympathy to earnest Puritans and the constant struggles between the minister and the governor were well known in New England. It was all very well for Lord Saye to talk of the staple commodities of the Main and their richness, but it would be difficult for him to point out one whereby the planters might make a decent livelihood. If the West Indies offered so fine a field for colonisation and for the investment of capital, why was it that the lords of Providence themselves had already sunk almost £120,000 without any material return?—a final question that with its bit of pardonable exaggeration must have been a hard nut for Saye and his friends to crack.

[10] The complete endorsement is as follows: (Mass. Hist. Soc. *Coll.*, 5th series, I, 303), "To my Lo: Brooke that their estates were gone already. Ask Mr. Gurdon, Dr. Darley, etc., what is borne of them. Mr. [illegible]. What content those have who be there. What Governor they [illeg.] with [illeg.] . What staple commodities for livelihood. What is become of their £120,000?"

Every effort was made by the governor and the ruling powers in Massachusetts to dissuade those colonists who thought of abandoning New England, and we can perceive the line which their arguments took in Winthrop's own words in his journal:[11] "Many men began to enquire after the southern parts, and the great advantages supposed to be had in Virginia, the West Indies, etc., made this country to be disesteemed of many, and yet those countries (for all their great wealth) have sent hither both this year [1640] and formerly for supply of clothes and other necessaries, and some families have forsaken both Providence and other [of] the Caribbee Islands and Virginia to come live here. And though our people saw what meagre, unhealthful countenances they brought hither, and how fat and well-liking they became soon, yet they were so taken with the ease and plenty of those countries as many of them sold their estates here to transport themselves to Providence. . . . Some considerations were proposed to them by the Court, which diverted some of them and made others to pause upon three points especially:

1. How dangerous it was to bring up an ill-report upon this good land, which God had found out and given to His people and so to discourage the hearts of their brethren, etc.
2. To leave a place of rest and safety to expose themselves, their wives and children, to the anger of a potent enemy, the Spaniard.
3. Their subjection to such governors as those in England shall set over them, etc. Notwithstanding these considerations divers of them persisted in their resolutions and set about to get some ship or bark to transport them."

[11] Winthrop's *Journal,* I, 333.

So firmly had some of the colonists set their minds upon abandoning Massachusetts, that two of them, Elijah Goose and Emmanuel Truebody, surreptitiously sailed for England to lay their views before the Providence Company and to arrange with them for the migration of a large number of New Englanders to the mainland of Cape Gracias á Dios, there to join in the building up of Pym's great English colony. The Providence leaders were only too pleased to receive an accession of settlers to their plantations, especially seeing that the new emigrants were strong Puritans who disliked the aggressively theocratic temper of Massachusetts' rulers. The reports of the state of affairs in Providence brought by Sherrard and Halhead and the other prisoners sent home by Capt. Carter, showed the company what a mistake they had made in appointing to the governorship a man like Capt. Butler; they resolved, therefore, to appoint as governor John Humphry, the leader of the new colonists, and to give him the fullest power over all their West Indian possessions, thus endeavouring to secure success by a return to the régime of a strongly Puritan governor and council.

Though Humphry found comparatively little difficulty in negotiating with the Providence Company, his arrangements with those desiring to leave New England proved a great deal harder to make. From a letter written by him to Lord Mandeville, that is still extant among the Manchester Papers,[12] we learn that he had persuaded between two and three hundred persons to leave Massachusetts with him. Although certain Providence planters had come to New England to paint the beauties and richness of Central America to recruits, neither they nor Humphry could prove to the emigrants that Cape Gracias á Dios was the best site for their new

[12] No. 424.

colony. Most of them had fixed their minds upon Florida for their home, and it was only when Humphry was able to promise them free transportation on two ships hired by Emmanuel Truebody at the Providence Company's expense, and to assure them of assistance in disposing of their surplus property in New England, that he succeeded finally in fixing their goal. Every possible obstacle was placed in their way by the Massachusetts rulers, and Fate herself proved unkind. We learn from Winthrop's journal that: "Mr. Humphry, who was now for Providence with his company, [and had] raised an ill-report of this country, was here kept in spite of all their endeavours and means to have been gone this winter [1640], and his corn and hay to the value of £160 were burnt by his own servants, who made a fire in his barn, and by gunpowder, which accidentally took fire, consumed all." However, at length, in May, 1641, the first party of emigrants, thirty men, five women, and eight children, left Boston for Providence in two small vessels under the command of Capt. William Peirce, being followed by Humphry with the main party in July.

CHAPTER XIV

CAPTURE OF PROVIDENCE BY SPAIN

The negotiations between the Providence Company and Truebody and Humphry had been conducted, not by Pym, but by Lord Mandeville, with the help and concurrence of Saye. Pym, who had been the moving spirit in the company for so long, had since the opening of the Short Parliament become so immersed in the direction of the struggle against absolutism that he could no longer spare time to carry forward his colonial schemes. Battle had at last been joined between two worthy foemen, the aristocrat, Strafford, fresh from the triumphs of his "Thorough" policy in Ireland, and the old parliament man, once more treading his familiar ground and determined to stake his life and all. With the closing of the Short Parliament all hopes of compromise between them were at an end, and Pym's energies throughout the summer and autumn months of 1640 were devoted to the organisation of the first electoral campaign that England had ever seen. His journeys from end to end of the country, his constant immersion in a tortuous web of intrigue that at any moment might lead him to the block, rendered all thoughts of Providence impossible and it was left to other hands to carry on the work. Warwick was devoting a great share of his attention to other West Indian schemes, and both he and Saye were in constant parley with the Scots, but Mandeville was still comparatively free and the Providence work fell to his share.

While the inevitable march of events towards an open struggle between king and people demanded the entire concentration of Pym's efforts, and thus deprived the Providence Company of his guidance at a critical moment, the fate that they had so long courted was hastening to overwhelm the Providence colonists. Their depredations upon Spanish towns and shipping, culminating in Butler's ransom of Truxillo, had at last reached such a pitch of audacity as to goad the Spanish authorities to the determination that Santa Catalina must be cleared of its pirate inhabitants at whatever cost. The failure of the attack of 1635 had been so great a disappointment as to demand the serious attention of the government at Madrid, in spite of its many preoccupations with the European situation. Special orders were issued to the Council of War, the Council of the Indies, and the Council of State to deliberate together and to determine on some means of redeeming the failure. The conclusions arrived at were recorded on December 11, 1636,[1] and though it was long before they were acted upon, they were the authority on which future action was taken, and therefore concern us. Two of the conclusions, voiced by the Duke d'Albuquerque and the Duke de Villahermosa, did little to help on matters, but the third, voiced by the Count del Castrillo, was more practical. The best moment for the expulsion of the pirates had passed since they had not taken advantage of the great military preparations to clear the Indies, when the Dutch were attacked at the battle of Curaçao. Funds were lacking for further preparations directed from Spain, so that it appeared to be the best course to give the governors of Cartagena, Panama, and Porto Bello a free hand to try and dislodge the English pirates with the means at their disposal and when there seemed

[1] Brit. Mus., Venezuela Papers, Add. MSS., 36323, fo. 297.

a likely probability of success. If the English were dislodged from Santa Catalina they would move on to some other undefended island, as they had done in past years, and would return to their original fastness when the danger was past. The only way of preserving Spanish rights intact was to maintain a great fleet in the Caribbean, ready for instant employment wherever required.

In these last words the whole root of the matter is expressed; it was impossible for the governors of the Indies to do anything effectual to clear out the foreigners, who had settled down on the Antilles like a plague of locusts, and who were swept from one place only to appear in another. Nothing but a great and powerful fleet, permanently stationed in the Indies and with some of its vessels constantly at sea, could effect the colossal task, but this fleet it was impossible for the impoverished Spanish government to supply. It has been the fashion among some writers to deride the Spanish colonial government and to accuse its officials of slothful ineptitude for their incapacity to maintain intact the inflated pretensions of the monarchy of Philip II, but nothing can in reality be more unjust. To guard the whole of a hemisphere would be too gigantic a task for any nation, and it is rather a tribute to the Spanish genius that the Castilian monarchy was able to maintain its American empire in the main untouched, than an occasion for derision that some of the smaller unoccupied islands on the edge of the Caribbean should have been lost to the foreigners.

The whole of the years 1637-1638 were occupied in Spain in the preparation of a great fleet for the supreme effort to recapture Brazil from the Dutch, and every Spanish or Portuguese vessel that could be spared was pressed into the service, special care being taken that ships, men, and stores should all be of the highest quality.

The fleet sailed from Lisbon in October, 1638,[2] and further reinforcements were despatched in January, 1639; but the Spanish government dared not weaken further their own coasts, owing to the constant fear of French attacks in the Bay of Biscay. Under these circumstances it was evident that nothing could be done towards the establishment of the required fleet in the Caribbean, and orders were therefore despatched to the governors of San Domingo and Cartagena to do the best they could against Santa Catalina with the means at their command. Nothing could be attempted till the summer of 1640,[3] when Don Melchior Aguilar, governor and captain general of the province of Cartagena, profiting by the arrival in that port of some reinforcements from Brazil, despatched Don Antonio Maldonado y Tejada, his sergeant-major, with eight hundred soldiers from the garrison and two hundred negroes from the local militia on board six frigates and a galleon of the armada. The expedition left Cartagena in May, 1640,

[2] State Papers, Foreign, Spain, Bundle XL, No. 150, Hopton to Coke. Also Hopton to Coke, 23 Jan., 1639, and other letters of about the same date.

[3] The information on the Spanish side concerning the attacks on Providence can be derived from three sources:

1. Alcedo y Herrera, *Piraterias y agressiones en la America Española,* edited by P. Zaragoza. Madrid, 1883. A very scrappy compilation from the eighteenth century works of A. de Alcedo and from Herrera's *Decadas.*

2. Cesareo Fernandez y Duro, *Armada Española,* 9 vols., Madrid, 1898. See tom. IV, 339. The most recent history of the Spanish navy.

3. José Wangumert y Poggio, *El Almirante Don Francisco Diaz Pimienta y su Epoca.* Madrid, 1905. An enthusiastic appreciation of the admiral based upon, and giving long quotations from, the original sources. For the capture of Providence these are:

a. ''Carta é informaciòn enviada por D. Juan Bitrian de Briamonte, 29 de Junio de 1640.'' Coleccion Navarrete, tomo xxv.

b. Memorial originally in the Chapel of the Pimienta family at Palma in the Canaries and now in the collection of the Marquis de Guisla y Ghiuselin.

c. A relation of the battle of Sa. Catalina, printed at Madrid in 1642 by Juan Sanchez and at Seville by Francisco Lyra.

and reaching Providence on Thursday, May 28, spent some time in attempting to find a passage through the shoals that form a barrier round the island.[4] Failing in this, attempts were made to reach the shore in shallops, and on May 30 the Spaniards succeeded in landing a large party of their best soldiers. Again and again were the island forts assaulted, but all attempts were unsuccessful and the attacking party was defeated in a pitched battle with great loss. Very few of the Spaniards succeeded in escaping to their ships, and finally on June 1, a gale springing up, the galleon and her consorts, which could find no safe anchorage, had to abandon the attack and return to Cartagena, having lost, either slain or taken prisoners, more than a hundred men and two captains. The rejoicings in Providence at the repulse of the attack were naturally great, and Thursday, June 11, was set apart as a day of thanksgiving for the great deliverance, but Gov. Carter marred his victory by putting to death the Spanish prisoners he had taken, though their lives had been promised them. It was the protest of Sherrard, Leverton, Halhead, and Lane against this cruelty that caused the governor's final excess of tyranny, which culminated in their despatch to England as prisoners in irons.

Maldonado returned to announce his discomfiture at Cartagena just as the armada for the silver had arrived from Spain under the command of Admiral Don Francisco Diaz de Pimienta. Pimienta was a man of great energy of character, who has earned for himself a considerable name in Spanish naval annals; leaving his vessels for their usual lengthy stay at Cartagena, he set

[4] A very full account of the attack and its repulse was sent home to the company in a sixteen-page letter signed by Henry Halhead, Richard Lane, Hope Sherrard, and Nicholas Leverton. It has been preserved among the Finch MSS., Vol. I, pp. 51-58, Hist. MSS. Comm., *Seventeenth Report*.

out in a swift barque for Spain to lay the state of affairs before the king and to demand permission to retrieve the dishonour to the Spanish arms. The permission thus demanded in person by a captain of Pimienta's merit could not be refused, and he was ordered to return immediately to the Indies and to dislodge the corsairs of Santa Catalina in the time that would elapse before the galleons had to commence their return to Spain with their precious freight. Pimienta lost no time and before the end of 1640 he was back in Cartagena, careening his ships, disciplining his infantry, and preparing his plans for the coming attack. It was evident to him that his task would be no easy one, for he was able to gather full information as to the strength of Providence from the Spaniards who had been permitted to land there from time to time. Fugitives from Spanish justice could find their most secure harbourage among the corsairs to whom their information as to local conditions was of much value, but they were always ready to make their peace with their own government, if they could do so at the price of their knowledge of the corsairs' retreats. One of the colonists' greatest complaints against Gov. Butler was that he so often permitted Spanish pilots to come ashore in Providence and thus allowed them to glean full information as to the defences of the island. From spies of this sort Pimienta learned that Providence was armed with fifty-six great pieces of artillery and one hundred and forty-eight smaller pieces disposed in fourteen forts and entrenched defences; there were about six hundred men capable of bearing arms. Feeling in Cartagena was excited in the highest degree on learning of the treacherous slaughter of the prisoners taken from Maldonado, and of the presence in Santa Catalina in strict confinement of several friars, who had been captured while proceeding in frigates on missionary journeys along the coast. For three months Pimienta diligently made his preparations and his biographer waxes eloquent over the earnest religious and crusading spirit in which these preparations were undertaken, his hatred against the natural enemies of his nation, and the care with which he had enquired into the hydrographic conditions of the island and with which he had organised his supplies. On the 6th of May, 1641, the expedition sailed from Cartagena, numbering in all two thousand men. The admiral was embarked in the galleon *San Juan* of four hundred tons, because she drew little water; his second in command, Don Jeronimo de Ojeda, sailed in the *Urca Sanson* of nine hundred tons, and accompanying them were the *Jesus Maria de Castilla* (four hundred tons), the *Santa Anna* (three hundred and fifty tons), the *Urca de S. M. San Marcos* (four hundred tons), the *Convoy* (three hundred tons), the *Teatina* (three hundred tons), the *Jesus Maria de Ajuda* (two hundred and thirty tons), the *San Pedro*, and three pataches of from seventy to eighty tons apiece. On the 17th of May, the armada first saw Santa Catalina, but it was not till two days later that attempts were made to penetrate the surrounding reefs. After sounding a passage in shallops, the vessels cast anchor within the outermost fringe of reefs at nine o'clock on the morning of Whitsunday. The *Urca Sanson* galleon, however, found that her draught was too great to enter even the outermost channel and she was therefore sent back to Cartagena. Pimienta was not content to entrust the reconnoitring of the island to a subordinate and set out himself with his most experienced captains in a felucca to try whether with the aid of a Moorish corsair, who had visited the island in a French vessel, it was possible to find a way into the harbour. The Moor proved a useless guide, but a Spaniard, who had long acted as pilot to the Providence ships and had lately fled from them to Jamaica, was sent to the admiralty by the governor of that island, and under his guidance Pimienta and the Conde de Castimellor with a force of some six hundred soldiers in nineteen lighters finally succeeded in effecting a landing on the 24th.

The spot chosen for the landing lay in the southeast of the island and was guarded only by earthworks. Fierce fighting took place round these works, but the English defenders were finally dislodged and took refuge in the hills. Neglecting to pursue them, Pimienta marched across the island to New Westminster and laid siege to the governor's house and the church, which were held by a few musketeers. These were unable to hold out for long against the overwhelming odds, and amid great rejoicings on the part of the Spaniards, their defenders were forced to surrender and the Dominican friars, who had been held captive in the island for three years, were set free. The remaining Englishmen with most of the women and children had taken refuge in the citadel-like peninsula that juts out from the northern part of the island, but in face of the great numbers arrayed against them, they willingly agreed to lay down their arms when Pimienta sent one of the liberated friars to them under a flag of truce to promise them their lives. Gov. Carter, Sergeant Major Hunt, and others of the principal English officers came in person to thank the admiral for his clemency and to deliver up possession of the remaining forts of the garrison.

On the 26th of May, solemn high mass was celebrated and a festal Te Deum was sung in the town square of New Westminster as a thanksgiving for victory in the presence of the whole of the Spanish force and of the four hundred captured heretics. Some of the English, who had fled to the woods at the first Spanish landing, had managed to make their escape in shallops to Henrietta and the Main, but almost all the principal colonists had been captured, and these were sent prisoners on board the fleet to be carried to Cartagena and thence to captivity in Spain. The women and children were permitted to take away a few of their personal belongings, and were placed on board an English ship and despatched to England. Nearly six hundred negroes and a great booty of gold, indigo, and cochineal, fell into the hands of the captors and the total worth of the prize was estimated at over half a million ducats. No attempt had been made to bring the ships into the harbour in view of the narrowness of the passage and of the disaster to the *Jesus Maria de Ajuda,* which, in attempting to find a safe anchorage, struck upon a sunken rock and was lost. The island was left under the command of Don Jeronimo de Ojeda with thirty-two pieces of artillery, many gunners, and some infantry, and the armada set sail for Cartagena, which was reached on the 6th of June, amid great rejoicings. The galleons of the plate fleet with Pimienta in command left Porto Bello on the 9th of July and reached Cadiz on the 7th of October with the English prisoners on board. The news of the capture soon got abroad in Spain and was received with the greatest satisfaction, but no official notice of the details of the fight was issued till the early part of 1642, when, in reward for his exploit, the king conferred upon Pimienta the habit of the Military Order of the Knights of Santiago. A full account of the battle was published in folio at Madrid and Seville[5] and it is from this account that most of the foregoing details have been derived.

[5] *Relaciòn del suceso que tuvo en la isla de Santa Catalina ó de la Providencia el Almirante D. Francisco Diaz Pimienta en que se da cuenta de como la tonió á los enemigos echándolos de ella y de la estimación de los despojos y número de prisioneros.* Madrid, folio, 1642.

Pimienta's sister in commemoration of his success ordered a picture of the battle to be painted from the descriptions of eyewitnesses, and placed this picture in the chapel of Santa Anna, the patron saint of the Pimienta family, in the parish church of Palma in the Canaries. An account of the battle was deposited among the archives of the church, but this has now found its way into private hands.

The outlook of Englishmen upon the capture was from a different standpoint and it would probably have caused greater stir had not men's minds been so disturbed and the country been arming for imminent civil war. The newsmongers, however, were not entirely silent on the matter and in March, 1642, the news appeared in print along with other miscellaneous information. The news-letter is now among the Thomason Tracts;[6] under the title, "Avisoes from several Places," it tells us of Cartagena: "The General of the galleons, named Francisco Diaz Pimienta, had been formerly in the month of July [sic] with above 3000 men and the least of his ships in the Island of Santa Catalina, from which he had taken and carried away all the English and razed the Forts, wherein they found 600 negroes, much gold and indigo, so that the prize is esteemed worth above half a million. This unexpected and undeserved act of the Spaniard in supplanting our Nation, will, I hope, ere long be requited when as in cool blood the Spaniard shall do us a mischief in demolishing and ruining that which another hath built and is not able or will not make use of it himself, supplanting our more industrious people, which endeavoured to do good both to the bodies and souls of men, and only to shew his greatness with his multitude to destroy a handful and to account that a victory which

[6] Thomason Tracts in Brit. Mus. (E. 141.10), "A letter [for N. Butter] from the Low Countries. 22 March, 1641½."

is rather a credilous [sic] treachery, but let him triumph that wins at last.''

In our previous chapter we left the colonists from New England setting forth in two small vessels, the *Salutation* and the *Sparrow* of Salem, for what they expected to be their new home in the West Indies. They arrived at St. Christopher early in June, 1641, and we may let Winthrop take up the thread of their story, for he must have received it from their own lips:[7] ''At Christopher's they heard that a great fleet of Spanish ships was abroad, and that it was feared they had taken Providence, so as the master, Mr. Peirce, a godly man and most expert mariner, advised them to return and offered to bear part of the loss. But they not hearkening to him, he replied, 'Then I am a dead man.' And coming to the Island,[8] they marvelled they saw no colours upon the fort, nor any boat coming towards them; whereupon he was counselled to drop an anchor. He liked the advice, but yet stood on into the harbour and after a second advice he still went on; but being come within pistol shot of one fort and hailing and no answer made, he put his bark a stays, and being upon the deck, which was also full of passengers, women and children, and hearing one cry out, 'They are traversing a piece at us,' he threw himself in at the door of the cuddy and one, Samuel Wakeman, a member of the church of Hartford, who was sent with goods to buy cotton, cast himself down by him and presently a great shot took them both. Mr. Peirce died within an hour; the other having only his thighs tore, lived ten days. Mr. Peirce had read to the company that morning (as it fell in course) that in Genesis the last,—'Lo I die, but God will surely visit

[7] Winthrop's *Journal*, II, 34. Hubbard repeats the story from Winthrop and Hutchinson summarises it.

[8] 21 June, 1641.

you and bring you back,'—out of which words he used godly exhortations to them. Then they shot from all parts about thirty great shot besides small and tore the sails and shrouds but hurt not the bark, nor any person more in it. The other vessel was then a league behind, which was marvelled at, for she was the better sailer and could fetch up the other at pleasure, but that morning they could not by any means keep company with her. After this, the passengers being ashamed to return, would have been set on shore at Cape Grace de Dios, or Florida, or Virginia, but the seamen would not, and through the wonderful providence of God, they came all home the 3rd of September following. This brought some of them to see their error and acknowledge it in the open congregation, but others were hardened. There was a special providence in that the ministers were sent prisoners to England before the Island was taken, for otherwise it is most probable they had all been put to the sword, because some Spaniards had been slain there a little before by the deputy-governor his command, after the lieutenant had received them upon quarter in an attempt they had made upon the island, wherein they were repulsed with the loss of 2 or 300 men.''

The vessel carrying out from England the new deputy-governor, Thomas Fitch, and the Rev. Mr. Leverton, also approached within gunshot of the island before they discovered that it was no longer in English possession. Calamy tells us:[9] ''[the prisoners] were kindly received by the lords planters or proprietors of the island and encouraged to return. Mr. Sherrard, being of a timorous disposition, chose to stay here, but Capt. Lane and Mr. Leverton returned plentifully furnished for their voyage and authorised with a new commission. At their approach to the island they found that the Spaniards

[9] Calamy, *Nonconformist's Memorial,* I, 373.

had seized it in their absence. However at Mr. Leverton's desire, they ventured an engagement with them, killed a great many of their men and forced their armed long-boats ashore." No landing, however, could be effected and Leverton and his companions had to sail away, leaving Santa Catalina in the Spaniards' hands. Leverton remained cruising in the West Indies for some years before he returned to England and met with many adventures and hardships. His landing in England after his travels is rather quaintly described by his biographer:[10] "Arrived at the Downs, he landed at Sandwich, where, as he was taking horse for London, the ostler says to him, 'Mr. So and so, you are somewhat like our minister. I believe you have lived in the hot countries, as well as he.' Upon enquiry he found the minister to be his old colleague, Mr. Sherrard, who was settled there, which brought them to an interview again to their mutual joy. Coming to London, he was received with great honour and respect by the Lords Proprietors of the Island of Providence, and soon after settled as minister of High Hedingham in Suffolk." After his ejection at the Restoration, he went out as chaplain to Lord Willoughby's plantation of Surinam, where he died. Sherrard in return for his services to the Providence Company had been presented by the Westminster Assembly with one of the sequestered livings at Sandwich, but his contentious temper allowed him to lead no more a peaceful life there than he had secured in Providence. Many disturbances arose in the town in consequence of his attempts to aggrandise himself at the expense of others, and his parishioners petitioned the House of Lords against him in very bitter terms.[11] After a great deal of trouble, Sandwich finally succeeded in

[10] *Ibid.*

[11] "House of Lords MSS.," 23 Oct., 1647, etc.

getting rid of him, and we last hear of him as being intruded upon the sequestered rectory of Melcombe in Dorset.[12]

The capture of Providence was a hard blow to the company as completing the loss of the capital they had sunk in the enterprise, but so engrossing were the preoccupations of the members in the national struggle that no attempts could be made to retrieve their losses. On February 8, 1642, a meeting of Pym, Warwick, Saye, Mandeville, and Brooke was held at Brooke House to straighten up the finances of the company as far as possible, and to notify each member the proportion of the company's debt for which he was personally responsible. The chaotic state of all business during the Civil War prevented any settlement of these debts, and it was not until the resumption of a more settled state of affairs in 1649 that the amounts due from each member were definitely ascertained. Then it was shown that Pym's estate still owed £1740, Saye £1190, and other members smaller amounts. No redress had been obtained from the Spaniards for the capture of Newman's ship by the Dunkirkers, and the company made this a pretext for demanding from parliament a share of the spoils of the rich Spanish ship, *Santa Clara,* which was seized with very doubtful morality in Portsmouth harbour in 1644. The case caused a great deal of stir at the time and was productive of a large amount of bitterness between the English and the Spanish governments. It was debated for many years and even till after the Restoration, and was productive of a large mass of documents which are still extant.[13] Its main interest for us lies in the fact that the Providence Company's journal was recopied as an exhibit in the case and

[12] *Lords' Journal,* X, 32.

[13] S. P. Dom., Car. I.

probably came into the State Paper Office among the *Santa Clara* papers. The Providence Company ultimately got little or nothing from the sequestered funds which dribbled away among the many venial employés of the Commonwealth.

The creditors of the company were not content to wait for their money, while the members were quarrelling as to how it should be paid. They began to take proceedings against members of the company in their individual capacity, though they had great difficulty in doing so owing to the fact that most of them were protected by parliamentary privileges. It is interesting to note that the permanent session of the Long Parliament acted as a bar to the recovery of debts from its members and their servants, and that full advantage was taken of this parliamentary privilege at the expense of the unfortunate creditors. Sir John Barrington, heir of Sir Thomas Barrington, who had died in 1643, was the only Providence adventurer who was unprotected from distraint by parliamentary privilege, and in 1645 we find him petitioning parliament[14] for protection against the Providence creditors, who were suing him for the whole of the company's debts. He was successful in his petition, and was compelled to pay only the debt owing by his father. On February 5, 1650, the last meeting[15] of the Providence Company of which we have any record took place and each surviving member assumed personal responsibility for the portion of the debts that was shown by Secretary Jessop to be due from him. With this step the company may be said to have dissolved.

We have now examined in detail the story of the Providence Company and its allied enterprises from their

[14] "House of Lords MSS.," 24 July, 1645, Hist. MSS. Comm., *Sixth Report*, App., p. 71a; *Lords' Journal*, VII, 506; Brit. Mus., Eg., 2648.

[15] Present Warwick, Rudyerd, Darley, N. Fiennes, Knightley, Graunt.

inception to their abandonment, and it behooves us to attempt to supply an answer to some questions that cannot fail to have suggested themselves in the course of our enquiry. Why did men migrate from England in the decade 1630-1640 by the thousand, with their wives, their families, and their whole possessions? Why did the then inhospitable shores of New England attract them, while only an insignificant number could be persuaded by the leaders of their party in England to sail for the balmy climate of the Caribbean?

It has been well said that revolts against tyranny arise, not when men are in the depths of misery, but when their prevailing prosperity is attacked. The Great Rebellion of the seventeenth century and the migration that preceded it, do something to bear out the truth of this statement, for the profound internal peace enjoyed by England for sixty years, had, by 1630, resulted in enormous progress in wealth and enlightenment. But while the nation as a whole was infinitely better off under Charles I than in the early days of Elizabeth, there was much in the condition of rural England to breed discontent in the hearts of the farming class.[16] The power of the nobility and greater gentry in the government of their counties was supreme, and though their rule generally commended itself to their poorer neighbours, yet there are many indications in the records of the time that English tenant farmers were not contented with their lot, but felt keenly that land hunger which so often besets the members of a rural community. In Massachusetts from the first it was possible for practically every man to own his own land in entire freedom from a landlord's oversight and from the heavy rents exacted in England. In Providence, on the other hand, in its earlier years the

[16] See Thorold Rogers, *Hist. of Agriculture and Prices,* Chaps. I and XXVII.

whole of the land was the property of the English company, and the half of all profits produced had to be paid over to them. At first the company would not even grant definite leases of the plantations, and this proved a terrible drawback in the eyes of men who left England, not merely to escape religious tyranny as they regarded it, but also to become their own masters and to own their own acres free from the overlordship of squire or noble.

We are familiar with the objections of the ruling classes to the obsolescent feudal rights of the crown, for they were loudly voiced during the debates in parliament on the "Great Contract." The pressure of feudal rights upon the tenant farmer class, though less heard of, must have been even more galling. For any proper understanding of the social conditions prevailing under the early Stuarts we must remember that however modern the tendencies of the time may appear, those tendencies had to work themselves out in a society bound and shackled in every direction by the rusty chains of the mediæval polity. The "Ancien Régime" died in a certain sense with an English king as much as it died with a French one, and there are many curiously exact parallels to be drawn between the last days of feudalism in both countries. The Stuart age was peculiarly one of lawyers, who, nurtured on the legal learning of Lancastrian precedents, could always find a way to prove that right lay on the side of the over-lord. Coke and Hakewill, Noy and Digges, may have laid the foundation of our modern liberties, but their rule was a hard one for the small man. To escape from the meshes of manorial pedantry to a community where practically all men were of equal rank, and where every freeman had a voice in the election of his rulers, must have been a most potent inducement to emigration to a generation that had begun to think for itself.

While New England could offer this prospect of freedom, Providence could hold out no such boon. The governor and the council were obedient nominees of the company at home, and their control of the planters was absolute, although in their selection no person in the colony had a share. The company's regulation of the trade of the island, and their requirement that the colonists should purchase all their goods from the stores, while they were compelled to dispose of their crops through the company's agents in England, contrasted ill with the entire freedom of trade enjoyed in Massachusetts, where commodities could be purchased in an open market and the fruits of the colonists' labours could be sold without restraint to the highest bidder. The conditions under which farming was carried on in New England and the crops to be raised there were familiar to every immigrant from a rural parish, but in the West Indies a man must learn to cope with an entirely new set of conditions in a climate unsuited to the exertion of the unremitting energy essential to success. In Massachusetts a man's whole labours might be devoted to his own concerns and very little danger was to be apprehended in the early years from the neighbouring Indian tribes; but in Providence a planter must be always ready to take up his pike or his musket, and was constantly being called away from his own plantation for hard work upon the fortifications. The constant dread of Spanish attack must have been one of the most potent causes in persuading an emigrant to choose Massachusetts as his goal rather than Providence, for while it might appear to men like Saye and Pym a most statesmanlike course to combine hatred of Spanish domination with hatred of English Arminianism, the course can hardly have presented itself in the same light to plain men, who had never had a share in politics at home, and who in emigrating to the West Indies laid themselves open to the prospect of ending their days in a Spanish dungeon. It was one thing to hate the Spaniard in the security of an English parish, but quite another to be prepared at any moment to join in repelling an overwhelming Spanish attack. Religious motives were far stronger in guiding the conduct of an Englishman in the seventeenth century than they are to-day, but it was only rarely that crusading ardour could be found combined in one personality with the patience, prudence, and persistence that are requisite in the founders of a successful colony. Not every infant community has been blest with the possession of a John Winthrop.

Some part of the reluctance of Puritans to emigrate to Providence may be attributed to personal causes. Looking back over the whole Puritan struggle, the Civil War, and the first years of the Commonwealth, we see the party groupings of the preceding years in a way quite different from that in which they appeared to plain men at the time. Warwick, Saye, Pym, and Barrington were the leaders of the opposition to King Charles I's ministers when parliament was sitting and they directed the policy of their party during the years of absolute rule, but their aims and their efforts were of necessity secret, and to the Puritan rank and file they must have appeared merely as somewhat distinguished members of the ruling classes, who, though having sound views upon religion, were yet acquiescent supporters of the absolute régime. To an Essex farmer the Earl of Warwick would appear only as the lord lieutenant of the county, keeping almost regal state at his seat of Leighs Priory, Puritan in his sympathies certainly, but carrying out obediently the orders of the government, appearing at the oppressive forest courts held by his brother, the Earl of Holland, as chief justice in eyre, anxious to maintain his rights against the king, but on his own estates insisting strongly upon his rights as landlord. Sir Thomas Barrington, as the lord lieutenant's trusty deputy, appeared in the same light as an agent of the government, and that he was not much liked by the lower orders in his own neighbourhood we can see from the many cases in the Domestic State Papers, where he was accused of illegally enclosing forest and common lands. Saye was more favourably known to the common people as an implacable opponent of the government, but Pym had made very little mark in public life before the opening of the Short Parliament, and he was always regarded by political observers of the time as a mere client of the Earl of Bedford, and a moderate, who, like Rudyerd, was hampered by his long connection with official life. Contrast this with the way in which men like John Winthrop and Thomas Dudley must have appeared to their humbler brethren. Both were men of decent family, but their religious fervour was strong enough to overcome their class feelings and to make them prefer to leave England forever, rather than submit to a church policy that they detested. They did not merely offer to send out emigrants to a distant colony, while they remained at home and weakly compromised with absolutism; in person they led the stream of emigrants across the Atlantic, shared their dangers and their hardships, and governed the colony they had founded with self-sacrificing care, foresight, and integrity. Such was the esteem in which the leaders of the rival colonies were held by the humbler folk. Can we wonder that while the colony succeeded abundantly that had but one member of the ruling classes, Henry Vane, among its leaders, Providence, essentially the creation of the Puritan members of those ruling classes, proved in the end and in every respect a failure?

CHAPTER XV

THE ABIDING INFLUENCE OF THE PROVIDENCE COMPANY'S ENTERPRISES

The Providence Company and its schemes had by 1641 come to a most unfortunate ending, as far as material advantage and success were concerned, but even in failure the efforts of the company prepared the way for future accomplishment. At the commencement of the present enquiry we stated that the Providence Company served as a connecting link between the Elizabethan seamen and Cromwell's "Western Design," between the exploits of Drake and Hawkins and the founding of Jamaica. With the chain of events that formed this connection we have been concerned throughout the foregoing pages, and it now only remains to look to the last of the links and to show briefly that the "Western Design" was no new creation of Cromwell's brain, but was an ordered attempt to carry to fruition the ideas of England's true foreign policy that Pym and Warwick had instilled into the minds of the members of the Providence Company and the Puritan party in general.

Throughout the whole life of the Providence Company the Earl of Warwick had maintained his private warfare against Spain and, in conjunction with certain London and Dartmouth merchants, had continued the privateering business that he found so profitable. He continued to take the greatest interest in all colonising schemes and when the Earl of Pembroke, seeing no likelihood of profit from his Caribbee patent, desired to dispose of it, Warwick purchased all his rights over the islands for a nominal sum. In 1638 he began to take steps to enforce these rights and founded small colonies in Trinidad and Tobago with emigrants from Bermuda under one of his old shipmasters, a Capt. Chaddock. After the capture of Providence certain of the settlers, who had managed to escape, took refuge with Warwick's colonists in Tobago and there carried on a precarious existence for a few years. Others fled to Cape Gracias á Dios and there mingled with the Indians, while others again took refuge with Claiborne's colonists in Ruatan and others of the Bay Islands. These last did not have a very long respite, for in 1642 they were attacked by a Spanish expedition from Honduras and either slaughtered or dispersed among the Indians. The most important group of fugitives, however, led by Samuel and Andrew Axe, escaped to St. Christopher and played a very important part in West Indian history in connection with the capture of Jamaica.

It will be recalled that Robins, the petitioner to the House of Lords against the tyrannical behaviour of which he had been the victim in Providence, complained in 1642 that Capt. Jackson, his persecutor, was bound to the West Indies on a voyage for the Earl of Warwick. This voyage we have already mentioned very briefly, and it must now again be noticed, for it was by far the most important event in the history of the West Indies between 1641 and 1655. The enterprise was financed by the Earl of Warwick and others of the Providence Company in conjunction with Maurice Thompson, and other merchants in the City of London. Jackson sailed from England in July, 1642, with three well-equipped vessels, having as his vice-admiral Samuel Axe, the old Providence colonist. Arriving at Barbadoes on the 27th of September, he made public proclamation of his commission from the

Earl of Warwick and of his intended expedition against the Spaniards, and called for volunteers. He was at once joined by large numbers of recruits both from Barbadoes and St. Christopher, and especially by very many of those who had escaped from the capture of Providence. By the beginning of November the whole force was complete, and consisted of seven vessels of various sizes and something over eleven hundred men. The land forces were divided into companies and placed under the supreme command of Capt. William Rous, who on his release from a Spanish prison had again found his way to the West Indies.

The first attack was directed against the pearl fisheries at the Island of Margarita, but little booty was obtained. After the capture and ransom of Maracaibo in December, other places in New Granada were pillaged and at the end of February, 1643, the expedition sailed over to Hispaniola to refit. On the 25th of March, Jackson landed his forces in the island of Jamaica and without any great difficulty captured its Spanish capital, Santiago de la Vega. For some three weeks Jackson held Jamaica at his mercy, and it was only on receiving a ransom of 7000 pieces of eight and very large stores of victuals for his ships, that he finally consented to retire on the 21st of April. Rous now gave up his command in the expedition and returned to England, having learned that he had been elected as a member of the Long Parliament. The expedition sailed next into the Gulf of Honduras under the guidance of the New England pirate, Capt. Cromwell. Truxillo was captured, but yielded little return, and the freebooters did not meet with much profit during the summer of 1643. In November a raid was made against the smaller towns of Costa Rica and the Isthmus, but again little booty was procured.

The winter of 1643-1644 was spent in raids upon the coast of Cartagena and the summer of 1644 in expeditions against Guatemala and the small towns in the Gulf of Mexico, and finally in September, Jackson and the remains of his fleet sailed out through the Straits of Florida without mishap and reached Bermuda on the 27th of October. After a long stay there to divide the booty, the expedition finally returned to England in March, 1645, and had its last fight off Plymouth with three Dunkirk men-of-war, one of its smaller vessels being sunk and a large portion of the crew drowned. For three years Jackson and his followers had kept the Indies in an uproar. It is needless to remark that the Spanish government had exhausted every means in their power to cause the English authorities to put a stop to his depredations; but when a country is plunged in the throes of civil war, little can be done, even by a willing government, to bring its disobedient subjects under control. As to the will of the parliament to bring Jackson's depredations to an end, we shall be more certain if we note briefly what happened in colonial affairs after regular government ceased in 1641.

The members of the Providence Company did not abandon their interest in colonial affairs when the events in England became so engrossing as to demand their whole attention. A lull in the civil strife appeared to have been reached, when, on September 9, 1641, both houses of parliament adjourned till the 20th of October, and once more we find an interest being taken in the West Indies. A committee was appointed by each house to look after affairs during the recess, and when we find upon the Lords' committee the names of Warwick and Mandeville, and upon that of the Commons' Pym, chairman, St. John, Gerrard, and Barrington, we are not surprised to learn that among the terms of reference is a direction "To consider of framing and constituting a West Indian Company."[1] Circumstances, however, were too critical for the committee to devote attention to the project and colonial affairs were left more and more to be dealt with by Warwick alone with the assistance of Jessop as his secretary.

With the outbreak of civil war in 1642, all formal governmental connection between England and her colonies ceased for nearly a decade. A body of so-called colonial commissioners was established by the Long Parliament, but though they contained among their number all the principal members of the Providence Company, they did very little business. In 1643 the Earl of Warwick was appointed governor-in-chief of all the American plantations and there seems to have been some understanding that he should submit important matters for consideration to the great Derby House committee. As a matter of fact, the parliamentary government was so overwhelmed with difficulties of all kinds, that no share of its attention could be paid to the colonies, and they were allowed to shift for themselves as best they could. An accurate investigation of the relations between the colonies and the mother country in those years of chaos would demand much patient and not very profitable research, but it would appear that our general conclusions are in the main correct, and that what small amount of communication was kept up, was carried out by the Earl of Warwick through William Jessop and practically upon his own authority.[2] Each colony was for the time being a little independent state, adherent nominally to either king or parliament as the case might be, and

[1] Clarendon, *Hist. of the Rebellion*, IV, 12; *Commons' Journal*, II, 288.

[2] A register of letters written to the colonies by Jessop in the name of the Earl of Warwick, 1645-1648, is in the British Museum, Stowe MSS., 184, fos. 114 sqq.

providing a haven for privateers of its own way of thinking, but in practice having very little to do with the struggle at home.

With the suppression of the second Civil War and the execution of the king in 1649, the reorganisation of government in England began to place affairs upon a more stable footing, and it became possible for the parliament acting through the Council of State to attempt to recall the colonies once more to an effective allegiance. A strong fleet was fitted out in 1650 and despatched under Sir George Ayscue to bring the royalists of Virginia, Barbadoes, and Bermuda into subjection. The task was practically completed by the early part of 1652, in time to deprive Prince Rupert of a refuge for his fleet in Barbadoes. The whole direction of the enterprise was supervised in a very spasmodic way by a committee of the council of state with William Jessop as its clerk and executive officer. Its guiding spirit, as far as colonial policy was concerned, was the Earl of Warwick, who even after his retirement from the position of lord high admiral had a very great influence in affairs, and we may claim with justice that through him and Jessop there was a direct connection between the colonial policy of 1652 and the Providence Company's West Indian enterprises that had failed in 1641.

On April 20, 1653, Oliver Cromwell, the chosen leader of the now all-powerful army, drove the Rump from the Parliament House and made the way clear for a new and definite course of policy in foreign affairs. Throughout the year the form which the new government was to assume was uncertain, but on December 16, 1653, a new written constitution, the Instrument of Government, was accepted, and Cromwell became Lord Protector. He was now free in great measure to fashion a definite foreign policy and to give to England once more a place of respect and influence in the European world. Either of two alternatives might be chosen as a policy, and each of them was supported by a party in the Council of State, with which under the Instrument of Government lay the deciding voice. On one hand, the Protector might adopt a policy of close alliance with the Spanish monarchy to curb the growing power of France, or on the other, he might take up that traditional policy of hostility to Spain that he and some of his most intimate friends[3] had been brought up from their earliest years to regard as England's heritage from the days of the great queen. Between these two alternatives the struggle raged in a tangle of confused negotiation that lasted until, in the summer of 1654, Cromwell was able to force his councillors to accept the decision to which his own personal feelings and his Puritan up-bringing had led him.

The modern mind, says Seeley,[4] is tempted to question this momentous decision and to ask why Cromwell wantonly plunged his country into war with the Spanish monarchy at a moment when she had scarcely emerged from a long, dark period of civil discord. He suggests that the guiding cause was Cromwell's emulation of the example of Gustavus Adolphus as the champion of Protestantism, rather than his foresight of the future colonial greatness of England and a desire to enrich her with the spoils of the declining Spanish empire. An American writer[5] has more justly ascribed Cromwell's motive to an emulation of the Elizabethans, but he imputes the connection of ideas to the inspiration of the renegade Dominican, Thomas Gage. The enquiry that has been carried through in these pages enables us

[3] For the intimacy of Cromwell with Warwick, see Carlyle's *Letters of Cromwell*, ed. Mrs. S. C. Lomas, III, 294, 338.

[4] Seeley, *Growth of British Policy*, II, 75.

[5] Strong, *Amer. Hist. Rev.*, Vol. IV, p. 233.

to offer a solution to the problem more prosaic than the one view, more natural than the other, and proof is not lacking that our solution is the true one, for it can be supported by evidence derived from Cromwell himself. For thirty years the foreign policy of the Puritan party had been to enrich England at the expense of the Spanish Indies, but only once within that time had it been possible to attempt this openly, and then its success had been foiled by royal bungling. At last the way lay open to carry the Puritan policy to fruition by Puritan means. Everything in Cromwell's personal and family history, everything in the counsels of his intimate friends, urged him to take up, now that he was able, the great cause of Protestantism in the Indies, that the Puritan leaders had attempted to uphold during the ten long years of absolute rule. Let him go on with the interrupted work to found, with the greater means at his command, Pym's English empire on the shores of the Caribbean—a blow at the realm of Anti-Christ and an extension of the Kingdom of God in the world.

In December, 1654, a great fleet sailed from Portsmouth under Adm. Penn and Gen. Venables with sealed orders to attack Hispaniola in prosecution of the "Western Design." In September, 1655, after having succeeded in capturing only that island of Jamaica which had fallen such an easy prey to Jackson's much smaller force twelve years before, they returned to England dejected, discredited, and in enmity one with another. So great an apparent failure seemed to demand an apology for the policy that had inspired the expedition, and on the 26th of October, 1655, there was published a lengthy Latin document entitled *Scriptum domini protectoris contra hispanos,* or in the English version of Birch, *a Manifesto of the Lord Protector, etc., wherein is shewn the Reasonableness of the Cause of this Republic against the Depredations of the Spaniards.*[6]

This manifesto has been always attributed to the pen of John Milton, then Latin secretary to the Protector. It recites at length the wrongs suffered by Englishmen at the hands of Spaniards since the beginning of the seventeenth century, and justifies the declaration of war and the despatch of the West Indian expedition as a retaliation for past injuries and an attempt to right the wrongs of Englishmen. It may be that the manifesto was merely an attempt to justify to the public an expedition that had been despatched by the Protector on quite other grounds, but this somewhat forced explanation seems exceedingly unlikely when we examine the list of wrongs charged against the Spaniards, and find how large among them loom the losses of the Providence Company, which had touched the pockets of so many among Cromwell's immediate friends and allies.

Ten instances of the unjustified seizure of English ships between 1605 and 1608 are dealt with in a general fashion in sixty-four lines of the manifesto, which then goes on to deal with the story of the Providence Company and the capture of Tortuga and Providence in a hundred and nineteen lines of accurate detail. With two or three very brief mentions of more recent attacks of the Dunkirkers on English ships the grievances of the Providence Company complete the list of wrongs. It is evident that Milton must have derived his information from someone entirely familiar with the history of the Providence Company, and this informant can be no other than the company's late secretary, William Jessop, now one of the clerks of the Council of State and in daily contact with Milton.

[6] Translated by Birch (1738) and printed in Bohn's edition of Milton's *Prose Works,* II, 342.

That the Protector himself was entirely familiar with the strategic situation and importance of Providence, we may learn from one of his own letters. Writing under date October 30, 1655, to Major-General Fortescue, then in command in Jamaica, he said:[7] "We think, and it is much designed amongst us, to strive with the Spaniards for the mastery of all those seas; and therefore we could heartily wish that the Island of Providence were in our hands again, believing that it lies so advantageously in reference to the Main, and especially for the hindrance of the Peru trade and Cartagena, that you might not only have great advantage thereby of intelligence and surprise, but even block up the same."[8] This mastery of the Spanish treasure route had been strongly insisted upon in the original instructions issued to Gen. Venables;[9] and, it will be remembered, was one of the most cherished designs of Pym and the Providence Company.

Not only were those in power in England familiar with the Providence story, but the leaders of the expedition themselves knew it well, and, if necessary, could refresh their memories from some of those who had taken part in it. Andrew Carter, the old deputy-governor of Providence,[10] was the leader of the fifth regiment, Anthony Rous, son of the deceased Providence minister, was serving in the army, and Kempo Sabada, the old Providence pilot, was one of the principal guides of the expedition.[11] A complete search through the records

[7] Carlyle's *Letters of Cromwell*, ed. Mrs. S. C. Lomas (1904), no. CCVI; old edition No. CXLIII.

[8] Carlyle emends "the same," which is in the original, to "Cartagena" and Mrs. Lomas allows the emendation to stand. It would rather seem that "the same" refers to the Peru trade.

[9] *Venables' Narrative*, ed. C. H. Firth, p. 113.

[10] For his later life see *ibid.*, Introduction, p. xxi.

[11] *Ibid.*, p. 20.

would doubtless yield other names, but it seems hardly necessary. The terms propounded to the Spaniards in Jamaica are sufficient to prove that revenge for the humiliations of 1641 was in every mind. Whistler tells us in his journal of the West India expedition:[12] "This morning came in to us eight Spaniards, they being the chief men of the Island [of Jamaica] to treat with us: and General Venables propounding to them the same compositions that they gave our English upon Providence, which was all to go off from the Island, each with a suit of clothes on his back: And to bring in all goods and all money and plate, with their negroes and all other slaves into the place appointed for the reviewing of it within ten days, upon pain of death, and so to be gone off the island."

Jamaica, having been captured, must be peopled and settlers sought on all sides. Again Cromwell followed the old lines and took up Saye's old project of obtaining settlers from New England. Saye's arguments and almost his very phrases were used to further his purpose. Again did Winthrop protest, again did the rulers of Massachusetts throw every obstacle in the way, and once again was the attempt to people the West Indies at the expense of New England a failure.[13] English and American Puritanism were divergent to the last. Other intimate links connecting Providence with the "Western Design" might be demonstrated, but even what has here been touched upon would seem sufficient to prove that it was from his own life-long friends, from those who, like Warwick, had made war upon the Spaniard a perpetual

[12] *Ibid.*, p. 164.

[13] Strong deals with the whole of this controversy in his article in the *Report* of the American Historical Association for 1898, pp. 77-94. See also correspondence with Daniel Gookin in Thurloe, *State Papers*, IV; *Life of Daniel Gookin*, Chs. IX, X.

duty, that Cromwell derived the inspiration for that "Western Design" and for that Spanish war, that formed so important a part of his foreign policy. He may have emulated Gustavus Adolphus, he may have talked with Thomas Gage, but it was the Elizabethan tradition, handed down through the members of the Providence Company, that decided his course.

It would be wrong to assume that the traditional policy of hostility against Spain had entirely expended its force when it led to the despatch of the Jamaica expedition. For a few years longer it continued to move the minds of men who had a large influence on England's colonial policy, and it was only with the restoration of the Stuarts and the advent to power of fresh men with a new outlook on world affairs that the long chapter was closed and it was seen that it was no longer the Spaniards but the Dutch whose commercial rivalry England had to fear in the western seas. In all his colonial administration Cromwell was personally influenced by a group of London merchants upon whom he constantly called for advice and whom he placed upon the many committees and councils established to look after trade affairs.[14] Among these men an important part was played by Martin Noell and Thomas Povey, to the last of whom more than to any one else England owes the beginnings of a definite colonial policy. In the "Overtures" of 1656-1657, that were drawn up by Noell and Povey and led to the formation of the Select Committee for Trade and Foreign Plantations, we find the following paragraph:[15]

"That [the proposed Council] do use their utmost industry and endeavour for the promoting those begin-

14 C. M. Andrews, *British Commissions*, etc., J. H. U. Studies, XXVI, 37.

15 Brit. Mus., Eg., 2395, fo. 99, Povey's draft. For all this matter see Andrews, *op. cit.*, pp. 38-60.

nings his Highness hath made at Jamaica both within itself and in order to further attempts upon the Spaniard. And that they do give encouragements (and rewards if they shall be deserved) to such as bring any considerable intelligence or information, and shall receive and debate and favour all such propositions as shall be tendered to them either for the making further discoveries or attempts upon any of the Spanish Dominions, or that shall desire by ships of war to make prize of any of his ships or goods in those Indias, that thereby Merchants and others may be invited either by themselves in their own ships and persons, or by a joint stock, to adventure upon some laudable undertaking in some of those parts.''

We have here a continuance of the old tradition that would give governmental sanction and support to such a warfare of privateers as that carried on by the old Providence Company. The merchants went so far as to propose the incorporation by Act of Parliament of a company, to be known as the West India Company, for the express purpose of attacking Spanish towns, interrupting the treasure fleet, and driving the Spaniards from their control in the West Indies and South America. The project went very far towards completion and among Povey's papers[16] we have many drafts and counter-drafts of projects that show what serious attention was paid to the matter. The proposals were presented to the Council of State after Cromwell's death, but the times were unpropitious[17] for their acceptance and

[16] Brit. Mus., Eg., 2395, fos. 89-113 and 202-237. See also Povey's Letter Book, Add. MSS., 11411.

[17] ''In 1659 business in the city was so poor that some merchants visited it only rarely; while through want of employment, a great number of poor families were in danger of perishing, and the burden of relieving them in some wards was found almost insupportable,'' Scott, *Joint Stock Companies*, II, 130.

after 1659 nothing more is heard of them. When in November, 1659, the harsh provisions of the Peace of the Pyrenees demonstrated to the world that the power of the Spanish Colossus was irretrievably at an end, a new era was opened in colonial affairs as in so many other branches of world politics. The newer maritime powers had definitely won their right to share in the exploitation of the Western Hemisphere and, although ten years were to elapse before Spain would acknowledge her defeat in the treaty of 1670, the further uselessness of the Elizabethan tradition was demonstrated to all Englishmen. It had long been felt by many that legalised piracy was compromising to the dignity of a great nation, and though Morgan and his ruffians were yet to sack Panama, and Esquemeling was yet to harrow the minds of Western Europe by his stories of the buccaneers and their exploits, it was as pirates that they fought—in defiance of their governments and with ever-increasing ferocity and a determination to profit not only at the expense of the Spaniards but of all honest men. As Major Robert Sedgwick wrote in 1655,[18] so after 1660 it became universally recognized that "this kind of marooning, cruizing West Indian trade of plundering and burning of towns, though it hath been long practised in these parts, yet is not honourable for a princely navy."

With the abandonment of Povey's project for a privateering West Indian company our enquiry comes to its natural close. It has ranged over the whole period of England's colonial beginnings from the earliest colonising of Guiana to the definite formation of a colonial policy, and though it has been mainly concerned with the history of a single colonising company it has, owing to

18 Col. Papers, No. 35, xxxii, Nov. 14, 1655, Maj. Robert Sedgwick to the Commissioners of the Admiralty.

the importance of the members of the company, had to touch upon many points in the history of the seventeenth century. Even if the story had dealt only with the details of the life of the Providence colony itself, it would have been worth the telling, for we have no such wealth of information concerning any other of the first West Indian colonies and only in a few cases so much concerning an early chartered company. But the main interest has not lain in this direction; it has rather been found in the light which the career of the company throws on the course of English history, at home during that lull of eleven years between the Petition of Right and the Long Parliament, when Charles I was endeavouring to establish his personal rule; and abroad in perpetuating the Elizabethan tradition of conflict with Spain for the control of America and the West Indies, which had not spent its course until in the days of the Restoration fear of the Spaniards passed permanently away. The purposes and activities of the Providence Company are not isolated forces operating in the backwaters of the historical current; they are factors contributing in no small measure to the outworking of important phases in the parliamentary and colonising influences of the time and as such deserve to take a sufficiently prominent place in the narrative as not to mask their historical significance.

The close relation between the leaders of the great migration to New England and the men who had directed the activities of the Virginia and Somers Islands companies has been demonstrated in many of our pages, and their intimacy with the principal English Puritans has also been made apparent. It has been shown that all these men were united by ties of relationship and by community of interest in a very near degree, and we have been enabled to cast some fresh light upon the careers of two men of commanding influence in the struggle against absolute monarchy. The obscurity that has veiled the life of John Pym from the dissolution of 1629 to the opening of the Short Parliament has been somewhat cleared, and we have shown that during that period he was playing a very active part in national life. In the management of the affairs of the Providence Company he was developing that massive breadth of judgment and that sagacious instinct for the right moment that were to make him for two crowded years "King Pym," the master of his country. The measure, the foresight, and the rare power in times of high contention of singling out the central issues and choosing the best battle ground,—all these were perfected in those eleven years; the industry, the patient persistence, and the tireless energy whereto he then had schooled himself, he could apply, when the time came, to some of the gravest problems that have confronted an English statesman. The work of Robert Rich, too, has been touched upon at many points, and we have noted how he had some share in the foundation of almost every English colony of his time. His great influence in the central government during the Civil War was the natural sequel to his activity in the Puritan councils during the period of absolutism. His inherited position as a great and wealthy noble made his house a rallying point for many of those who disliked innovations in church and state, while his natural abilities and adventurous spirit made him take the lead in many directions where Lincoln's natural timidity and Saye's disagreeable and radical temper debarred them from success. His true importance as an actor in the historical drama has hardly yet been properly appreciated, and some day, no doubt, Warwick will receive his due meed of recognition as an important figure in the action of his time.

The field of West Indian history after the period of the Spanish conquest is as yet almost virgin soil and we have here been able only in the briefest way to indicate the movements that were going on where they were of importance to our immediate subject. The Caribbean, that under Philip II was a Spanish sea, became during the first half of the seventeenth century a seething cauldron into which were poured the most adventurous spirits from every western nation; therein worked all the passions that could no longer find their outlet on their native soil. Huguenot and Leaguer, Puritan and Arminian, Hollander, Swede, and Courlander, all could hope for fighting, adventure, and booty from the Spaniard. Their hopes of riches might be disappointed and they might be compelled to take to peaceful planting in the islands they had wrested from him, or to smuggling with his colonists and slaves, but the end of the struggle was the same for all. When with the pacification of Europe peace came to the western seas, Spain had lost all she was to lose for a hundred and fifty years and the other nations were fixed in the outer ring of islands, which from barren volcanic rocks they were to convert during the eighteenth century into some of the richest and most populous spots in the world. Throughout our pages this theme has never been far away and it has provided, perhaps, the principal justification for their writing. If the work has contributed anything to illustrate the development of the policy of hostility to Spain from its full vigour to its final close, its purpose has been achieved.

INDEX